TRIBAL IDENTITIES

TRIBAL IDENTITIES
Nationalism, Europe, Sport

Edited by
J.A. Mangan

FRANK CASS • LONDON

First published in Great Britain by
FRANK CASS & CO LTD
Newbury House, 900 Eastern Avenue
London IG2 7HH, England

and in the United States by
FRANK CASS
c/o ISBS
5804 N.E. Hassalo Street, Portland, Oregon 97213-3644

Copyright © 1996 Frank Cass & Co. Ltd.

Library of Congress Cataloging-in-Publication Data

British Library Cataloguing in Publication Data

Tribal Identities: Nationalism, Europe, Sport
I. Mangan, J. A.
306.483094

ISBN 0-7146-4666-0 (hb)
ISBN 0-7146-4201-0

Printed in Great Britain by
Antony Rowe Ltd.

This group of studies first appeared in a Special Issue on 'Tribal Identities:
Nationalism, Europe, Sport' in *The International Journal of the History of
Sport*, Vol.12, No.2, published by Frank Cass & Co. Ltd.

Contents

Backwards into the Future

A very few weeks after the Barcelona Olympics had quite successfully presented a generally uplifting view of the potentialities in the New Europe to contrast with the bleak events in the Balkans, the old Europe also bubbled up out of the western hemisphere of its collective unconscious, tribal as ever. The triggers though not in any sense the causes, were the currency market developments leading to Black Wednesday, and the French referendum on Maastricht.

Neil Blain et. al., *Sport and National Identity in the European Media* (Leicester: Leicester University Press, 1993), p. 189.

Introduction

In the autumn of 1990 the International Society for the Study of European Ideas held its second international conference at the Catholic University of Leuven, Belgium. Its theme, 'Towards a Future Europe: A Comparative History of European Nationalism', celebrated the current attempts at a deliberate forging of a new European political, cultural and social consciousness.

The premise underpinning the conference contributions was that the past was giving slow and determined birth to the future. Historical identities shaped by national demands had now been found wanting and were replaced by identities shaped by wider and pressing geopolitical needs. A supra-national social Darwinism was dictating the end of European nationalism as it has been known. It was therefore time to revisit the past – to locate precisely the impetus to the future.

The conference had four 'workshops' – Politics, Economics, Culture, Philosophy – and each workshop had a substantial number of themes. Culture, for example, included contributions on 'Language and Nationalism and the University' – and 'Nationalism and Sport'.

As the convener of this latter theme, I invited ten contributors from Europe, the United States and Australia who were asked to consider one or more of the following sub-themes:

1. Sport as a mechanism of national solidarity promoting a sense of identity, unity, status and esteem.
2. Sport as an instrument of confrontation between nations stimulating aggression, stereotyping and images of inferiority and superiority.
3. Sport as a cultural bond linking nations across national boundaries, providing common enthusiasm, shared empathic experiences, the transcendence of national allegiances, and opportunities for association, understanding and goodwill.

So that the session had a distinct focus and a common purpose, it was suggested that these contributors reflect on the relevance and validity of these three themes in a recent historical context.

Well before the conference word of the workshop spread to academics who were attracted by its themes but who were unable, for one reason or another, to attend the conference. Later others found the themes appealing and came forward with their ideas. The result was a long but, it is hoped, worthwhile gestation period before the eventual publication of these essays.

This volume is, therefore, the consequence of extended circumstances. It certainly offers a fuller opportunity than was available at Leuven for the conference contributors to present their ideas. And in addition, it also offers a forum for those who were unable to attend the conference, and those who, even later, were interested in involvement, to provide their reflections on the issue of nationalism, sport and Europe. The outcome, is a rich, diverse and original explorations, within European (and European influenced) nations, cultures and societies, of the historical role of sport and its capacity to assert, establish, reinforce and deny national consciousness.

The opening chapter, by J. A. Mangan, focuses on the nature of the indoctrination of a chauvinistic self-sacrificial elite within the late Victorian and Edwardian public school system and, in particular, explores the combined role of 'poetry, prose and pictures' in the indoctrination process. The chapter develops perspectives and arguments presented in several publications in recent years and offers further and fresh evidence, despite strenuous denials at the time, of at least partially militaristic society, a partially militaristic public school community and a sustained process of socialisation into the role of self-sacrificial imperial subaltern within the schools. In these institutions, argues Mangan, masculinity, to a considerable extent, was viewed as a martial concept and the male body represented a political icon symbolizing institutional commitment to ethnocentricity, racism, militarism and imperialism with sport as the pre-eminent instrument of the socialization process.

Richard Holt draws attention to the fact that the popular nationalism of the late nineteenth century expressed itself through sport in sharply differing ways in Britain and France. The French saw sport, especially the gymnastics movement, as a source of national regeneration and a proper concern of the centralized state. French sporting divisions were largely political and religious with the Church and State either setting up or subsidising rival organizations. There was little tolerance of separatist movements based upon the strong traditions of French regional identity and autonomy; the most important sporting phenomenon was a explicit source of national integration: the Tour de France.

In Holt's view this contrasted sharply with the United Kingdom. Here the federal nature of the constitution, the revived historic nationalisms of Ireland, Wales and Scotland as well as the 'small state' approach of the Victorians combined to produce a striking alternative to the Third Republic. Democracy in France, despite its seemingly cosy provincialism, was driven by older traditions of centralism as well as newer forms of racial nationalism and militarism. English sporting nationalism, as opposed to the more easily recognizable Celtic varieties, was ambiguous, seeming to deny crude chauvinism yet remaining deeply imperialistic. This was especially true of cricket with its distinctive colonial bonds and moral vocabulary which provided the English with a national identity allegedly based not on crude national interest but on moral principle – hence 'perfidious Albion' and the British reputation, especially amongst the French, for hypocrisy.

Of course, Holt has insufficient space for consideration of this perspective, but it was equally true that the English supposedly chivalrous concept of 'fair play' was widely praised in France and in other Continental countries.

The representational symbol of this ethical phenomenon, the late Victorian and Edwardian Games Ethic of the English Public School, was hugely admired by influential Continental Europeans. their endorsement aided its ascendancy an also helped promote within the schools themselves an arrogant, complacent and confident ethnocentricity. A seldom appreciated consequence of this ethnocentricity was the transformation of the famous concept of 'fair play' from an internal utilitarian instrument of control into an external moralistic doctrine 'peculiar' to the upper and middle-class English schoolboy. In turn, this doctrine became for some Continental Europeans and many British a symbol of the superiority of the English Gentleman. Fair play was seen as his largely exclusive property and, to an extent, one source of his imperial success.

It was only after the Great War that public school priorities were widely challenged by British and other critics and the Games Ethic was increasingly derided and eventually became defunct. However the ideal of fair play was above suspicion and beyond criticism. It remained a source of admiration and envy in mainland Europe and elsewhere. One indication of the longevity of its appeal was its adoption as an official exhoration in the European Cup of 1990! Its origins were never scrutinized, its original purpose never probed and its adoption as a symbol of ebullient chauvinism never understood.

H. F. Moorhouse briefly reviews the historical complexities of a 'cultural nationalism' associated with soccer in the United Kingdom. More importantly, however, he suggests that for the British, sport as exemplified by soccer, a game of great cultural significance, may be a force to be reckoned with in the continuing process of defining the four British nations, being 'an institution of great emotional power in the reproduction of cultural nationalism'. However 'four nation nationalism', he points out, is now threatened by other nations in FIFA who seek to reduce the historic over-representation of the four countries of the United Kingdom, and he argues that in conjunction with this diminution of international power and prestige and in the wake of other forces such as Europeanization, traditional patriotic allegiance associated with the old soccer nations may well come under increasing scrutiny – and perhaps threat. This is an interesting scenario and we must wait and see what transpires on soccer fields and terraces and in cultures and societies – a more assertive, cosmopolitan Europeanization of an even more defensive, insular nationalism.

Jan Tolleneer reviews the c lose association of gymnastics, militarism and nationalism in Belgium in the nineteenth century. Since 1830 Belgium has been an independent kingdom comprising a Flemish (Dutch-speaking) and Walloon (French-speaking) population. Belgium's history of sport is characterized by different gymnastic federations which followed the German model of 'turnen' (gymnastics). With the foundation in 1892 of the National Federation of Catholic Circles for Gymnastics and Military Exercises, the Catholics reacted against the more liberal attitudes of the Belgian Federation of Gymnastics founded in 1865. Like the Belgium Federation, this independent Catholic federation had an obvious nationalistic character. This nationalism was apparent in the federation's periodical, *Belgica*. National Songs, flags and other symbols also came to the forefront in festivals and processions. The attachment to the nation became even more evident through the rationale and the implementation of the gymnastic programme. Through gymnastics and military exercises young people were prepared for the defence of the country. These motives appeared clearly in 1910 when the Catholic federation became a member of the Association of Belgian Physical Education Federations for Preparation for Military Service. While some of the gymnasts were also involved in the Fleming-nationalist movement which was more outspoken in the Belgian Federation than in the Catholic Federation, this ethnic-nationalist reaction did not detract from the 'Belgian' character of both federations. The Catholic federation, especially, was strongly embedded in the Belgian national movement. The Catholic political party, in power from 1884 to 1914, stood for a united Belgium. For the Catholic gymnast, consequently, 'God' and the 'fatherland' were always mentioned in the same breadth.

Jean Michel Faure is convinced that sport is a representation of the latent violence of the Western mind and, frequently, a state instrument of preparation for legitimate military violence in the pursuit of state ends. As competitiveness is the essence of political existence, so true sport equals competitive sport: ' Life, belongs to those who fight'. And over time such sport 'has tightened its grip on physical culture' and become *its* essence. In France, sport is an affair of state. Its extensiveness is a product of the energy, efficiency and the organizational capacity of the ruling class. And its purpose is to 'bind the individual to the state and to enrol him in society'. Furthermore, asserts Faure, the management of sport is 'a class prerogative'. Competitions, for their part, 'offer the proof of their own legitimacy in their ability to mobilize the crowd around the ritual representations of confrontation which they provide'. They promote social cohesion and offer possibilities for national identification, and for the mobilization of the masses. In short, sport produces a social order in which trials of strength are seen as part of the natural course of things. In France, therefore, and often elsewhere, states Faure, sport is not a substitute for war, but a permanent preparation for it.

Henning Eichberg locates a unique tripartite role for Swedish Lingian gymnastics in late nineteenth-century Denmark. Denmark is the only country in Europe, he declares, where the gymnastics of the Swedish Lingian type have become popular; a broad cultural movement based on voluntary grassroots associations. An explanation for this cannot be found in gymnastics itself. It must be sought within a framework of cultural revolution, class conflict and the formation of a national identity in the years between 1848 and 1902. And it raises questions about the relations between Danish nationalism and the 'body culture movement' and the relationship between the 'movement' and popular ('folkelig') nationalization. Other Nordic countries have certainly favoured other physical cultural representations as symbols of national identity, for example, traditional dance in Greenland. However, Eichberg suggests that a study of 'the body culture movement' in Denmark symbolized by Lingian gymnastics offers a unique case study of political modernization through sport.

Matti Goksøyr examines the rising national-political consciousness that influenced sport as well as other cultural expressions in Norway from the middle of the nineteenth century. Nationalism offered a new legitimacy for some sports, while others were given a new role in a new political situation. The breakup of the union between Norway and Sweden in 1905 caused hostilities to spill over into sport, and led to the first Norwegian political boycott of an international sports event in the same year, when the Nordic Winter Games in Stockholm were left without Norwegian skiers – a symbolic gesture of national autonomy. Goksøyr leaves us in no doubt that sports helped define Norwegian nationalism in the second half of the nineteenth century.

Sverker Sörlin is concerned with skiing and the part it has played in establishing a Swedish national consciousness and a consciousness of nature. Both, in his view, melded in the earlier part of the nineteenth century in consequence of a growing appreciation of the spiritual role of the winter wilderness of forests, waterfalls and mountains. Then in the late nineteenth century skiing became a sport, and shortly after, a theme of art, literature and history. At a time of fierce competition with other nations skiing also became a symbol of both the manly and militaristic. Later there was a reappraisal of nature as a nature resource against a backdrop of industrialization. At the same time there was also a growing realization of nature as a location for spirituality, leisure and recreation as Sweden moved from a rural agrarian to urban industrial economy. a nationalism of nature was reinforced by the establishment of organzations concerned directly with the 'outdoors' – the Swedish Tourist Association (1885), the Swedish Boy

Scout Movement (1908) and the Swedish Nature Conservation Society (1908), but particularly by the Swedish Ski Association founded in 1892.

Skiing, suggests Sörlin, was a central part of the nationalism movement. The Swedish Ski Association had strong patriotic overtones up to the Second World War. Both then and later the Association was a prism through which attitudes to nature in Sweden were refracted. While initial attitudes were patriotically nationalistic and remained so for some fifty years, shortly before the Second World War, with numbers spiralling upwards, the Association embraced a wider role – one for all seasons and all places – under the title of the Swedish Ski and Outdoor Life Association. In the 1980s this wider role was made more evident when the term 'ski' was dropped altogether.

When after the 1945 the emphasis shifted from the militaristic to the recreational, the enthusiasm with which this shift as greeted was stimulated in part by a string of publications providing both a rationale for, and an impetus to action. In the wake of this change the Association declined in significance – neither patriotism nor social welfare were no enough. Environmentalism, among other things, created new priorities.

In essence, the Association, as the mirror through which nature might be viewed in Swedish society, has three phases: 1892–1930, with its emphasis on nationalism, patriotism and militarism; 1930–45, with its stress on individual and family well-being; and the 1950s onwards, with its increasing concern with the environment and its preservation. The Association thus possessed three ambitions over time: nationalism, social welfare and environmentalism. Through its skiing, nature and life in nature became inseparable from Swedishness. To understand the Swede, and indeed for the Swedes to understand themselves, claims Sorlin, it is necessary to know the story of their physical, mental and spiritual involvement in the activity of skiing.

Interestingly in the light of recent political developments in the former Soviet Union, John D. Windausen traces the close relationship between national identity, international image and modern sport in late Imperial Russia. As in the early twentieth century, the character of Russian sports was marked by national organizations and international competition. These developments made possible the Russian participation in the Fifth Olympiad in Stockholm in 1912. At that time, Russians, rather like the Chinese today, felt left out of world competition and exhibited a somewhat frantic effort to catch up and demonstrate their modernity. Stockholm was clearly intended as another of those Petrine leaps into the future that characterizes the Russian psyche. By 1912 Russians regarded themselves as members of the world athletic community.

Windhausen observes that recent Soviet historians mock the few medals won by Russian athletes at the Fifth Olympiad and refer to the Stockholm Games as a kind of 'Sports Tsushima'. By contrast they boast that the Communist regime opened up sport to the masses and the result has been world athletic dominance. However, in Windhausen's view, the Russian experience at Stockholm was far from a sporting disaster. The nation was provided with athletic heroes, involvement in the European sports movement constituted a source of national pride in modernity, and partial athletic success at Stockholm brought a further modest measure of national well-being.

Arnd Krüger examines the forms of nationalism surrounding the Olympic Games of 1908, 1912 and 1916. He shows with the help of archival sources, parliamentary debates and newspaper analysis that the clashes between the United States and Great Britain, but more particularly Germany and France, were instrumental in bringing about the international endorsement of the Games and that in this way modern athletic contests served early in modern world history as a keen instrument of national aggrandisement. Krüger uncovers the extent of government involvement and financial expenditure in preparing national teams, for the early twentieth-century Olympic Games. The arguments in the German parliament in 1931, for example, concerning the value of national teams for national prestige, claims Krüger, are now widely heard today throughout Europe and indeed the world. Nationalism with official government endorsement was an early fellow-traveller of modern European national identity.

Eduardo P. Archetti, in his discussion of national identity and football, suggests that the search for identity in Argentinian football is tied to style. Football, in his view, constitutes a symbolic arena for reflection about the nature of national identity. He explores the character of the Argentinian style of playing football as it has evolved in the twentieth century and in the context of its European antecedents. The national identity of Argentinian football, he argues, has leaned heavily on outstanding individuals and their self-projected image. In footballing terms Argentinian history has been, therefore, the product of 'lucky accidents and unexpected events' as much as the product of any stable, corporate continuity; yet out of the unpredictable emergence of gifted individuals a mythology of a predictable collective stylistic tradition has been constructed that offers the security of perceived permanence. Of course, the reality of football, as of life, is complex, and in fact an actual, as distinct from mythical, identity constructed through football is similarly complex. Tantalizingly Archetti suggests, in the briefest of asides, that the logic that has produced a footballing identity for Argentina (erratic individualism transmuted into mythical collectivity) offers an appropriate interpretative model for the 'stormy and difficult' evolution of Argentinian history as 'an unrealized modern nation on the periphery of the world'.

Finally, Joseph L. Arbena analyses, citing examples covering several different sports and countries, the role of sport in promoting national identity and national integration in post-independence Latin America, often in reaction to the legacies of former colonisation and/or to later European and North American neo-colonial domination and concomitant Latin American dependency. In some instances, sporting events almost incidentally captured public attention and stimulated national pride and identity. More commonly, physical educators, sports administrators and government officials consciously promoted a variety of sports activities to shape national identity, to make healthier and more disciplined populations, to achieve international recognition, and/or to consolidate support for incumbent regimes. In some cases, sport also generated external confrontations, building a nation's own identity in part through the negative presentation and rejection of other nations. In a few situations, such as the hosting of international sporting events, Arbena asserts, sport has served to enhance nationalism while simultaneously strengthening positive transnational ties with other countries. but, always and ironically, success in sport has meant success in promoting and performing 'European' sports – beating the masters at their own game – in order to achieve nationalist goals likewise defined primarily in European terms. Sport has proved to be a potent form of neo-colonialism!

The contributors to this volume make a strong case for a further consideration of the role of sport in structuring modern nations, cultures and societies. Most of the contributors point to the significant contribution of sport in the making of modern European nations, both intentionally and unintentionally, internally as an agent of consolidation stressing similarity and externally as an agent of confrontation emphasizing difference. Furthermore, the influence of European forms of sport on nationbuilding has spread far beyond Europe as the brief consideration above of Latin American nationhood reveals.

In the period of national reassertion in Eastern Europe, and, to an extent, in no way to be exaggerated, national non-assertion in Western Europe, and in an era when sport, transmitted instantly and widely by the media, can graphically and powerfully reach huge audiences, its role in the making and unmaking of national, cultural and social allegiances merits the most serious inquiry. Truistically it is far more than a national and international entertainment: it is a source of political identity, morale, pride and superiority. It also sustains political antagonisms, hatreds and prejudices. Elie Kedourie once referred to nationalism as 'doctrine invented in Europe at the beginning of the nineteenth century...[which] holds that humanity is *naturally* [emphasized added] divided into nations'. He added that it serves a basic human need to be part of a stable, coherent, and it could be appropriately added, successful community. To what extent can sport be used then to promote a stable, coherent and successful supranational European community? To what extent can it be used to sustain smaller national identities within that larger community? To what extent will it serve to deny attempts at a European community with a common identity? Can it and should it be used, calculatedly, to merge the nations in Europe into a new corporateness which could claim a meaningful communality?

This volume demonstrates that sport has been effectively used, both calculatedly and uncalculatedly, to forge feelings of national oneness. It has been responsible, with other political agents, for creating national 'tribalism' in modern Europe. Arguably its potency in this regard, in Europe and indeed elsewhere, is increasing rather than diminishing as a product of new technologies, nascent national defensiveness and bewilderment with complexity. It might yet prove to be one stumbling block to future European supranational ambitions, especially if nationalistic political forces begin to appreciate its emotional hold over polutions, the significance for them of emblems associated with athletic allegiance and its in-built capacity for separateness rather than 'togetherness'.

The point is simply made: the potential of sport for unity and disunity should never be underestimated.

Duty unto Death: English Masculinity and Militarism in the Age of the New Imperialism

J. A. MANGAN

E. P. Thompson's[1] *The Making of the English Working Class* is widely known throughout the academic world, and indeed beyond; justifiably so, as it has many virtues. Among other things, it is an impressive synthesis of the ideas of the 'good and the great' of the social sciences. In it we hear echoes not only of Gramsci but of Weber and Durkheim, and we see references not only to classes but to codes and values.[2] Thompson, of course, was concerned, first and foremost, with the creation of 'community'. In the eighteenth century, he argued, in traditions which revolved around the 'code' of the self-respecting artisan – decency, regularity, mutuality – were to be found the seeds of the 'highly organised and self-conscious working class' of the Industrial Revolution. This code promoted a secure, ordered, cultural milieu and ensured a viable working-class culture. As this culture evolved, it linked to the artisanal code the languages of religious brotherhood and socialist idealism. The outcome was a collectivist culture, propagated by political theory, by new social organizations and by cohesive rituals.[3] This cultural transformation, Thompson insisted, ensured political recognition. In Thompson's view, the emergent autonomy of working-class culture 'was a historical and political necessity'[4] – an interesting viewpoint with period application elsewhere.

The attraction here of Thompson's analysis, albeit briefly outlined above, is that it appears relevant at the other end of the social class continuum of Victorian England – especially late Victorian England and the Era of the New Imperialism. Among the upper middle class of the period there was also concern with the creation of a 'community', albeit smaller; a 'self-sacrificial warriorhood' – a small elite of sacrificial subalterns conditioned to accept the responsibility, if necessary, of martial martyrdom. This elite had its 'code' which ensured a militaristic culture – one which also emerged out of perceived historical necessity.

David D. Gilmore's *Manhood in the Making: Cultural Concepts of Masculinity*[5] is concerned with the way different cultures conceive and experience manhood:[6] 'the approved way of being an adult male in any given society'. Gilmore is intrigued by the fact that so many societies construct an exclusionary image of manhood through trials of skill and endurance, by the fact that there seem to be 'parallels in male imagery around the world' constituting 'a ubiquity rather than a universality', and finally, by the fact that there appear to be continuities of masculine expectations across cultural boundaries; in particular, the demand made upon males to 'be a man' or 'act like a man' – an expectation of aggressive assertion.[7]

Gilmore's attention has been caught by the apparently similar and the often dramatic manner in which cultures, past and present, non-literate and literate, define manhood. Can we speak, he asks, of a global masculine archetype born of trials and testing . 'If there are archetypes in the male image,' he surmises, 'they must be largely culturally constructed as symbolic systems, not simply as products of anatomy, because anatomy determines very little in those contexts where the moral imagination comes into play. The answer to the manhood puzzle must lie in culture; we must try, therefore, to understand why cultures use or exaggerate biological potentials in specific ways.'[8]

It is appropriate at this point to note the conclusions of Clark McCauley in *The Anthropology of War:*

> ... Twenty years ago, Lortenz and Ardrey ... popularised the idea of an aggressive or killer instinct for aggression in warrior societies, but which was present to some degree in all humankind ... Anthropologists then and now find the hypothesis of a killer instinct not so much wrong as irrelevant to the kind of facts they want to explain. The Vikings of some hundreds of years ago are the notably peaceful Danes of today. The horse and gun made some people of the Shoshonean Basin – the Utes and Snakes – into warriors, and other people of the same basin – the poor Diggers – into fearful refugees. The gun and the market for sales made both the Miskito kingdom and its Sumo victims 'out of identical aboriginal material'.[9]

In these examples, the rate of cultural change is too great to be a function of genetic differences. So McCauley advances the notion of *pre-adaptation*:[10] ecological change that leads to cultural adaptation mediated by human choice based on pre-existing culture. Historians of culture, claims McCaulay, 'are confident that the speed and direction of cultural change in relation to changed ecology could only be understood in terms of change consciously directed by the perceptions of human actors'.[11] Both directly and indirectly such arguments lead back to Gilmore who argues, unremarkably, that culturally endorsed ideals of manhood make an indispensable contribution both to the continuity of social systems and to the psychological integration of men into their communities. To understand the meaning of manhood from a sociological point of view, and, on occasion, as I hope to demonstrate, from a historical point of view, therefore, it is important to understand its social rather than individual functions *and* causes. And to Gilmore, it is clear that acts of manhood are frequently related to the extent of disciplined aggression required of the male In his opinion this simply demonstrates that life is mostly hard – and men, historically, have been given the dangerous tasks in the interest of the survival of the group. Thus while there may be no 'Universal Male' it is possible to speak of a Ubiquitous Male – a quasi-global personage: 'Man-the-Impregnator-Protector-Provider'.[12]

These three moral injunctions 'seem to come repeatedly into focus' whenever and wherever the 'word' manhood is valued. They represent danger: 'they place men at risk on the battlefield, in the hunt, or in confrontation with their fellows.'[13] Consequently if the group is to survive, boys must steel themselves to undertake such activities, must be prepared by various sorts of tempering and toughening, *and* must accept the fact that they are expendable Thus, states Gilmore, in a crucial passage, men too, nurture their society 'by shedding their blood, their sweat, their semen..., by producing children, by dying if necessary in faraway places to provide a safe haven for their people'.[14] In short, manliness is a cultural construct with the important concomitant of martial expendibility. And in Gilmore's words – most apt for our immediate historical purpose here (the relationship to contemporary society will be discussed later) – 'in Victorian England, a culture not given over to showy excess, manhood was an artificial product co-axed by austere training and testing'.[15] In other words, an imperial masculinity consonant with empire building became a sexual imperative.

The making of masculinity is the focus of this study. It is concerned with the cultural creation of a self-sacrificial warrior – an imperial elite – and with the conditioning of this elite – on the public school playing fields of the privileged; those important locations of an indoctrination into martial, moralistic manhood with eventually serendipitous global ramifications.

II

Correlli Barnett has suggested that 'to hear politicians and constitutional historians holding forth on the virtues of parliamentary democracy, it is easy to forget that ours is a civilisation largely born out of war and devoted to it'.[16] War, symbolized in the metaphors of war used so widely and so frequently, is deeply embedded in our institutions, thinking, recreations.[17] Nevertheless, throughout the nineteenth century, there was a marked reluctance among the British to see Britain as a militaristic nation: the myth of British anti-militarism was pervasive: 'Almost all nineteenth century writers on the army and the State, prior to the Boer War at least, agreed that Britain was not a military nation.'[18] This was a belief reiterated full in the face of jingoism!

However, all was *not* as was claimed. The Victorians, early, middle and late, were as addicted to playing at soldiers as any of their continental counterparts. For many people, different and gorgeous uniforms, badges and helmets of Volunteers, Militia and Yeomanry in the magnificent displays in British military museums may seem a puzzling collection for so small a military power, says Geoffrey Best, but soldiering, he adds, appears to have been 'the hobby of the aristocracy and gentry'.[19] Hugh Cunningham has described Volunteering as the spectator sport of mid-Victorian Britain.[20]

Furthermore, at the level of what Michael Howard has termed High Culture, emphasis on military matters was intense. It amounted to the worship of war as a sacred path to moral purity, ascendancy and domination. In the second half of the nineteenth century war came to be seen as a moral mandate.[21]

There were several schools of thought in support of war.[22] There was the school which considered war desirable on evolutionary grounds, exemplified particularly well by the American Hover Lea, who was widely read in Britain. For Lea war was inevitable due to the contact of nations 'in the convergence of their expansion.' For G. F. Wyatt in his book *God's Test by War*, 'efficiency at war represented God's test of a nation's soul'. Field Marshal Lord Roberts lectured the length and breadth of Britain on 'war as a tonic of character'. J. A. Cramb, sometime Professor of History at Queen's College, London, declared, 'War is the supreme act in the life of the State.' Sir Garnet Wolseley stated that 'War .. .exercises a healthy influence on all classes of society.'[23] As early as 1865, John Ruskin lectured on 'War' at the Royal Military Academy, Woolwich – seemingly an incongruous combination of an improbable speaker, at an improbable place on an improbable theme for here was an impotent, aged aesthete captive in a cage of virile, young philistines lecturing on a decidedly unaesthetic theme.[24] The irony, to the modern liberal, seems even more pointed when Ruskin's words are noted: 'All the pure and noble arts of peace are founded on war; no great art ever yet arose as art, but among a nation of soldiers.' Ruskin's ideas harmonized with Wyatt, Cramb, Wolseley and others: 'War, by eliminating the unfit, determined who were the best – those highest loved, most fearless, coolest of nerve, swiftest of eye and hand.' And for good measure Ruskin added that war was the source of all virtues and facilities while peace was the source only of sensuality, selfishness and death. 'All great nations,' he told his audience, ' ... were nourished in war, and wasted in peace, taught by war, and deceived by peace; trained by war, and betrayed by peace – in a word, they were born in war, and expired in peace.'[25]

By the turn of the century virtually everyone in Britain, claims John Gooch, seemed to be interested in war. 'The periodicals, in particular, turned ever more attention to 'the glorification of war as a theatrical event of sombre magnificence' with the young public school officer as 'juvenile lead'.[26] War now became an integral part of the Social Darwinist thinking widely prevalent at the time, so much so that on the eve of the Great War *The Nineteenth Century* published an article in which it was asserted:

> ... Victory in war is the method by which, in the economy of God's providence, the sound nation supersedes the unsound, because in our time victory is the direct offspring of a higher efficiency, and the higher efficiency is the logical outcome of the higher morale ... victory is the crown of moral quality...[27]

To the adherents of this Darwinism, 'healthy organisms were unrelentingly at war with competitors in their environment – whether on the battlefield, the stock exchange, or the playing field'. These beliefs had their effect. Late Victorians passed their militaristic inclinations and preoccupations to the Edwardians. And while Edwardian Christianity was not particularly martial or bloodthirsty, claims Anne Summers, it adopted militarism with an apparent uncritical enthusiasm.[28]

The self-indulgent myth of nineteenth-century Britain as an anti-militaristic society, then, will not bear scrutiny.

In the view of one commentator, 'the origins of the strident militarism so common in nineteenth-century Britain still lie largely hidden'.[29] This militarism, suggests another, has escaped the attention of many social historians – misled by those long-standing 'conventional wisdoms' that Britain was a nation of seafarers not soldiers and that socialist pacifism ensured a hostility to militarism. In consequence, the rush to the colours in the Great War still requires adequate explanation and there still exists a lack of real understanding of the political, cultural and social basis of British patriotism of the pre-war period.[30] The fact that Great Britain produced 1.5 million volunteers in its first two years disposes Anne Summers to the view that Britain 'must have developed, over a long period, a very wide and pervasive range of military or militaristic modes of thinking' somewhat different from the more conventional and obvious forms of militarism – conscription, garrison towns, duelling manias and the like – which characterised other European societies before the Great War.[31] So what were they?

In 'The Language of Patriotism 1750–1914'[32] Hugh Cunningham offers one clue. In the third quarter of the nineteenth century racial patriotism called for loyalty to the State, an essential element of imperial ideology. In the Age of this New Imperialism, says Cunningham, the English were continually exhorted to be patriotic. Conservatives of the 1870s constructed a patriotic measuring rod: 'the patriot was above class, loyal to the institutions of the country, and resolute in defence of its honour and interests.'[33] Patriotism was now inseparable from conservatism, militarism, royalism and racialism.

At one point in his argument Cunningham doubts whether among the working class this new emphasis had the effect which was intended: 'There was a sense of the irrelevance of patriotism to most of working-class life.'[34] Later, however, he considers that it was illusory to consider that neither minority criticism nor proletarian interpretation immunized the working class 'in any thorough going way from the virus of right-wing patriotism'.[35] He adds two thoughts of interest to the theme of this chapter; first, patriotism was effectively a classless phenomenon. In chapels, especially Wesleyan Methodist chapels across the land, he remarks, the congregation was now more likely than earlier in the century to hear patriotism being preached from the pulpit. (Thompson's working class community was drawing nearer to the upper middle class community), and second, there was now continuous speculation about the relationship between patriotism and playing field.[36]

III

Within this new climate, a rhetoric of jingoistic conceit in poetry, prose and printing now coalesced into a triadic instrument of propaganda in which the subject of this essay, *the self- sacrificial subaltern* – was celebrated. The sons of the upper middle class could not escape, even if they wished, which was often unlikely, its sustained attack.[37] In *Before the Lamps Went Out*, his autobiography of the years before the Great War, Esmé Wingfield-Stratford provides graphic and startling evidence of the impact of a rampant militarism on the young:

> ... the whole atmosphere of the time seemed to be faintly redolent of gunpowder; ... among those who professed and called themselves gentlefolk in the *fin de siècle* – and I think this would apply to an even wider circle – everybody seemed to be talking about those two linked attractions of war and empire.'[37]

What Thomas Carlyle had insisted, many had come to believe. The national hero was now a warrior and a patriotic death in battle was the finest masculine moral virtue.

Unsurprisingly, therefore, in popular British culture, the image of the military was transformed by the end of the century. Execrated as vicious in 1800, it was eulogized as virtuous in 1900.[38] A shift in role from repressive internal agent of conservatism to external agent of liberalism, a public perception of being sinned against rather than sinning, endorsement by a new confident Christian militarism after 1860, institutional reform after 1870 and imperial expansion account for much of the change in public perception.[39] In the Age of Empire, senior officer, junior officer and common soldier became popular heroes in the public imagination for the basic reason that the perceived nature of imperialism had altered:

> The dominance of soldier heroes ... in popular culture in the last decades of the nineteenth century represented a distinct change of emphasis and accompanied a change in the nature of imperialism. In mid-century 'free trade imperialism' was dominant, the concept of a commercial and maritime empire with minimum territorial responsibilities and maximum profit. But by the time Disraeli proclaimed Queen Victoria Empress of India in 1876 the mood was changing.[40]

There was a practical basis to this change in emphasis from 'free-trade imperialism' to 'militaristic imperialism'. With Russia, France and Germany as challengers, strategically Britain was now on the defensive. In addition, following the Crimean War, the Indian Mutiny and the Jamaica revolt there was a new need for military readiness.[41] Both developments enhanced war and the military in popular culture.

Even more significant to the change in emphasis, however, was the fact that British society was increasingly characterized by a belief in the morality of imperialism.[42] The empire was to be extended as an ethical imperative – and an endorsed militarism was to be the means of extension. Influential imperialists such as Curzon, Balfour, Milner and Rosebery articulated a fully formed imperial creed, with militaristic overtones: 'a creed compounded of the concepts of destiny, duty and service'.[43] They personified the politics of conviction. This conviction grew stronger as the century grew older. Colonial conquest was approved because it would Christianize the pagan and civilize the savage. The military now became an instrument of imperial moral design.[44] A few out of step radicals booed but most, including schoolmasters, academics, artists, poets and novelists, cheered. It was John Ruskin who provided an acceptable moral argument for colonial warfare. His ethical system united art, colonizer, colonized and warrior. Art was a route to moral order, managed landscape depicted in art was order out of chaos, empire was a large-scale managed landscape – 'and force through the colonial campaign was the means to that management'.[45]

The imagery of chivalry penetrated deeply into the fabric of late Victorian culture. The subaltern – the instrument of imperial force? – was now frequently portrayed as a mystic pre-medieval paladin. Imperial heroes were regularly compared to Knights, and Empire was the Holy Grail. Baden Powell's *Scouting for Boys* is heavy with chivalric images. He had originally intended to call his scouts 'The Young Knights of the Empire.'[46] Romantic impulse led Ruskin also to espouse colonial rather than modern war. It offered greater opportunity for individual chivalric heroism. In this view, he was at one with many of his contemporaries.[47] In one regard, Ruskin, however, was quite out of step. In his view 'the knight has a shield and sword, not a bat and ball.' For Ruskin sport was not war and war was not sport. Many differed with him – not least the plethora of public school officers who considered colonial wars more or less as sporting events. Colonial battlefields were exotic versions of the playing fields of Eton and elsewhere.

War for many subalterns was a game:

> It would be a mistake to imagine that this light–hearted playing with fire had anything in common with the grim blood lust of Continental militarism. Nations with open frontiers, and every fit man a soldier, did not think of war as a game, played between professional teams for the entertainment of the ordinary civilian. But that was just how we, in those roaring 'nineties, did think of it. And though the best, it was only one of many games.[48]

And while the Boer War and the subsequent military reforms of Lord Haldane from 1906 onwards, especially his creation of a Territorial Army reserve, stimulated more extensive and systematic military training in the public school, as E. S. Turner has explained there was little danger of officers becoming boringly professional:

> Year after year they were going in for an ever-widening range of sports ... If in this period, as General Fuller would have it, sport developed into a 'pestilence', then the blame must fairly be laid on the officers. Many others have criticised the British officer on the ground that his obsession with games encourages him to look on war in a sporting light ... [but] Such critics have usually minimised the effect played by sport in creating *esprit de corps*, and in revealing those individuals – both officers and men – with stamina and mettle. Other nations failed abjectly to understand the British officer's attitude to sport.[49]

IV

Highly influential agents of indoctrination into militarism, however difficult it may be to measure their influence with any precision, were the prose, 'poetry' and painting that enveloped the public schoolboy at school and at home. The 'triad' preached the glorious virtues of militarism – and projected the sanctified image of the sacrificial subaltern – an elite of martial martyrdom; they were pervasive, smothering, unrelenting. Nowhere, to my knowledge, has there been an attempt to consider at any length and in any systematic way the combined potency of these three elements in the martial mythology of masculinity. It is an overdue task, but first a caveat.

Ours is not an age in any way sensitive or sympathetic to the potency of the militaristic mythologies of late Victorian and Edwardian Britain. Perhaps then it is time to attempt, however inadequately, to understand the passion, power and persuasiveness of the Victorian myths, mythologies and myth-makers as part of a wider attempt to comprehend the nature of common processes of cultural conditioning into masculinity. The lead should be taken from Roy Porter, who attempted in his elegant biography of Gibbon 'to probe the problems and principles of history as they appeared in Gibbon's own time' rather than simply assess him in terms of today's values.[50]

It is a truism to observe that all men, women and children are products of their time as well as of biology and psychology. To appreciate their cultural indoctrination from infant to adult they must be set carefully in the context of their times:

> And the Late-Victorian public schoolboys had grown up at a time when Britain was at her apogee ... They would have been brought up in the nursery on the patriotic verse of Robert Southey and Thomas Campbell. At school their minds would have been moulded by men with the robust and simple-minded patriotism of Charles Kingsley and of William Johnson Cory, that vehement enthusiast who taught so many future members of the ruling class at Eton, not least among them Lord Rosebery and Lord Esher. From schools where they came under the influence of such teachers, this generation passed to universities where they came in contact with professors like John Ruskin.[51]

John MacKenzie claims that the central subjects of major imperial myths such as Henry Havelock, Charles Gordon and T. E. Lawrence were 'essential elements in the culture of imperialism'.[52] They symbolized absolute conviction, collective will and spiritual legitimacy, but above all they were 'iconic figures representative of a masculinity that was martial in essence'. The heroic myths of empire were essentially militaristic and were used to seduce the young into appropriate attitudes and actions. These mythical imperialists were moral symbols, in life and in death. In the eyes of their contemporaries they expanded the moral universe through the defeat of 'barbarism', the rule of Western law, and the extension of Christendom.

They were inspirational stereotypes embodying self-sacrificing service, personifying national nobility, justifying the grandeur of imperialism, and they were model prototypes 'committed unto death, taking on forces, natural or human, that called forth the exercise of an indomitable will, superhuman physical stamina ... an almost miraculous courage'.[53] Finally, in accordance with the Christian paradigm, they secured their ultimate conquest through martyrdom.

In the process of transformation into mythical status, states MacKenzie, 'the most potent hero is the dead hero'. As such he becomes:

> ... an archetype, representing a set of personal qualities and heroic characteristics that are not only supremely valued by his society but are seen by contemporaries and succeeding generations as having major instrumental power. One of the defining aspects of the myth is that it is constantly used in a didactic context, in training the young ... The hero thus becomes not only a moral paradigm but also the exemplar and advocate of policy ...[54]

In the hagiography of imperialism Havelock, Gordon and Lawrence were individual icons, but no less important was the collective icon of the 'sacrificial subaltern' – the subject also of sustained imperial mythology. The Age of the New Imperialism was, as E.S. Turner has reminded us, the period of the subaltern's wars. In Turner's exotic phraseology: 'Dacoit and dervish, mullah and monk and mandarin, fakir and khan, slaver and pirate, the obscene kings of Africa, the chivalrous Maoris, all these defied, and then accepted, the Pax Britannica'.[55] He has remarked, without intentional hyperbole and with perhaps more than a grain of truth,

> It was, as Lord Elton has pointed out, 'an age in which, it almost seemed, any stray detachment of the British Army could be relied on, should occasion demand, and almost as a matter of routine, to produce a junior officer capable of pacifying a frontier, quelling a rebellion or improvising and administering an empire'.[56]

and then added: 'In each subaltern lurked a hope that he, some day, might be able to rule a fierce, proud family with as sure and unchallenged a touch.'[57] True or not, there certainly existed the expectation if not the ambition. It was a myth of some potency.

The source of such imperial myths was not the official mind of imperialism but in its enveloping culture.[58] And it was the culture of the 'community' comprising upper middle class society, the parents of the public schoolboy, and the public school and its masters which created and sustained the image of the sacrificial subaltern as a sacred icon of the late imperial age. This heroic cult required mediators – priests who constructed, interpreted and sustained the myth.[59] These existed inside and outside the schools – as we shall now see. They mastered the presentation of a powerful and simple iconography and passed it passionately on from one generation to the next. It is now time to consider at least some of them.

IV

Certain important aspects of the pre-Great War *Weltanschauung*, it has been suggested, have been lost from sight;[60] in particular, the extent to which British society was *conditioned* to accept militarism as necessary and desirable. Consideration of this conditioning requires a long overdue examination of the ideal of self-sacrificial service inculcated in schools and universities through an investigation of the 'advocative impact' of serious literature.[61]

War, militarism, imperialism and sacrifice are nowhere more idealized than in J.A. Cramb's *Reflections on the Origins and Destiny of Imperial Britain*.[62] In few other period examples of 'serious literature' can the assured conviction of the militaristic imperial zealot be found in more extreme form. For Cramb, the Anglo-Saxon race 'dowered with the genius for empire is compelled to dare all, to suffer all, to sacrifice all for the fulfilment of its fate-appointed task'. And this task was nothing less than 'to subdue the world, to establish there her peace, governing all in justice.[63] Cramb preached this Mandate of Destiny to his students and to the wider public. With bombastic confidence – in style and vision – he recited to them an allegorical fantasy:

> There is an Arab fable of the white steed of Destiny, with the thunder mane and the hoofs of lightning, that to every man, as to every people, comes *once*. Glory to that man, to that race, who dares to mount it! And that steed, is it not nearing England now? Hark! the ringing of its hoofs is borne to our ears on the blast![64]

Imperialism, he told them, is the supreme form of political organization – the acme of a historic linear progression: 'The civic, the feudal, or the oligarchic ... passes into the national, the national into the imperial ... irresistibly, as by a fixed law of nature.'[65] He lost no time in praising the radiance of military martyrdom in pursuit of imperialism. It was not the 'diamonds of the mines' that took British soldiers to South Africa to die: 'No man can believe that,' he wrote, 'The imagination recoils revolted ... it was simply not British.' Cramb saw them 'self-evoted to death, with a courage so impetuous, casting their youth away as if it were a thing of no account, a careless trifle ... to bring imperial justice to the world as a natural presence as normal as air.'[66] Then followed a passage of quite extraordinary euphemistic, credulous and sanguine martial mysticism:

> Fallen in this cause, in battle for this ideal, behold them advance to greet the great dead who fell in the old wars! See, through the mists of time, Valhalla, its towers and battlements, uplift themselves, and from their places the phantoms of the mighty heroes of all ages rise to greet these English youths who enter smiling, the blood yet trickling from their wounds! Behold, Achilles turns, unbending from his deep disdain; Rustin, Timoleon, Hannibal, and those of later days who fell at Brunanburh, Senlac, and Trafalgar, turn to welcome the dead whom we have sent thither as the *avant-garde* of our faith, that in this cause is our destiny, in this the mandate of our fate.[67]

Britain's unique empire up raised by the sword and valour, Cramb warned, could be maintained only by the sword, a death-defiant valour and a heroic self-renunciation.[68] Not only did Cramb acknowledge the existence of militarism, he justified it: 'There is nothing in our annals which warrants evil presage from the spread of militarism, nothing which precludes the hope, the just confidence that our very blood and the ineffaceable character of our race will save us from any mischief that militarism may have brought to others.'[69] Safe, therefore, from the militaristic excesses of lesser races, the Anglo-Saxon would wage war for freedom and justice, exalted by the ideal of Empire and conquering less for herself than for humanity. In turn, the ideal of empire would exalt the soldier – 'hallowing the death on the battlefield with the attributes at once of the hero and the martyr'.[70]

J.A. Cramb addressed students, Sir Henry Newbolt addressed schoolboys; but the message was the same: struggle is inevitable, imperial war is righteous, only the warrior is truly fulfilled. Newbolt's *The Book of The Thin Red Line*, published in 1915, contained 'A Letter to A Boy'. Newbolt wrote, 'I have written you ... a book about soldiers ... all of them were boys, and they took war as boys take their games, with a mixture of fun and deadly earnest: like Ulysses, they enjoyed greatly and suffered greatly.'[71] In his later work, *The Book of the Happy Warrior*,[72] a title borrowed from Wordsworth's famous lines,

> Who is the Happy Warrior? Who is he
> That every man in arms should wish to be?

Newbolt addressed himself 'To All Boys' informing them that he had made available to them, for the first time in the English language, stories of some of the great warriors of history including Roland, Richard Coeur de Lion, St. Louis, King of France, Robin Hood, Bertrand de Guesclin, the Black Prince and Bayard. In reality, however, these stories were merely a means to make a point about modern chivalry and the modern English public schoolboy who, in Newbolt's view, in the admirable pursuit of empire, had 'fought without hatred, and conquered without cruelty, and while doing so had preferred death, and even defeat to the deliberate use of foul means'.[73] There were two great principles of chivalry, Newbolt told his boys of the empire, service to country and membership of a warrior caste – a brotherhood, past and present – founded on chivalrous team games because their great merit was that they made men not bookworms.

This, of course, was a common belief at the time. It was not the exclusive ideological property of Newbolt. In *The New Elizabethans* celebrating the lives of heroes of the Great War, published after it, E. B. Osborn wrote:

> Cricket and football and the other English team-games are modern substitutes for the hard exercises of the mediaeval knights, and if either the hardness or the chivalry goes out of them, then they cease to provide the training in *moral* which is the most vital part of true education. The fact remains that the most important element in war – and in peace for that matter – and the most difficult to make sure of, is the moral element, and for that there is nothing like the old English school tradition which makes so much use of the hard, exhilarating discipline of team-games.[74]

In a chapter entitled 'Chivalry of Today' Newbolt argued that it was left instinctively to the boys outside the classroom to 'keep the traditions of the Knights alive for nearly all English boys are born to a love of fighting and service'. However, with the Boer War a sad truth was out: 'You may get from the playing fields the moral qualities such as leadership and endurance and fair play which are indispensable for war, but you cannot get the scientific training which is also indispensable.'[75] He concluded that if games were to be a thorough training for war they would have to include throwing the bomb as well as the cricket ball and racing not only in boats but in aeroplanes and armoured cars.[76]

Newbolt, like Cramb, was both an admirer and advocate of War. The soldier, providing he is chivalrous, he advised his readers, could find tranquillity, probably for the first time, from 'the sense of service, of brotherhood, of self-sacrifice':[77]

> The time may come when fighting will be infrequent, but so long as there remain in the world wild beasts, savages, manias, autocrats and worshippers of Woden, there will always be the possibility of it, the necessity for the indignant heart and the ready hand. And even if the possibility were done away, man must still keep the soldier's faith, for human life itself is a warfare, in which there is no victory but by the

soldier's virtues, and no security but in their transmission. Peace is given only to the Happy Warrior, in life or in death.[78]

Newbolt ended his book with a typical Newboltian militaristic verse that summarized his message to the young:

Hic Jacet
Qui in hoc saeculo fideliter militavit.
He that has left hereunder
The signs of his release,
Feared not the battle's thunder
Nor hoped that wars should cease;
No hatred set asunder
His warfare from his peace.
Nor feared he in his sleeping
To dream his work undone,
To hear the heathen sweeping
Over the lands he won;
For he has left in keeping
His sword unto his son.[79]

VI

The glorification of war in juvenile fiction was a feature of late Victorian and Edwardian Britain and has been extensively discussed. It requires only relatively brief consideration here. Throughout the last quarter of the nineteenth century and later it was unquestionably a powerful means of disseminating messages of intoxicating militarism in an imperial setting. Few sources of imperial sentiment were as inspiring. Throughout the year the ardour of young imperialists was fanned by dozens of illustrated periodicals containing an enticing array of imperialistic articles and stories. And every Christmas hundreds of adventure stories appeared which 'romanticised and glorified the exploits of British empire builders'.[80]

The novels sold in their thousands while the periodicals sold in their millions.[81] The incredible popularity of juvenile militaristic fiction is made very clear by Wingfield-Stratford:

It was extraordinary what an amount of matter came from the press to feed this craving for bellicosity. I took in, at different times during this period, no less than three sumptuously illustrated fortnightly publications, bound volumes of which I still have – *British Battles, Battles of the Nineteenth Century,* and *Wars of the 'Nineties.* Such literature must have commanded a huge sale before it could have become a paying proposition; I never remember anything of the kind having been attempted since.[82]

Popular literature for boys was a medium as much as a mirror. It promoted as much as reflected imperial involvement. It developed an awareness of an imperial responsibility. And it was a responsibility boys accepted. It excited their imagination; and offered them instruction in a faith that was at one and the same time reassuring and stimulating.[83]

Magazines and weeklies for boys of the middle and upper middle classes containing serialized novels of England and Empire with tales of war, sport and adventure first appeared in the 1860s.[84] They were introduced as an antidote to the allegedly sensational and unacceptable weekly 'penny dreadfuls'. They included *The Boys' Own Magazine, Young England, Chatterbox, The Boy's Journal* and *Every Boy's Magazine*. In the 1870s *The Boys' Own Paper* appeared. It became 'something of a national institution'[85] and it has been described 'as the most important and influential children's periodical ever to have appeared in Britain'.[86] It employed the most famous children's writers and illustrators of the time and had 'the highest circulation of any boy's paper in the Victorian age'.[87] The first number of *B.O.P.* – indeed the first pages – contained a short story 'My First Football Match'. It concerned the initiation of a new boy at his public school 'into the code of behaviour of an elite'. It was certainly no accident 'that the qualities informing this story – courage, determination, team spirit – were presented in the context of the playing-field of a public school.'[88] Here, of course, was the famed location of training in imperial leadership. In time, the great writers of the period novels for boys – W. H. Kingston, R. M. Ballantyne, G. M. Fenn and G. A. Henty – and indeed many more, wrote for the B.O.P. and 'many of their serialised novels were set in far-flung corners of the Empire where might was right, duty was duty, and native unrest was put down by the application of 'the glorious British upper-cut coupled with the glorious English maxim gun'.[91] In the early 1890s *Chums* was published by Cassell and Company and became 'a paper with a strong pro-Empire line in both its fiction and non-fiction departments'[90] and with the self-appointed task of expatiating upon 'the soldier-like instincts of British Boys'.

Other story papers for boys appeared in the 1890s were published by Alfred Harmsworth, who by virtue of modernity and price, eventually dominated the market: *Marvel* (1893), *Union Jack* (1894), *Pluck* (1894) and *The Boy's Friend* (1895). *Pluck*, with its emphasis on the deeds and bravery of founder of the empire and those still expanding its borders, and with its plea for a course of Empire-related studies and cadet training for all boys, was an efficient mouthpiece for the jingoism of the age.[91] However, *The Boys of Our Empire* published between 1900 and 1903, was arguably the most jingoistic of all the juvenile periodicals, and exuded a 'bellicose, boisterous mood of imperialism'.[92]

During the Boer War, a flood of new periodicals appeared while the established periodicals were replete with details of the campaign. It is an interesting fact that the violence so abhorred by the middle and upper middle classes in the Penny Dreadfuls seemed wholly acceptable – indeed legitimate – in their approved magazines in an imperial setting![93] The most famous of the boys' writers was G. A. Henty. Few would disagree with Roy Turnbaugh's description of him as 'a publicist for the British Empire, [and] a recruiting officer for a generation of schoolboys'.[94] The main features of Henty novels, says Turnbaugh, is his preference for killing rather than wounding (more final, less troublesome), the cool, casual nature of the violence and the aggressive nationalism: for Henty the Empire was 'won and held by force of arms'[95] and the purpose of conquest was the 'unrestrained quest for glory'.[96]

Not all of Henty's young heroes are public schoolboys but they are all well-born, strong and courageous. Henty was a publicist for robust and reticent masculinity as much as empire. 'He had a horror of a lad who displayed any weak emotion and shrank from shedding blood, or winced at any encounter.'[97] For Henty, at least in his stories, the empire was essentially a ritualistic theatre of war. His heroes, after passing through the trial of battle, invariably return successful from Empire to England. Imperial wars in effect were 'rites of passage' into manhood.[98]

Henty's books are, therefore, militaristic romances, as Jeffrey Richards states,[99] conforming to the timeless qualities of the Romantic novel, as outlined by Northrop Frye – sensational, unambiguous, hierarchical, conservative, mystical, chivalric with a clear, moral message and a strong didactic purpose – in this case to perpetuate an Anglo-Saxon imperial cadre committed to domination at home and abroad in the moral interest of itself and others. It alone had access to a chivalric code. Henty was an unabashed racist[100] who subscribed to the view that the Anglo-Saxon was superior in all important aspects to any other comparable racial or cultural group in the world The Empire was where the young Briton fulfilled his destiny as 'schoolboy master of the world' – more often than not behind the barrel of a revolver or the blade of a sword. Henty was 'in step with the mood of an age in which militarism and hero-worship marched hand in hand. Britain's imperial wars supplied an endless succession of military heroes who became household names. Henty deployed them in his books as imperial icons, blessing and promoting, praising and preserving his boy heroes: Gordon, Wolseley, Kitchener, Roberts, Baden-Powell.'[101]

As propagandist for a cause, Henty had the essential quality of confident certainty:

> Henty's imperialism suffers from no sudden doubts about the
> legitimacy of violence; his conviction of English superiority is visited
> with no qualms about the failure of most Englishmen to live up to their
> Christian profession, and his racial generalisations make a simple
> dichotomy between 'us' and 'them' untroubled by any Christian
> conviction that all men are equal.[102]

He gave his young readers a sure sense of the moral, cultural and racial duty
of what Cecil Rhodes called 'the first race in the world' and they responded
'by devouring his works with relish'.[103]

Henty, says Richards, is the acknowledged king of boys' writers of the
late Victorian period. Memoirs are full of references to his centrality to
boyhood reading. And since literature exposes the inward thoughts of a
generation, Henty is essential reading for the social historian.[104] Huttenback
claims that Henty was read by virtually all boys who grew up at the turn of
the century and by most of the generation that followed. Consequently his
books are significant as social commentary if not literature.[105] The juvenile
literature of 1880s and 1890s was saturated in heroic military imagery.
Henty was one of many who were products of, propagandists for, and
monuments to a concept of empire that emerged then and, contrary to what
is often alleged by historians, survived at least into the Thirties.[106]

A war paranoia gripped the Britain of the late Victorian–Edwardian
period. Symptomatic of this and a feature of the time were invasion novels.
The most famous and by far the earliest of which was Sir George Tomkyns
Chesney's *Battle of Dorking*, published in 1871, written to expose the
inadequacies of Britain's defences. By the turn of the century dozens
appeared every year.[107] Invasion stories became frequent ingredients of Lord
Northcliffe's Amalgamated Press juvenile periodicals. Northcliffe shared
his obsession of invasion with Dr Gordon Stables, one of the most famous
of all writers for boys on the themes of empire, militarism and adventure,
who at one time was more popular than Henty. In his book *The Meteor Flag
of England: or, The Story of a Coming Conflict* serialized in *The Captain* in
1905, the combined strengths of the Boys' Brigade and the Church Lads
Brigade rebuff the invasion force of French, German and Prussians who had
defeated the British army. As Patrick Dunae remarks, 'The prospect was
unlikely, but the message was clear. Since adult authorities were unwilling
to take the lead it was up to boys to prepare for the impending crisis.'[108]

To a degree lack of preparation for a European war characterized the
juvenile press in the Edwardian era. Young patriots had new responsibilities
and new anxieties. There were, says Dunae, important differences between
late Victorian and Edwardian adventure stories: 'The former were assertive

and confident, while the latter were insular and xenophobic.'[109] The explanation lay in social tensions in Britain, political unrest in Europe, and the growing naval and military strength of Germany. These factors, coupled with the memory of Britain's military reverses in South Africa, contributed to the anxious, self-conscious mood which pervaded the spy stories, the aerial adventures and the futuristic tales of invasion. Vigilance was the key word in boys' literature during the years which immediately preceded the Great War, and readers must have realized that they were being exhorted to prepare for the defence of Great Britain – not for the expansion of Greater Britain.

Before leaving the world of juvenile literature it should not be overlooked that the success of the publishing enterprises for boys of Samuel O. Beeton, Routledge, Ward, Lock and Company, George Newnes, Cassell and Company, the Religious Tract Society and the Harmsworth Brothers was made possible by rapid industrialization between 1850 and 1914 which 'brought with it a doubling of population, a rise in living standards, a nearly universal literacy and an increase in leisure time'.[110] And with these developments 'came an explosion in printing technology – steam power, rotary presses, mechanical typesetting, wood pulp paper'.[111] The result was the reduced costs of books and newspapers, an increase in readership and more time for reading, and in consequence 'the printed word assumed a paramount role in moulding opinion. With paper production in England up sixfold between 1860 and 1900, with posters running off presses at 10,000 copies per hour, with the cost of a pulp-paper book dropping to as low as one penny, only a blind man or an illiterate could escape the bombardment of words.'[112]

VI

In the late Victorian and Edwardian Britain 'military heroism and the martial spirit, service and sacrifice suffused popular poetry'.[113]

This poetry of martial patriotism was written by an extraordinary wide group of patriots – including, in not always exclusive categories, major poets, minor poets, poet laureates, schoolmasters and schoolboy poets, obscure citizen poets and hitherto mostly neglected women poets. They are numbered in their hundreds. The most famous included Kipling, Newbolt, Conan Doyle, George Barlow, Francis Doyle and W.E. Henley and the poet laureates Alfred Lord Tennyson, Alfred Austin and Robert Bridges.[114]

It is seldom appreciated how complete was the support for martial masculinity by those 'unacknowledged legislators of the world', as Shelley once called poets. *Lord God of Battles*, a war anthology compiled by A.E. Manning Foster in 1914, contained poems on warriors and war by

Tennyson, Campbell, Wordsworth, Austin and Gerard Manley Hopkins.[115]
Hopkins, Jesuit ascetic, contributed a verse entitled 'What Shall I Do?':

> Where is the field I must play the man on?
> O welcome there their steel or cannon.
> Immortal beauty is death with duty,
> If under her banner I fall for her honour.[116]

While Alfred Austin, in the same volume, asserted:

> So long as flashes England's steel,
> And English trumpets shrill,
> So long as One Flag floats and dares?
> So long as the One Race dares and grows?
> Death – what is death but God's own rose?
> Let the bugles of England play
> Over the hills and far away![117]

Well into the Great War, and indeed after it, ordinary and obscure men and
women, deeply moved by tragic events, struggled to put a naive and intense
patriotism into verse – of a sort, that owed nothing to the perceptions and
experiences of the celebrated war poets, but spoke still of a sacrificial,
obligatory duty:

> For he died for England's sake
> If thou so live
> If thou so give
> That road thyself shall take.[118]

and the nobility, honour and fearlessness of 'golden boys':

> These happy boys who left the football field,
> The hockey ground, the river, the eleven,
> In a far grimmer game, with high elated souls,
> To score their goals.[119]

The icons were preserved. Perhaps they needed to be. For the many, rather
than the few, their retained sacredness was a means of existing with horror,
death and loss.

   Women versifiers of the Great War were numerous but have been mostly
ignored. *Scars Upon My Heart*,[120] edited by Catherine Reilly and published
in 1981, sought to remedy this situation. Her voices from the past all mourn
for the dead. Reilly admits, perhaps reluctantly, that 'sentimentality and
patriotism certainly went together during the Great War years'. Now, she
states correctly, 'we have less time for Rupert Brooke and his solemn young
heroism'. We hear only Sassoon and Owen – 'reluctant heroes [who] both
stayed submissive to the high-minded macho ethic of the English officer'.[121]

The self-protective emotional reticence of male combatants draws far less sympathy from Reilly than the expressed emotions of female non-combatants. In their verse, she writes, patriotism and religion became inter-changeable. The soldier became Christ crucified, as in Alice Meynall's elegiac 'Summer in England, 1914' which ends:

Chide thou no more, O thou unsacrificed!
The soldier dying dies upon a cross,
The very cross of Christ.[122]

'This,' remarks Reilly, most perceptively in my view, 'is the poetry of England, inalienable from Honour, Duty, God, Christ and Sacrifice', celebrating not war but the sacrifice of youth – a sacrifice expressed with gratitude: 'All flows from Duty'. Reilly herself read many of these patriotic poems with mixed emotion. They read to her of neither superficiality nor hypocrisy but of 'fearsome desperate nobility'. She fails to make the point, however, which should be made – that this acceptance of 'the rightfulness of Sacrifice' was the legacy of history.

Reilly offers us poems of both patriotism and protest – and, as she says, 'many thoughtful stirring in between'; but patriotism received her closest attention – there is simply more of it, and she seems to find it inexplicable. She gives little space, however, to Katherine Tynan in her volume, yet she is in 'the purest chantress of war' as a source of patriotic sacrifice. For Tynan the Great War offered the fullest opportunity for the exercise of chivalric heroism:

Pinks and syringa in the garden closes,
And the sweet privet hedge and golden roses,
The pines hot in the sun, the drone of the bee,
They die in Flanders to keep these for me.[123]

Her war verse is suffused with a Malorian neo-medievalism:

Paradise now has many a Knight,
Many a lordkin, many lords.
Glimmer of armour, dinted and bright,
The young Knights have put on new swords.[124]

While her public schoolboys are Arthurian heroes from the pages of Tennyson's 'Idylls of the King':

As they pass without a sound, there is many a red wound.
Oh, pale they are and faint they are, these warriors renowned!
Yet smiling all together in the calm sweet weather,
As they ride home together.[125]

and

I hear his impatient charger neighing,
I hear the trumpets blow afar!
His comrades ride, as to a Maying,
Jesting and splendid to the war.[126]

For others, like Nora Griffith in her verse 'The Wykamist', however, the public school subaltern had a more immediate historical reality:

... A year ago your heard Cathedral's chime.

You hurried up to books – a year ago;
Shouted for 'Houses' in New Field below.
... You ... 'died of wounds' ... they told me
... yet your feet
Pass with the others down the twilit street.[127]

One year after the end of the Great War, John S. Arkwright published a small volume of verses, *The Supreme Sacrifice and Other Poems in Time of War*.[128] It was unusual in that it contained both words and illustrations – jointly epitomizing a militaristic ethos that had come to maturity in 1914. Most of the verses were written in the *concluding* stages of the war – but all were written during it – and were reprinted in the order of their date forming 'a loosely connected series', which he wrote, 'may serve to recall something of the successive emotions felt by the Nation at home during the progress of the struggle'. These emotions were a mixture of admiration, sorrow and acceptance. The first poem, from which the volume takes its title, 'The Supreme Sacrifice', was predictable in its romantic imagery of martial courage and contentment in sacrificial death:

These were His servants; in His steps they trod
Following through death the martyr'd Son of God:
Victor He rose; victorious too shall rise
They who have drunk His cup of Sacrifice.[129]

Equally predictably in *The Supreme Sacrifice* the soldier became a seraphic Knight of Christ:

He lifts the Cross, he draws the blade,
He gives his manhood – scarce begun;
God shield him till the set of sun
On this the holiest, last Crusade![130]

His Bunyonesque progress through his Valley of Despair, in God's safe-keeping, was through the battle-scarred roads of Flanders:

But Truth and Honour nerve his arm,

And Faith is yet his shield and stay;
And God will save his soul from harm
Who dares to tread the Pilgrim's Way.[131]

These versifiers, largely unknown, have their place in history. They are not to be dismissed by virtue of their crude metre, stilted language or conventional expression. Whatever their literary qualities, they are genuine voices of period idealism. It can only be fully understood by reference to them, and others like them.

VIII

'The visual is sorely undervalued in modern scholarship', Camille Paglia has claimed, with the result that literature and art remain unmeshed.[132] Whatever the present relationship between literature and art, throughout the second half of the nineteenth century, 'the heroic image of the army and of war conjured up by the words of the war correspondents was given visual life by the work of war artists and battle illustrators'.[133] Literature and art were one in their depiction of the heroic dead. Furthermore, the period from 1874 until 1914 witnessed a marked increase in the number of battle paintings in public exhibitions, while the period 1885 to 1914 saw a graphic increase in the production of celebrations of the military glory of the empire.[134]

War artists, studio painters, campaign painters and engravers depicted the images of imperial war for public consumption. These images, as befitted an age besotted with Camelot, presented the young officer in empire as an Arthurian knight errant. However, he owed as much to the playing field as the tilting yard. A boyish British officer appeared in quantity in Academy paintings in the 1890s. The works of Richard Caton-Woodville, for example, who painted the Zulu War of 1879, the Invasion of Egypt of 1882, the Sudan expeditions of 1885 and 1896–98, the Matabele and Boer Wars and the Chitrel campaign, portrayed the schoolboy officer, 'exhibiting sporting dash'.[135]

And among some of the most striking examples of the 'manliness' genre typical of the period were pictures of sport and sportsmen carrying an 'unspoken assumption that sport is the best preparation for battle'.[136] As Wingfield-Stratford has recorded:

To anyone born in the twentieth century it must seem incredible that there was actually a time, within living memory, when war was regarded almost in the light of a glorified test match – a thrill of all thrills, more to be looked forward to than feared.[137]

The Victorians greatly respected and invariably required earnest moral messages. War, as depicted by the war painters, was valued largely for 'its expression of warrior qualities' portrayed in scenes of individual heroism, sacrifice, glory and pathos.[138] Two of the most famous paintings of the sacrificial subaltern were Elizabeth Thompson, Lady Butler's 'Floreat Etona' and Alphonse De Neville's 'Saving the Colours'. 'Floreat Etona!' (the title is the motto of Eton College) was painted in 1882 and depicts two Etonian subalterns in a charge at Laing's Neck in the First Transvaal War. Alphonse De Neuville's 'Saving the Colours' records the efforts of Lieutenants Melville and Coghill to save the colours of the 29th at the Battle of Isandhlwana. Both paintings deal with disasters – Elwes, Melville and Coghill were all killed. Bravery in death was what mattered: it led to ultimate triumph – for others, and the dead.

War as pictorial journalism appeared first in the *Illustrated London News* in 1842. It was also a feature of *The Graphic* founded in 1869. Both gave extensive coverage to British colonial wars which became the most important single subject in both papers: 'Military scenes formed nearly 40 per cent of all illustrations in an average year from 1875, and almost every issue carried news and illustrations of the campaigns being fought in outposts of empire.'[139] Although photography pre-dated pictorial journalism, artists continued to paint war and battle, partly, R.T. Stearns has suggested, 'because they could fulfil the public's expectations of the heroic'.[140] He added that illustrated news items were, in all probability, the most influential of painted scenes of war. Artists such as Melton Prior, Frederick Villiers, Archibald Forbes and Frank Viozetelly shared and presented the conventional view of war, based on 'a warrior ethos and acceptable attitudes to heroes and to death'.[141] Images of war were dramatic. In sketches with both brush and pen they portrayed dead and wounded in a style that omitted the horror and the suffering. Stearns reports that Villiers, wrote of the dead highlanders at Tel-el-Kebir as 'resting in easy attitudes on the desert as if in deep slumber'.[142] These deaths, and the stylized deaths of Melville and Coghill, were acceptable to the public, the public schoolboy and his parents. Pacifists, remarks Stearns, alleged that they misrepresented war![143] And there is no doubt that there was deceit in the depiction. The prose, poetry and painting of subaltern self-sacrifice presented a carefully sanitized view of warfare. It adhered to stylistic conventions – a euphemistic imagery distancing, reader and viewer from the reality of conflict.

The boys' magazines of the period frequently borrowed from the illustrated news weeklies. Consequently illustrations in the magazines included pictorial representations of Victorian officer heroes of fiction and fact. In *Chums* (volume 2, 1893–94) the frontispiece was of an officer standing, revolver in one hand and sword in the other, defending a wounded comrade in a desperate last stand. This illustration, in adapted form, was carried on the spine of *Chums* annuals from 1893 to 1908.[144] In the view of Robert H. MacDonald, the illustration symbolized imperial masculinity: manhood is fighting, fighting means dying, dying is sanctified by chivalric brotherhood. Through such imagery, courage, loyalty, duty and patriotism were given iconographic form. It constituted a visual vocabulary of martial patriotism.[145] MacDonald is convinced that *Chums* attempted through its constant heroic images of battle 'the social reproduction of aggressive virility linking 'the battles of the playing field to the glorious sport of war, repeating the familiar theme of Newbolt's Vitaiï Lampada with its twinned scenes of the cricket match and the last stand in the desert'.[146]

There is a final set of martial images to be reviewed before the consideration of visual indoctrination is complete. The illustrations in books for boys. One example must suffice – Newbolt's *The Book of The Thin Red Line*. The pictures of The Charge of the Scots Greys (at Waterloo), The Third Light Dragoons Charging the Sikh Guns (at Aliwal), The 78th Highlanders at Lucknow and The 9th Lancers at Chillean Wallah are all 'close ups' of apparently fearless officers – images for imitation, and models for life. Mary Cowling has suggested that much of the appeal of Victorian art, painting and illustration was anthropological – in the sense that the physical man revealed the moral man. To this end, the human face and figure were invested with a special significance – which today we no longer recognize.[147] It is a point of view worth reflecting upon.

IX

Alan Swingeword has argued that it is literature, in literate societies, that carries a major responsibility for establishing and sustaining the communal symbolism necessary for the survival of ideologies: 'the 'styles' and 'forms' of living, dying, fighting and mating, is taught us in modern society through literary depictions'.[148] The argument may also be usefully extended to include art – and now the media. Structuralists like Roland Barthes have argued that the 'language' of a culture, defined as its *whole* system of signs, reflects the culture. However, it has been suggested that 'refraction' with its implications of a more subtle relationship, is a more useful term than 'reflection'. Others, yet again, press for a more active role of 'language' in society, as an agent of change, conservation, dominance or resistance. All these points of view are concerned with cultural 'signs' as forms of power – both direct and indirect: Levi-Strauss's aphorism, 'we do not think with myths but myths think themselves in us', is apposite here.

These brief reflections raise the issue of the role of system of signs in creating social reality. More specifically, it raises the question of the influence of the militaristic 'language' of late Victorian and Edwardian Britain. There is no way, of course, to measure with any accuracy the impact of images of war as a game, battlefields as playing fields and conflict as a match on schoolboy minds just as 'there is no way to measure precisely ... the effect of militant literary [and artistic] outpouring upon actual historical events'.[151] C. D. Eby suggests that probably in most cases the writer, and we will add the painter, like sensitive radar, responds to frequencies already pulsating in the ether[152] – and that in the period before 1914 popular literature, and we will add art, was so steeped in militant nationalism that the Great War, when it finally arrived, came like an ancient prophecy at last fulfilled.[153] Whatever the truth of this assertion, the intention here has been to present the ideals, arguments and images of the writers and painters of late nineteenth- and early twentieth-century military patriotism rather more fully than is customary today, but much more than this, to suggest that they played a not insignificant part in the indoctrination of an elite community of sacrificial subalterns from the upper middle class, and imbued them with an uncomplicated concept of patriotism, imperialism and masculinity.

Of course, within the elite and within society some responded avidly, some less avidly, some remained unconvinced, some became disenchanted, but it is reasonable to claim that many were convinced of the appropriateness of the projected martial image of masculinity.

And this image was functional in at least three critical respects: it produced young men confident of their duty to fight and die; it offered psychological support for the bereft; it provided a martial culture to facilitate and sustain imperial expansion.

It could be argued that in the age of empire the imagery of militarism was a cultural imperative and the nature of the imagery of militarism was a necessary deception; to revisit Gilmore, it socialized upper middle-class schoolboys into a 'male nurturing role' appropriate to the period, and it disguised, sanctified and glorified their death in battle, assuring society of the appropriateness of their sacrifice.

NOTES

1. E. P. Thompson, *The Making of the English Working Class* (New York: Vintage, 1963).
2. Jeffrey C. Alexander, 'Analytical Debates: Understanding the Relative Autonomy of Culture', in Jeffrey C. Alexander and Steven Seidman (eds.), *Culture and Society: Contemporary Debates* (Cambridge, 1990), p.21.
3. Ibid.
4. Ibid.
5. David D. Gilmore, *Manhood in the Making: Cultural Concepts of Masculinity* (New Haven: Yale University Press, 1990).

6. Ibid, p.1.
7. Ibid., p.90.
8. Ibid. p.23.
9. Clark McCauley, 'Conference Overview', in Jonathan Hass (ed.), *The Anthropology of War* (Cambridge: Cambridge University Press, 1990), p.2.
10. Ibid., p.7.
11. Ibid., p.8.
12. Gilmore, *Manhood in the Making*, p.223.
13. Ibid.
14. Ibid., p.230.
15. Ibid., p.18.
16. Correlli Barnett, 'The Education of Male Elites', in *Journal of Contemporary History*, 2, 3 (1967), 15.
17. Ibid., p.15.
18. See John Gooch, 'Attitudes to War in late Victorian and Edwardian England', in Brian Bond and Ian Roy (eds.), *War and Society: A Year Book of Military History* (London: Croom Helm, 1975), p.87.
19. Geoffrey Best, 'Militarism and the Victorian Public School', in Brian Simon and Ian Bradley, *The Victorian Public School* (Dublin: Gill and Macmillan, 1975), p.130
20. Anne Summers, 'Militarism in Britain before the Great War', in *History Workshop Journal*, 2 (1976), 107.
21. Michael Howard, 'Empire, Race and War in pre–1914 Britain', in Hugh Lloyd Jones *et al.* (eds.), *History and Imagination, Essays in Honour of H. R. Trevor Roper* (London: Duckworth, 1981), p.343.
22. Gooch, 'Attitudes to War', p.88.
23. See Jeffrey Richards, 'Popular Imperialism and the Image of the Army in Juvenile Literature', in John M. MacKenzie (ed.), *Popular Imperialism and the Military 1850–1950*, pp.5–6 (Manchester: Manchester University Press, 1992), pp.85–6.
24. John M. MacKenzie, 'Introduction' to *Popular Imperialism and the Military 1850–1950*.
25. Quoted by Richards in 'Popular Imperialism and the Image of the Army', p.86.
26. Gooch, 'Attitudes to War', p.91.
27. Quoted by Richards in 'Popular Imperialism and the Image of the Army', p.86.
28. Summers, 'Militarism in Britain before the Great War', p.120.
29. O. Anderson, 'The Growth of Christian Militarism in Mid–Victorian Britain', in *English Historical Review*, 86 (1971), 46.
30. Summers, 'Militarism in Britain', 105–6.
31. Ibid., p.105.
32. Hugh Cunningham, 'The Language of Patriotism 1750–1914' in *History Workshop Journal*, 12 (1981), 8–33.
33. Ibid., p.24.
34. Ibid., p.23
35. Ibid.
36. Ibid., p.24.
37. Esmé Wingfield-Stratford, *Before the Lamps Went Out* (London: Hodder and Stoughton, 1945), p.74.
38. MacKenzie, 'Introduction', p.1.
39. Richards, 'Popular Imperialism and the Image of the Army', pp.84–7.
40. Ibid., p.84.
41. Ibid, p.85.
42. Ibid.
43. Richards, 'Popular Imperialism', p.88.
44. MacKenzie, 'Introduction', p.5.
45. Ibid.
46. Richards, 'Popular Imperialism', p.87.
47. MacKenzie, 'Introduction', p.6.

48. Wingfield-Stratford, *Before the Lamps Went Out*, p.78.
49. E. S. Turner, *Gallant Gentlemen: A Portrait of the British Officer 1600–1956* (London: Michael Joseph 1956), p.269.
50. Roy Porter, *Edward Gibbon: Making History* (London: Weidenfeld and Nicolson, 1988), p.iv.
51. Howard, 'Empire, Race and War', p.341.
52. John MacKenzie, 'Heroic Myths of Empire', in MacKenzie (ed.), *Popular Imperialism and the Military*, p.134.
53. Ibid., p.113.
54. Ibid., p.112.
55. Turner, *Gallant Gentlemen*, p.246.
56. Ibid.
57. Ibid., p.250.
58. John MacKenzie, 'Heroic Myths of Empire', p.109.
59. See J.A. Mangan, 'Moralists, Metaphysicians and Mythologists: The 'Signifiers' of a Victorian and Edwardian Sub-culture', in Susan J. Bundy, *Coreobus Triumphs: The Alliance of Sport and the Arts* (San Diego: SDSU Press, 1988), pp.141–62.
60. Gooch, 'Attitudes to War', pp.88–93.
61. Ibid., p.89.
62. J.A. Cramb, *Reflections on the Origins and Destiny of Imperial Britain* (London: Macmillan, 1900).
63. Ibid., p.17.
64. Ibid., p.35.
65. Ibid., p.132.
66. Ibid., p.35.
67. Ibid., p.36.
68. Ibid.
69. Ibid., p.154.
70. Ibid., pp.160–1.
71. Sir Henry Newbolt, *The Book of The Thin Red Line* (London: Longman's Green and Co, 1915), pp.v–vi.
72. Sir Henry Newbolt, *The Book of the Happy Warrior* (London: Longmans, Green and Co, 1917), p.256.
73. Ibid., p.256.
74. E.B. Osborn, *The New Elizabethans* (London: John Lane, 1919), p.2.
75. Newbolt, *The Book of the Happy Warrior*, p.222.
76. Ibid., p.274.
77. Ibid., p.275.
78. Ibid., p.279.
79. Ibid., p.283.
80. P.A. Dunae, 'Boys Literature and the Idea of Empire 1870–1914', *Victorian Studies*, 24 (Autumn 1980), 105.
81. Dunae, 'Boys' Literature', p.106.
82. Wingfield-Stratford, *Before the Lamps Went Out*, p.76.
83. Dunae, 'Boys' Literature', p.106.
84. *Penny Dreadfuls and Comics* (London: Victoria and Albert Museum, 1983), p.41.
85. Ibid., p.42.
86. Patrick Dunae, *'The Boys' Own Paper:* Origins and Editorial Policies', in *The Private Library,* Vol. 9 (Winter 1976).
87. *Penny Dreadfuls,* p.42.
88. *Penny Dreadfuls,* p.43. The story was by Talbot Baines Reed.
89. *Penny Dreadfuls,* p.43.
90. Ibid., p.42.
91. Ibid., p.52.
92. Dunae, 'Boys' Literature', p.112.

93. *Penny Dreadfuls*, p.43.
94. Roy Turnbaugh, 'Images of Empire: George Alfred Henty and John Buchan', *Journal of Popular Culture*, 9 (1975),.734.
95. Ibid., p.736.
96. Ibid., p.735.
97. Jeffrey Richards quoting Henty's contemporary, friend and biographer George Manville Fenn in 'With Henty to Africa', in Jeffrey Richards (ed.), *Imperialism and Juvenile Literature* (Manchester: Manchester University Press, 1989), pp.70–1.
98. Turnbaugh, 'Images of Empire', p.735.
99. Richards, 'With Henty to Africa', p.75.
100. Turnbaugh, 'Images of Empire', p.735.
101. Richards, 'With Henty to Africa', p.82–8.
102. J. S. Bratton, *The Impact of Victorian Children's Fiction* (London: Croom Helm, 1981), pp.197–8.
103. Richards, 'With Henty to Africa', p.103.
104. Ibid., p.73.
105. A. Huttenback, 'G. A. Henty and the Visions of Empire', *Encounter*, 35 (1970), 47.
106. Richards, 'Popular Imperialism', p.81.
107. Dunae, 'Boys Literature', p.119.
108. Ibid.
109. Ibid., p.121.
110. Cecil Debrotte Eby, *The Road to Armageddon: The Martial Spirit in English Popular Literature, 1870–1914* (Durham, Duke University Press, 1987), p.4.
111. Ibid.
112. Ibid.
113. Richards, 'Popular Imperialism', p.81.
114. Tennyson (1850–92), Austin (1896–1913), Bridges (1913–30).
115. A. E. Manning-Foster, *Lord God of Battles* (London, Cope and Fenwick, 1914).
116. Gerard M. Hopkins, 'What Shall I Do', in Foster, *Lord God of Battles*, p.35.
117. Alfred Austin, 'Is Life Worth Living', in Foster, *Lord God of Battles*, p.51.
118. H. Fielding-Hall, 'The Heroes Road', in *For England* (London: Constable, 1916), p.108.
119. W. M. Letts, *The Spires of Oxford* (New York: E. P. Dutton, 1917), p.16.
120. Catherine Reilly (ed.), *Scars Upon My Heart* (London: Virago, 1981).
121. Reilly, *Scars*, p.xvi.
122. Ibid., p.xviii.
123. Katherine Tynan, 'High Summer' in *The Holy War* (London: Sedgwick and Jackson, 1916), p.43.
124. Katherine Tynan, 'New Heaven', in *The Holy War*, p.48.
125. Tynan, 'Riding Home', in *The Holy War*, p.49.
126. Katherine Tynan, 'The Bride' in *Flower of Youth: Poems in War Time* (London: Sedgwick and Jackson, 1915), p.20.
127. Nora Griffiths, 'The Wykhamist', in Reilly, *Scars Upon My Heart*, p.44.
128. John S. Arkwright, *The Supreme Sacrifice and Other Poems in Time of War* (London: Skeffington, 1919).
129. Arkwright, *Supreme Sacrifice*, p.18.
130. Ibid., p.79.
131. Ibid., p.26.
132. Camille Paglia, *Sexual Personae* (Cambridge: Yale University Press, 1990), pp.33–4.
133. Richards, 'Popular Imperialism', p.83.
134. J.W.M. Hichberger, *Images of the Army: The Military in British Art 1815–1914* (Manchester: Manchester University Press, 1988), p.75.
135. MacKenzie, 'Introduction', p.17.
136. Paul Usherwood, 'Officer Material: Representations of Leadership in Late Nineteenth-Century British Battle Paintings', in John M. MacKenzie, *Popular Imperialism and the Military 1850–1950*, p.173.

38   TRIBAL IDENTITIES

137. Wingfield-Stratford, *Before the Lamps Went Out*, p.78.
138. R.T. Stearns 'War and the Media in the 19th Century: Victorian Military, Artists and the Image of War, 1870–1914', in *Journal of the Royal Military Service Institute for Defence Studies*, 131 (Sept. 1986), p.61.
139. Hichberger, *Images of the Army*, p.75.
140. Stearns, 'War and the Media', p.56.
141. Ibid., p.58.
142. Ibid.
143. Ibid.
144. Robert, H. MacDonald, 'Signs from the Imperial Quarter: Illustrations in Chums 1892–1914', in *Children's Literature*, Vol.16 (1988), pp.31 passim.
145. Ibid., p.33.
146. Ibid. p.46.
147. Mary C. Cowling, 'The Artist as Anthropologist in Mid-Victorian England ...' *Art History*, 6, 4 (Dec. 1983), 461.
148. Peter Burke and Roy Porter, *The Social History of Language* (Cambridge: Cambridge University Press, 1987), pp.12–17.
149. Eby, *The Road to Armageddon*, p.7.
150. Ibid., pp.7–8.
151. Ibid., p.1–8.

Contrasting Nationalisms: Sport, Militarism and the Unitary State in Britain and France before 1914

RICHARD HOLT

Comparing the role of sport in the development of nationalism in Britain and France one is immediately struck by the diversity of forms of national feeling and the flexibility of sport in expressing such differences; the late nineteenth century saw the emergence of the 'new nationalism' based upon a potent cocktail of forces: better education and literacy combined with the rise of popular politics; the new racial theories of 'the survival of the fittest' nations based upon a crude social Darwinism; the massive growth of imperialism; and the increasing threat of German power in Europe. However, this kind of 'ethnic' or 'popular' nationalism, which differed from older forms of patriotism, or state-led nation-making, in its open hostility to others and its use of crude racial language, was not a simple or homogeneous phenomenon. All too often historians of sport as well as mainstream historians treat *fin-de-siècle* nationalism as if it were similar throughout Europe. Sport offers a useful way of correcting this misunderstanding. Nationalism, as we shall see, was not the same in Britain and France. Nor, however, was it totally different. The task of a comparative history is to explore not only the distinctiveness of a national political culture by reference to opposed tendencies but also to recognize similarities. Sport offers an unusual and sensitive way of looking at the changing identities of these old enemies as they insidiously turned into new allies – examining the tension between what they did and what they did not share in the drive towards a new kind of popular collectively: the nation.[1]

Although both states shared the preconditions for the new nationalism in terms of popular education and a mass press, the historical traditions and national interests of Britain and France remained very different and this was reflected in sport and reinforced by it. The distinctiveness of British and French nationalism is evident in the first place in terms of the role of the army in particular and militarism in general; to what extent did these two liberal democratic states use sport as a means of preparing young men for military service? Secondly, there is the question of the structure of the state itself. To what extent did sport promote the idea of the unitary national state? How did sport embody the differing traditions of centralism and federalism within Britain and France? Finally, how important was the admiration for sport expressed by anglophiles such as the Baron de

Courbertin and other promoters of athletics? Despite the clear-cut differences in terms of national defence and cultural nationalism, was there not a sense in which much of the effort of the French in promoting 'athletic' sports also involved accepting British ideals of 'fair play' and imperial endeavour? The Anglo-French contrast starts out as quite stark in the 1880s but becomes rather less marked as the impact of popular Darwinism, imperialism and Germanophobia in both countries becomes increasingly important in the pre-1914 era.

Traditions of Militarism

Looking at the role of militarism in sport, the difference in the nature of nationalism within France and the United Kingdom is striking. In France there was an explicitly patriotic purpose behind the development of organized competitive exercise, which did not exist in the same form in Britain. Gymnastics, which was the largest sporting activity until at least 1900, was organized as a movement openly and explicitly in order to assist military revival and was frequently linked with shooting clubs; it took as its motto the words of a French general – 'Faites moi des hommes, nous en ferons des soldats' – and was supported by the state both through subsidies, education and through the granting of honours to officials in the movement. It became directly involved in political conflict through the threat to the Republic from 'Boulangisme'. This has been carefully documented in the extensive researches of Pierre Arnaud and others.[2] In Lyon, for example, there was substantial support for the *bataillons scolaires*, the school-based gymnastic groups set up under a law of 1881 which permitted 'any public educational establishment, primary or secondary, with between 200 and 600 pupils aged over 12, to assemble pupils for gymnastic and military exercises'.

This permissory legislation, following in the wake France's catastrophic defeat at the hands of Prussia, was quite unlike anything which existed in Britain at the time. Patriotic authorities soon availed themselves of the subsidies on offer. In Lyon the Mayor reminded the boys that 'the first duty of a French citizen is to respond readily to the call of the *'Patrie'*; in Lyon the two battalions which were set up received about 50,000 francs a year and had about 1200 members in the 1880s.[3] Official statistics claimed as many as 146 groups in France including 24 in Paris by 1886.[4] Though these figures are of limited value, they serve to give an indication of the scale of a phenomenon which had no equivalent in the state schools of Great Britain, where a little 'drill' involving children waving their arms around by their desks or in the playground seems to have been the only concession to a system of mass physical education. It was not until after the Pyrrhic victory of the Boer War that the British began to think about promoting the health of the troops by exercise at school.[5]

However, this moment of ultra-patriotic consensus in French military and educational history did not last long. When General Boulanger tried to use popular nationalism as a means of overthrowing the Republic in 1889, the municipality of Lyon withdrew its support and the school-based military gymnastics movement in the city collapsed. This pattern was repeated throughout France, where the need to protect the new democratic state from the Right temporarily took precedence over the need to build up a powerful force to defeat Germany and take back Alsace-Lorraine.[6] However, the failure of the *bataillons scolaires* ('un erreur patriotique' as the democratic forces described the movement) only temporarily weakened the militaristic thrust of French sports, especially gymnastics. After 1905 there was a sharp revival in military preparation through sport; this arose partly as a result of international tension arising from fears of German expansionism, and partly because the separation of Church and State in 1905 gave a much sharper edge to competition between them for the adherence of the young: both Church and State wanted to play the patriotic card.[7]

France was politically distinctive from Britain not simply because it was a democratic Republic as opposed to a liberal monarchy but because of its turbulent and conflicting political traditions. France lacked a constitutional consensus, with a good part of the Catholic Church broadly committed to an anti-Republican position. It was as if Britain had abolished the monarchy and the Tory landed interest had sided with the Church of England to discredit the new institutions and set up rival organizations in all spheres of life including sport. No wonder the Baron de Coubertin so admired the durability, solidity and flexibility of British values and institutions, part of the success of which he ascribed to the sporting education of the elite.[8] In France the patriotic thrust of popular education, notably the *bataillon scolaire*, had produced an immediate and hostile clerical response. In Dijon the bishop complained that 'no sooner had the bells rung for the service, than the drums would sound in front of the church door and the *bataillons scolaires* would parade and exercise every Sunday'.[9] The maxim of the highly influential anti-clerical Ligue de l'Enseignement was 'Pour la patrie, par le livre et par l'épée'; they supported a secular and patriotic system of popular education aimed at the regeneration of France and the recovery of the lost provinces of Alsace-Lorraine.[10] As the Catholics themselves took up the cause of sport from their own perspective of a re-born France of the faithful, a 'Republican crusade' to counter their influence took shape. This division became very important after the introduction of formal qualifications for military preparation through sport in the form of the Brevet d'Aptitude Militaire in 1907, which supported school and post-school gymnastic and rifle clubs. The Catholic gymnastic body, the Fédération Gymnastique et Sportive des Patronages de France (FGSPF) had 234 clubs in 1907, 480 in 1908 and 1250 in 1912. The consequence of this was that the chauvinist and militarist tone of gymnastics – and especially that of the rapidly expanding number of rifle clubs which were often linked to gymnastics – became more and more strident as Church and secular clubs tried to outdo each other in vehemence and rhetoric.[11]

This chauvinist tone was significantly more muted amongst those who took up 'Anglo-Saxon' sports. Despite the adoption of athletics and football by the Catholic 'gym' clubs in the immediate pre-war years, the Anglo-Saxon sports largely avoided the explicit Germanophobia of gymnastic clubs with names like 'La Revanche' and 'La Patriote'. The ideology of the dominant sporting organization, the Union des Sociétés Françaises des Sports Athlétiques (USFSA), was never as stridently militaristic or chauvinistic as that of the gym clubs; yet their underlying values, modelled on those of the British, were broadly Darwinian and patriotic. Like their mentors across the Channel, however, the athletic elite who ran the USFSA, graduates of the smart Parisian *lycées* for the most part, were careful to encourage 'fair play' and amateurism, and not to infuse sport with too openly a nationalistic programme. Their ideal, as we shall see later, was similar to that of Coubertin's famous dictum: 'rebronzer la France', i.e. build a dynamic elite who would succeed economically, colonially and politically;[12] that such a reinvigorated nation would then be able to challenge its rival across the Rhine was a largely unspoken assumption. However, the relative lack of chauvinism at the official level may not have been representative of the membership. A famous survey of Parisian students published in 1913 observed a close link between a liking for athletic sports and a bellicose attitude, especially towards Germany; as one contributor remarked, 'La guerre ... c'est sport pour le vrai'.[13]

Even in sports events organized ostensibly for profit there was no escaping the imperatives of national pride and national unity; consider for example the ideological impact of France's major spectacle: the Tour de France. The Tour was designed not just as a commercial event to sell newspapers but as an ideological tool, an expression of the unity of France as conceived by its conservative backers who were staking their claim to ownership of the national idea. By passing through all of France the Tour could teach the French public about the riches of their own nation. On one occasion the Tour was granted permission to pass through German-controlled Alsace-Lorraine and not surprisingly this provoked anti-German demonstrations. On the eve of the First World War, *L'Auto*, the newspaper which organized the Tour, ran a ferociously anti-German article using sporting rhetoric for the purposes of chauvinism and militarism: 'The

Prussians are a bunch of bastards ... You've got to get them this time ... this is the Big Match that you have to play and you must use every trick that you learned in sport ... No more Kaiser! No more Agadir! No more nightmares! No more bastards ["salauds"]'.[14]

Interestingly, this kind of national vehemence began to find expression in football in the immediate pre-war years. In his most valuable and wide-ranging documentary history of French football, Alfred Wahl noted the 'rise in chauvinism' which identified the fortunes and characteristics of the French race with their performance as a national team on the football field. 'Good blood never lies' ('le bon sang ne savait pas mentir') remarked *L'Auto* on the performance of France against Belgium in 1914, whilst a few years earlier *Les Jeunes* had ventured to suggest a parallel between the playing style of French teams and the national character of the French, especially of the French army. France would attack fiercely, the 'furia francese' against opponents who were calmer and better organized, absorbing the heroic assault to hit back decisively at the end when the French were exhausted, rather like the knights at Crécy had charged the English archers, or searching even further back, Vercingetorix had faced the Roman cohorts. Like the Celtic element in the Scots or the Welsh, the Latin self-image in France in footballing terms turned upon the idea of inspiration, courage and impulsiveness – better the 'petit français' than the brute force of the German or the machine-like superiority of the English.[15]

Most societies develop their own myths of national character and identity expressed in sport, which may have little or nothing to do with less subjective external assessments. 'Le petit français', after all, was a member of a large country, which straddled the Mediterranean and the northern European world, and had dominated Europe from the sixteenth to the nineteenth centuries. National self-image, however, may be crucially determined through the perception of the ethnic qualities of rivals; and here the French, despite their geographical size, revealed their inferiority complex in relation to the victors of Sedan whose ever-increasing demographic and economic superiority was the source of profound national anxiety. This was something which the British, even with their manifest unease about German naval building and manufacturing after 1900, could hardly comprehend. It must be remembered that the closer understanding between France and Britain in the form of the Entente Cordiale of 1904 was no more than that: an understanding and *not* a treaty. There was no alliance before 1914; no solemn agreement to commit troops to defend the territorial integrity of France; only a growing awareness of the need to maintain the balance of power in Europe and a rather weaker sense of the moral duty of one democracy to defend another. The fact that Britain and the British Empire in the event did make an unwavering contribution to the defence of

France should not obscure the fact that no one, least of all the French, could have been absolutely sure of this in advance. Protected by a huge fleet and with air power still insignificant, neutrality was always an option, if not an honourable one, for Britain. Hence the French needed to shore up their position with the Russian alliance, the cornerstone of their diplomacy despite its ideological incongruity, to outflank Germany. The point here is simple: France, despite having the largest army in Europe, felt vulnerable, aggrieved and aggressive; Britain did not.

These strategic differences between Britain and France help to explain the striking contrast between the primacy of gymnastics in France and its obscurity in Great Britain. After the Boer War the British did become more concerned with the issue of conscription but this never became more than a minor theme in the history of sport. By 1903 only 2.7 per cent of males aged between fifteen and forty-nine were in the Volunteer Force, a body set up to promote military preparedness after invasion scares in the middle years of the nineteenth century inspired by the spectre of Bonapartism.[16] The main role for gymnastics in Britain was to provide a little rudimentary exercise for schoolchildren – 'drill', as it was called, was brief, basic and by no means uniformly practised – and specifically to provide what was considered more suitable exercise for women. In Britain, in fact, gymnastics came to be primarily associated with female physical education. European gymnastics was mostly directed towards promoting the strength of the conscript through German-style group exercises whereas in Britain women's gymnastics took the lead in developing and adapting Swedish forms of individual exercise for good posture, grace and agility.[17]

Popular British sport, therefore, was not particularly interested in European national rivalry and played a very minor role in military preparation. Of course, as Mangan has stressed, elite sports were rather different. Whilst denying any overt military purpose in the name of 'fair play' and 'character-building', the boys who played games most afternoons on the playing fields of the public schools were imbued with a fiercely patriotic and Darwinist ideology.[18] This kind of British nationalism was subsumed within the wider framework of imperialism. 'The Gattling's jammed and the colonel's dead, ... the sands of the desert are sodden red', and so on, entered the national consciousness through Newbolt's famous poem linking cricket to the idea of fighting the savages. As we shall see later, the French athletic elite also linked sport and Empire, though not to the same extent as the British who effectively disguised English nationalism under the cloak of imperialism. This allowed the public school elite to look down on the cruder forms of popular chauvinism whilst simultaneously promoting a vigorous cult of Empire from Queen Victoria right down to the syllabus of elementary schools. The belief that the British were best, that the

Empire was a 'good thing' was more deeply entrenched in a very wide swathe of public opinion than some imperial historians and others have suggested.[19] It was not so much that Britain lacked the kind of deep sentiment found in France; it was rather that national feeling took different forms. In France stress was laid on the nation-state ('la République une et indivisible') whereas in the United Kingdom of Great Britain and Ireland – to use its full name – it was the wider Empire and the different elements of the federation itself which acted as foci for national feeling.

Centralism and Federalism

It is all to easy to overlook the federal character of the British Isles. The lack of a very visible English nationalism makes it easy for the English to neglect the strength of national feeling in other parts of the United Kingdom.[20] Yet France was a centralized Republic and the United Kingdom a federal monarchy. The role of the monarchy was to provide a focus and symbol for the British Isles, including Ireland. Whereas French state education castigated dynastic territories in the name of the free citizen, in Britain the monarchy did not have the same repressive 'feudal' associations. A considerable effort, moreover, went into reviving the popularity of Victoria both as Empress of India and through such invented traditions as the annual Scottish visit to Balmoral. The crown expressed a dual sense of identity which was simultaneously imperial and federal. Royal attendance at sports events, which increased after 1900, acknowledged this just as the presence of the president in France symbolized 'indivisibility':[21]

What is clear is that sport in Britain was less centralized than in France and that national teams were not used in the same way to promote the idea of a unitary national state. Although the federal system of sport in Britain may ultimately have achieved the same end as the rigorously centralist one in France – that is, both structures in different ways promoting a sense of belonging to a kind of national community – the means were quite distinct. In France separate sporting structures for historic 'states' like Provence, Burgundy or Brittany were avoided. Regional committees were, of course, set up but they were never given much power. The USFSA took it upon itself to withdraw from the Fédération Internationale de Football Association – the setting up of which in France in 1904 was incidentally further evidence of the British indifference to international competition – without properly consulting its own members, who were as a result effectively deprived of international contacts. This 'centralizing obsession' cost the USFSA the control of football in France.[22] Paris remained far too dominant. Even the early football championships were run on the basis of a knock-out provincial competition, the winners of which then played the best of the Parisian teams, whose officials were key figures in the Union. English football may have been nominally centred on the London headquarters of the FA but the actual running of the spectator side was done by a northern-based Football League which was dominated by northern teams. Only one southern team won the FA Cup between 1883 and 1914 and there was even a separate Southern League. Arsenal apart, London was marginal to English football before 1914.

The sense of national consciousness within England in this period has begun to attract serious attention, although in terms of sport at least it remains difficult to analyse.[23] The English cricket team won vast support, especially in the bi-annual Test matches against Australia that became a sporting institution from the late nineteenth century. But the English national football team does not appear to have been followed with the same enthusiasm. Cricket was the true 'national' sport in England in the sense of crossing all social strata. After the professionalisation of representative football in the 1880s middle-class interest in the Home internationals seems to have declined. Nor were urban industrial workers noticeably strident in their support of England (unlike some of their descendants) and clung tenaciously to regional and local identities expressed in derbies or in the North versus South games that were a feature of the period.[24] However, proper research is needed in this area; for crowds were large – very large by French standards – at English national games and the impression of tepid national feeling for the England team may be misleading. England had a distinctive national style which encouraged restraint, team work and understatement – and this was a positive if muted expression of identity; this liking for 'ordinariness' has come out in English heroes, of whom Stanley Matthews and Bobby Charlton in football and Jack Hobbs in cricket are the supreme examples. Great English footballing heroes before 1914 are hard to come by. Perhaps amateur selectors were disinclined to create English national personalities; Steve Bloomer of Derby probably comes closest in the pre-1914 era; the most controversial, gifted and passionate player, Billy Meredith, was born just across the border in Wales and never played for England.[25]

The great stress on national unity found in the Tour de France and elsewhere in French sport was needed because France remained in many ways so strongly regionalized. The Republican education system, conscription, the press and the expansion of the national economy and transport networks were designed, in the words of Eugen Weber, to turn 'peasants into Frenchmen', but the task was still incomplete by 1900 and it was part of the function of sports and gymnastic clubs as viewed by the State to finish it.[26] In contrast, Britain was a state where a national economy and good communications had created a highly integrated economic and political formation in which Wales and Scotland could exist as distinct 'nations' in a cultural sense. In fact, the sports system favoured this kind of 'subcultural' nationalism over the broader notion of 'Britishness'. The four 'Home' nations – England, Scotland, Wales and Ireland – played against each other in football, rugby and most other sports; it was only at the Olympics where the French in the person of Coubertin and others refused to recognize anything but a single team that the British played as a unified nation state (the United Kingdom). The division of sport into competing sporting nations was not an expression of the weakness of the United Kingdom; in fact, it strengthened the union by giving it a sporting dimension which allowed supporters to affirm their loyalty both to their 'cultural' nation and to the federal state which provided the framework for competition.[27]

France had nothing like the system of 'home' internationals which dominated the two winter team sports of the United Kingdom. When France took part in representative rugby it was as a unitary state competing with the historic nations of the United Kingdom. The role of rugby in Wales has been particularly well studied by Gareth Williams and Dai Smith.[28] It seems clear that rugby achieved a special place in Welsh culture as part of a broader shift away from the older world of distinctive dress and language. As the bardic culture declined and south Wales attracted huge numbers of migrants to the coalfields, there was a need to create a new, more inclusive, kind of Welsh identity. In the 1890s a Welsh national side recruited from miners as well as from the sons of merchants and the liberal professions found they could hold their own against the English. England was weakened by the geographical and social split in rugby in 1895 between the Northern Union (later to become the Rugby League), which accepted semi-professionalism and the Rugby Union run by public school men from the comfortable suburbs of London. Rugby in Wales became increasingly identified with a reinvention of Welshness on the basis of an interest in ethnicity, which was as a feature of the new nationalism. As Hobsbawm has noted, the popular nationalism of the post-1880s put no threshold on the size that could be considered a 'nation' (as state-builders like Cavour and Bismark had done), and accepted the importance of a shared 'folk-identity' which could exist without necessarily requiring a formal independence movement.[29] This was precisely the case in Wales where alongside religious revival, trade unionism and vigorous choral and educational traditions, rugby came to play a central role in the building or national identity. 'We all know the racial qualities that made Wales supreme on Saturday,' enthused one observer. 'The great quality of defence and attack in the Welsh race is to be traced to the training of the early period when powerful enemies drove them to their mountain fortress. There was developed, then, those traits of character that find fruition today. "Gallant little Wales" has produced sons of strong determination, invincible stamina, resolute, mentally keen, physically sound.'[30]

Here the discourse of racial nationalism with its clear undertones of social Darwinism was used for the purposes of the cultural nationalism of the Welsh. This popular sense of Welshness did not regard the United Kingdom with hostility, although there was a certain antagonism towards the English which was partly historical and partly class based on account of the solidly public school nature of the English teams. The climacteric of this process of building national identity through rugby in Wales came with the defeat of an otherwise undefeated New Zealand team in 1905. Beating the All Blacks gave Wales not only a special place in the United Kingdom but within the British Empire as well. 'Wales is proud of this victory', remarked the *Western Mail*. 'She is particularly proud of the fact that Welsh peers and Welsh labourers – with all the intervening stratas of society – were united in acclaiming and cheering the Welsh team. It was … a victory for Wales in a sense that is "probably" impossible in any other sphere.'[31] Proud as he was of being a Welshman, as one supporter put it on St David's Day in 1900, he confessed to a still greater pride that Wales was part of the British Empire.[32]

Sport played a similar, though by no means identical, role in Scotland. Scottish sport was sharply class-divided with the public school liberal professions, especially strongly concentrated around the legal and administrative centre in Edinburgh devoting themselves to rugby, whilst the industrial working class, especially the miners of Lanarkshire and the engineering and shipbuilding trades of Glasgow, took to football with a passion unequalled elsewhere. The middle classes of England and Scotland had their polite, if hard fought, annual confrontation in rugby for the Calcutta Cup. Middle-class nationalism expressed in a fervent amateurism and a strong interest in the imperial dimension to rugby accorded well with the Act of Union, which Nairn has described as 'a peculiarly patrician bargain between two ruling classes – the bargain whereby a nationality resigned statehood but preserved an extraordinary amount of the institutional and psychological baggage normally associated with independence'. Scotland, according to this reasoning, was 'a decapitated state rather than an ordinary assimilated nationality'.[33] However, it was a state that had voluntarily resigned its political autonomy and showed no particular desire to get it back either at the level of the political elite or in more popular terms. Nineteenth-century Scottish democracy was Liberal; twentieth-century popular politics have been Labour; neither party until relatively recently was associated with the creation of separate political institutions for Scotland.

Hence the real business of building a popular Scottish consciousness through sport took place elsewhere, most notably around the annual confrontation between England and Scotland. As an Edwardian observer remarked, 'One has only got to be in Glasgow on International Day to realise adequately how tremendous is the hold the game has on the Scottish mind.'[34] Beating England was a way of asserting equality, even superiority, over 'the auld enemy', by using the new materials to hand. The national football team, as Moorhouse has shown, has become a central 'part of a sturdy subculture of symbols, slogans, heroes and myths which sustains an apolitical, inverted but palpable subnationalism which combines a strong identity of being Scottish with a very weak national project'.[35]

Scotland asserted Scottishness by playing the same game whilst the Irish nationalist movement understood that taking part in the network of Anglo-Saxon sport in fact embedded them in British culture; they would be offered national recognition *only* in sport by the English, and in return they would *de facto* have to accept their place within the United Kingdom. This was acceptable to the Scots and the Welsh, whose elites shared in the running of the Empire alongside the English. But the Irish saw matters quite differently. They saw themselves as victims of British imperialism and hence their militant opposition to Anglo-Saxon sports. Archbishop Croke, a leading Irish Catholic nationalist, complained of 'the ugly and irritating fact that we are daily importing from England not only her manufactured goods … but her fashions, her accents, her vicious literature, her dances and her pastimes to the utter discredit of our grand national sports, and to the sore humiliation, as I believe, of every son and daughter of the old land'.[36] It was this thinking that lay behind the establishment in 1884 of the Gaelic Athletic Association (GAA), which promoted hurling and Gaelic football and banned its members from playing any English sports. The GAA established itself as the most important sporting body in Ireland providing a dramatic and successful example of the use of sport for the specific purposes of nationalism. As a result Ireland developed two sporting systems: that run by the GAA and the alternative of 'British' sports such as football, rugby and athletics.[37]

Of course, it would be quite wrong to think that French and British sport had nothing in common. There were significant similarities as well as differences between France and the United Kingdom. As we saw, the anglophile Union des Sociétés Françaises des Sports Athlétiques, which regulated the Anglo-Saxon sports, adopted broadly the same set of attitudes (though not the same national structure) as its British counterpart. Initially it rejected the popular nationalism of men like Pascal Grousset, who like the Irish openly sought to re-discover forgotten indigenous sports and to popularize them through student festivals around 1890.[38] Pierre de

Coubertin in particular opposed the 'new nationalism' with its emphasis on hostility to other races. The Olympic ideal was patriotic but not nationalist, loving one's own country rather than hating someone else's.[39] Pierre Arnaud catches the difference nicely between the clubs organized around the idea of preparing the conscript and those involved in middle and upper class athletic sports clubs. In Lyon not only the gymnastic and rifle clubs were fiercely Germanophobe but the swimming clubs too, which were important in the city at the confluence of the Rhône and the Saône. Behind the bland progressiveness of their proclaimed purpose of 'Hygiène, Patrie and Humanité' lay the more practical ambition of teaching potential recruits to swim so that 'they could cross the Rhine, when the moment came'.[40] However, the rugby and football players as well as the athletes of Lyon were urged in a rather different direction. Their journal avoided all nationalist rhetoric and subscribed to the dictum of Coubertin that 'le sport est fait pour viriliser et non pour militariser'.[41]

Coubertin, then, was unusual in the extent to which he took the idea of internationalism but not in his cultured unwillingness to embrace the new nationalism with its loathing of Germans and crude assertions of French superiority and self-interest. The elite sportsmen of *fin de siècle* France were less interested in re-crossing the Rhine than in expanding French dominion throughout the wider world. It is easy to overlook the remarkable success of the French imperialists in the late nineteenth century, especially in north Africa and Indo-China. As every schoolboy used to know, this led to a very dangerous confrontation with the British at Fashoda and some wild talk of war. The British and the French were playing the same imperial game and French sportsmen seem to have supported their side. Coubertin had no doubts about the benefit of sport for imperialism. 'Sport can play a role in colonialism, an intelligent and effective role ... sports are an instrument of vigorous discipline. They promote all sorts of good social qualities, health, cleanliness, order, self-control'.[42] Here they were at one with the imperial priorities of their British counterparts. Eugen Weber picked up this theme in his pioneering article on French sport written over twenty years ago but which has, as yet, not spawned major studies of the kind that J. A. Mangan and others have done for the British Empire.[43]

The French leftist critic Jean-Marie Brohm has made much of Coubertin's nationalism and imperialism, stressing the racist discourse which underlies his assumptions, and outraging respectable Olympians with his accusations. However, one does not have to cite Coubertin – mistakenly and quite unhistorically in my view – as a precursor of fascism, to accept that he held many of the same views about the supremacy of western culture taken for granted by the public school men he admired on the other side of the Channel. Mangan has shown how deeply racist notions, partly derived from Darwinism and partly no more than rationalizations of the needs and realities of Empire, dominated the thinking of elite British sportsmen.[44] Here was a discourse of nationalism shared by both the French and the British. Contrary to some of the received ideas about the nature of French imperialism, which has traditionally been seen as overwhelmingly cultural with a strong educational and linguistic focus, it may be that there was less difference in styles between the Blues who ruled the Blacks and the colonial administrators of the *grandes écoles*. Perhaps the natives sweated no more over Molière and Racine than they did over Shakespeare. Certainly, the interesting recent research of Phyllis Martin on youth and football in French equatorial Africa suggests that the French – the missionaries in particular – were active in promoting sports; the Director of a Catholic Mission, quoted by Martin, holds forth like a prep schoolmaster: 'the team spirit that comes from working together can start from the activities of group sport. This in turn can bring out a flourishing spirit of unity which can spill over into other spheres of activity.'[45] Martin's research certainly suggests that sport was a success in terms of relations with subject peoples. Many of the best football teams of contemporary Africa, after all, come from formerly French colonies.

There was clearly some convergence too in the area of domestic public opinion in the immediate pre-war years. Mass politics and culture were shaping new forms of public opinion in both countries. Britain became increasingly anti-German; there was widespread acceptance of the idea of racial struggle ('Social Darwinism') and the demand on behalf of groups like the National Service League, founded in 1901 and claiming 200,000 members by 1912, that Britain should also have a conscript army like France.[46] There was growing emphasis on supposed racial and historic qualities of the British as a single nation or 'an island race' which could join together to sing 'Rule Britannia'. Although in the British case the spread of the new popular racial nationalism did not lead to the use of sport for military preparation as in France, the link between sport and 'national efficiency' was coming to be more widely accepted. A good example of this was the dismay on both sides of the Channel which greeted the relative failure of both Britain and France to perform well in the 1912 Olympic Games and the alarm at the prospect of German success in the next Games scheduled for Berlin in 1916.

So French and British sport shared certain common tendencies whilst also reflecting profoundly different historical traditions. It is the tension between what was shared and what separated the two nations which is of historical interest and which reveals the importance of sport as an indicator of the complexity of national identity. Sport can be a way of making specific comparisons between states – a difficult task which both historians of sport and historians more generally have been reluctant to undertake – but one which in turn can throw light on some of the most important themes in modern history. Thus, a comparison of the characteristics of sporting nationalism in Britain and France before the First World War shows not only the impact of the new nationalism in both states – that is, wider social forces promoting convergence in the forms of national expression – but also the fact that in Britain the force of the new mass culture was mediated by a range of factors including the strength of internal sub nationalism, the continued reliance on the Royal Navy for national defence and the ideological priority accorded to the Empire and to 'fair play' amongst the amateur leaders of British sport. Such were the peculiarities of the British; as for the French, they could point to divisions between gymnastics and athletes, between Church and State, democrats and authoritarians – all of which combined to shape the different character of their sporting nationalism around the turn of the century.

NOTES

I am grateful to the Institute of Physical Education, K.U. Leuven, for their assistance in preparing this article.

1. Recent studies have tended to dwell on the preconditions for mass nationalism – the anatomy of 'imagined communities' in Benedict Anderson's frequently cited phase – rather than on the role of the state in nation building. E.J. Hobsbawm, *Nations and Nationalism since 1870: Programme, Myth and Reality* (Cambridge, 1990) provides a valuable general survey and bibliography. This nicely complements E. Hobsbawm and T. Ranger (eds.), *The Invention of Tradition* (Cambridge, 1983), which broke new ground in the exploration of nationalism from a socio-cultural perspective, including the analysis of sport as one of the means for the definition of national identity. French works, such as that of Michael Winock *Nationalisme, anti-semitisme et fascisme en France* (Seuil, Paris 1982) and the continuing publications of Zeev Sternhell on the revolutionary right, have been more concerned with question of the ideological similarities between the racial populism of pre-war nationalism and the development of facism in the interwar years. The latest Anglo-American work, however, has seen a marked swing back to the 'older' approach centred on the state and contingent strategic factors; see, for example, J. Breuilly, *Nationalism and the State* (Manchester University Press, 1993) and L. Greenfield, *Nationalism: Five Roads to Modernity* (Harvard University Press, 1993) as well as the case studies such as Linda Colley's *Britons: Forging the Nation, 1707–1837* (Yale University Press, 1992). Greenfield looks specifically at the role of military defeats in promoting movements for national regeneration – a line of inquiry with obvious relevance for sport and physical culture – whilst Colley stresses the way in which the long military conflict with France up to 1815 helped to create a new kind of 'Britishness' that was to provide both a structure for the internal nationalism of the United Kingdom and the British identity that underpinned Victorian imperialism.
2. P. Arnaud (ed.), *Les athlètes de la République: gymnastique, sport et idéologie républicaine* (Toulouse, 1987) is the key work; for a summary of the main themes in English, see R. Holt, 'Ideology and Sociability: A Review of New French Research into History of Sport, 1870–1914', *International Journal of the History of Sport*, 6,3 (Dec. 1989).
3. P. Arnaud, 'Un exemple de militantisme municipal', in Arnaud (ed.), *Les athlètes*, p.76.
4. A. Bourzac, 'Les bataillons scolaires en France', in Arnaud, *Les athlètes*, p.62.
5. P. McIntosh, *Physical Education in England since 1800* (London, 1968) gives a useful

outline but the lack of a new standard work reflects the relatively low priority of gymnastics in British sport and history.

6. Bourzac, 'Les bataillons', pp. 82–4; see also R. Holt, *Sport and Society in Modern France* (London, 1981), pp. 47–8, 192.

7. E. Weber, 'Gymnastics and Sports in fin-de-siècle France: opium of the classes?' *American Historical Review* (Feb. 1971) opened up this discussion and remains of great value.

8. J.J. MacAloon, *This Great Symbol: Pierre de Coubertin and the Origins of the Modern Olympic Games* (Chicago, 1981), esp. Ch.3; this work was the first to compare British and French traditions through an historical analysis of the personality and programme of Coubertin.

9. Bourzac, 'Les Bataillons', p.50.

10. B. Maccario, 'Gymnastique, sport et éducation populaire: le combat de la Ligue d'Enseignement', in Arnaud, p.182.

11. J.-L. Gay Lescot, 'Les sociétés sportives scolaires et post-scolaires de tir dans le département de l'Ile et Villaine, 1907–14', in Arnaud, pp.125–40.

12. MacAloon, *This Great Symbol*, esp. pp.71–3.

13. 'Agathon', *Les jeunes gens d'aujourd'hui* (Paris, 1913), pp.33, 143.

14. E. Seidler, *Le sport et la presse* (Paris, 1964), pp.58–9.

15. A. Wahl, *Les Archives du football: sport et société en France, 1880–1980* (Paris, 1989), pp.159–60; this work is unique in being simultaneously a source book and an acute general history.

16. A. Summers, 'Edwardian Militarism', in R. Samuel (ed.), *Patriotism: The Making and Unmaking of British National Identity*, Vol.1 (London, 1987), p.237; H. Cunningham, *The Volunteer Force* (London, 1976) shows that gymnastics was not part of military preparation.

17. K. McCrone, *Sport and the Physical Emancipation of English Women* (London, 1988), and S. Fletcher, *Women First: The Female Tradition in English Physical Education* (London, 1984).

18. J.A. Mangan, *Athleticism in the Victorian and Edwardian Public School* (Cambridge, 1981) is the key work.

19. J.M. MacKenzie (ed.), *Imperialism and Popular Culture* (Manchester, 1986), pp.1–13 gives a good introduction.

20. K. Robbins, *Nineteenth-Century Britain: Integration and Diversity* (Oxford, 1988).

21. D. Cannadine, 'The Context, Performance and Meaning of Ritual: The British Monarchy and the "Invention of Tradition", 1820–1970', in E. Hobsbawn and T. Ranger, *The Invention of Tradition* (Cambridge, 1983).

22. A. Wahl, *Les Archives du Football*, p.108.

23. R. Colls and P. Dodd (eds.), *Englishness: Politics and Culture 1880–1920* (London, 1984) is stimulating but surprisingly neglects sport, as do Samuel's three volumes of articles on *Patriotism* (London, 1989).

24. For a tentative framework see R. Holt, *Sport and the British: A Modern History* (Oxford, 1989), pp.262–79.

25. In comparison to the rich literature on cricket the paucity of full-length football biographies of any real quality is very striking; J. Harding, *Billy Meredith* (Derby, 1985) is worthwhile but there is little else apart from what can be found in Tony Mason's outstanding *Association Football and English Society* (Brighton, 1979).

26. E. Weber, *Peasants into Frenchman: The Modernisation of Rural France* (London, 1977).

27. Holt, *Sport and the British*, pp.236–61.

28. D. Smith and G. Williams, *Fields of Praise: the Official History of the Welsh Rugby Union, 1881–1981* (Cardiff, 1980).

29. Hobsbawm, *Nations and Nationalism*, p.102.

30. Smith and Williams, *Fields of Praise*, pp.173–4.

31. Cited in D. Smith, 'Focal Heroes: A Welsh Fighting Class', in R. Holt (ed.), *Sport and the Working Class in Modern Britain* (Manchester, 1990), p.201.

32. G. Williams, *1905 and All That: Essays on Rugby Football, Sport and Welsh Society* (Gower Press, 1991), p.82; outstanding on the creation of a national identity.

33. Tom Nairn, *The Break-Up of Britain* (London, 1981 ed.), p.129.

34. H.F. Moorhouse, 'Shooting Stars: Footballers and Working Class Culture in Twentieth Century Scotland', in Holt (ed.), *Sport and the Working Class in Modern Britain* (Manchester, 1990), p.259.
35. Moorhouse cited in R. Holt, *Sport and the Working Class*, p.259.
36. Holt, *Sport and the British*, p.238.
37. W.F. Mandle, 'The IRB and the Beginnings of the Gaelic Athletic Association', *Irish Historical Studies* (Sept. 1977).
38. E. Weber, 'Pierre de Coubertin and the introduction of organized sport into France', *Journal of Contemporary History*, 2 (1970).
39. MacAloon, *This Great Symbol*, p.268: 'To ask the people of the world to love each other is merely a form of childishness. To ask them to respect one another is not in the least utopian.'
40. P. Arnaud, 'Diviser et Unir: sociétés sportives et nationalismes en France (1870–1914)', *Sport Histoire*, 4 (1989), p.39.
41. Ibid., p.40.
42. 'Le sport et la colonisation', in *La Revue Olympique*, Jan. 1912, cited by J-M Brohm, 'Pierre de Coubertin et l'avènement du sport bourgeois', in Arnaud (ed.), *Athlètes de la République*, p.295.
43. E. Weber, 'Gymnastics and Sports in fin-de-siècle France'.
44. J.A. Mangan, *The Games Ethic and Imperialism* (London, 1986). Apart from Martin (below) see recent articles by J-P. Augustin and B. Deville-Danthu in P. Arnaud and A. Wahl, *Sports et Relations Internationales* (Metz, 1994), pp.187–208.
45. P.M. Martin, 'Colonialism, Youth and Football in French Equatorial Africa', *International Journal of the History of Sport*, 8,1 (May, 1991), p.59.
46. A. Summers, 'The Character of Edwardian Nationalism', in P. Kennedy and A. Nicholls, *Nationalist and Racialist Movements in Britain and Germany before 1914* (London, 1981) – a pioneering comparative effort but with the exception of the introductory essay all the contributions, which are of a very high standard, deal with only one of the two nations.

One State, Several Countries: Soccer and Nationality in a 'United' Kingdom

H.F. MOORHOUSE

Introduction

The Football Association of Ireland
80, Merrion Square
Dublin
27th April 1959

Sir Stanley Rous, CBE, JP.
Football Association
Lancaster Gate
London W2.

Dear Sir Stanley,

My Association has had under consideration recently the matter of our endeavouring to obtain some International games with the British Associations. We do realise the many International calls all have, but request your Association, in the best interests of the development and progress of the game in our part of Ireland, to give sympathetic consideration and we trust agreement, to the following proposal:

(1) That England, Scotland and Wales, each agree to play an evening International match in Dublin, every three years in turn, in late September or early October, on half gate terms, less match expenses. We would also very much like to include, if they consider it feasible, the Irish Football Association. It will be understood there might be difficulty in the two Irish Associations playing an International match, but we feel and trust we can get over any difficulties and have a game also with them, if they so desire.

(2) We have suggested this period because (a) the League Clubs will have finished their evening games, (b) a very good attendance and receipts would be obtained at this time, and (c) this extra fixture (only one every three or four years) would not interfere with or cut across present or future other International matches.

(3) We do not ask for any agreement for return away matches to be played, so as not to present difficulty, as our main request is, to have this one home game, with the Associations in turn to keep our public interested. It will be understood, that our people are much more conversant with and interested in players playing in the British Leagues than they are in even the most famous of Continental players. In addition, of course, many of our best players are playing in Britain. Nonetheless, if any of the Associations found at any time, that they could offer us a return International fixture in their country, we would be very glad to accept.

We would like to stress again the need for these games especially in view of our proximity and interest in each other and the belief that such games could be instrumental in increasing friendship between our peoples. While our Continental matches are attractive, our public would like, even occasionally, to see the 'home' countries as they do in other codes......

> Yours sincerely,
> Jos. I. Wickman
> Secretary.[1]

Mainstream sociological analysis tends to ignore sport, including football. While there is a lively sub-discipline, centring on football 'hooliganism', most social analysis does not bother with one of the great pastimes of the people, one which has divided and united groups in socially significant ways, and one which commands popular attention in ways that institutions which are regarded as more socially important (and are much more studied) do not. For example, we are told that in an Edwardian railway factory, 'Politics, religion, the fate of empires and governments, the interest of life and death itself must all yield to the supreme fascination and excitement of football.'[2] However, in much sociology such everyday truths are smiled at, then quickly forgotten in the 'real' business of getting down to serious social analysis. Yet if understanding consciousness, meaning, perception and subjectivity is a vital key for decoding patterns of social structure and action then it seems reasonable to insist that consideration of at least the most popular sports should be aligned more closely with many of the recurrent themes of social analysis than it is, and should not be ghettoized as a marginal field of study.

This essay uses the records of one of the most important of the ruling bodies of the sport – The International Football Association Board – to discuss how the development of the organization of soccer as a world sport related to the nature of tensions within the union of a 'United' Kingdom, and to sketch the relationship of football to the maintenance of identities within that union that are ethnic and 'national'.

There has been a tendency for British academics to treat the relationship of football, popular culture and the production of values only in terms of some (ill-defined) 'class' with, more recently, a nod towards gender divisions and racism encapsulated in some all-too-encompassing assertions about the effects of 'norms of masculinity'. The tendency to downplay lines of conflict stemming from ethnicity and culture has meant that, usually covertly but sometimes quite arrogantly, most scholars have talked about *England* when they claim to be uncovering the social meanings of soccer in *British* society.[3] This fits quite well with a general, taken for granted, cultural hegemony in the United Kingdom where 'Britishness' is either taken as equivalent to 'Englishness' or, vaguely, assumed to be a 'mixture' of all 'elements', with the 'Celtic fringes' acting as sources of lovable, if eccentric, noble savages or, the obverse of that particular cultural coin, of uncivilized brutes when they appear in the guise of Irish bombers or Scottish football supporters.[4] In his influential discussion of nationalism Anderson notes 'the fact that the Soviet Union shares with the United Kingdom of Great Britain and Northern Ireland the rare distinction of refusing nationality in its naming.'[5]

Yet within this bland union forms of 'nationalism' are promoted. In sport the 'United' Kingdom, the Royaume 'Uni', often but not always, fragments into four countries, such that, quite uniquely in terms of world football, one political state is allowed to contain four 'nations', and have three major leagues which send teams into continent-wide club competitions. Moreover, adding to the complexities and tensions, these 'nations' and leagues have been structured in relations of dominance and subordination, both in terms of wider political and economic forces *and* in terms of football finance, so that the top stars of all countries have tended to gravitate to just one of the leagues, the English.

Not surprisingly, then, there are many currents which eddy around football, group identity and 'nationality' in the two large islands off the coast of Continental Europe which turn on the effects of *English* imperialism. Holt has pointed to the significance of sport in symbolizing and sustaining the particular 'cultural nationalism' which tends to define the non-English parts of the Kingdom: 'sports were shared with the English and used as a means of asserting claims for the recognition of special ethnic and national qualities'.[6]

It is certainly true that sporting competition is one of the main processes which serve to designate membership in some groups and not others, but it can have some sharper edges than Holt allows. In addition, if what I have been alluding to concerns what might loosely be called the cultural consequences of 'internal colonialism',[7] the soccer relationship of the United Kingdom with another, now apparently separate, political state – the Republic of Ireland – is quite complicated, such that possession of the very term 'Ireland' has been as vigorously contested as any goal, while at the present time a club from Northern Ireland, part of that 'United' Kingdom, plays in the league of the other, apparently distinct, political entity. Overall, a major element in the symbolism produced by the routines of football in the United Kingdom is a resentment of English power and pretensions, an element which echoes in many other places in the world. It is part, an important part, of the 'tradition' of football and one which still plays a role in refurbishing a particularly mournful strand found in some of the 'nationalities' contained in the British Isles.

Wales

Here the story is quickly told. In sporting terms national allegiance in Wales tends to be linked to rugby. Soccer is relatively unimportant culturally. The major professional clubs in Wales play, and historically have played, in the English league. At different times six Welsh clubs have played in the Football League. There has been the occasional, and much celebrated, success, but by and large Welsh clubs have not been major forces in the game. Even the biggest clubs in the Principality have been relatively poor, and famous Welsh players, from Billy Meredith through John Charles to Ryan Giggs, have tended to make their fame, and sometimes fortune, with English, if not Continental, clubs. This, as in the case of Scotland, has tended to mean that their availability for international fixtures has often been in doubt and so their 'nationalism' has been questioned. But this has been less significant in Wales where rugby is the real game of the masses.

Ireland

Here the situation is more complex for at least three reasons:

1. All of Ireland was part of the United Kingdom until the 1920s, so the achievement of independent statehood by part of that island after much of the international organization of football had been established created problems about just what 'Ireland' *was* in football terms, and which organization was to control it.

2. Soccer was so intertwined with imperialism that in Southern Ireland it used to be regarded much less favourably by state and moral authorities

than other 'indigenous' Gaelic sports, while in Ulster (Northern Ireland) clubs have tended to have 'Protestant' or 'Catholic' labels, one of whose effects is that some clubs have sought to play, or have played, in competitions based in the other political state.

3. Clubs in both 'parts' of Ireland have remained rather small, and there has been a constant migration of players, so that soccer fans often have quite strong allegiances to clubs in the Scottish or English leagues, and indigenous teams have often served as overt feeders of talent to these clubs.

The four football associations which represented the 'countries' of the United Kingdom set up an International Football Association Board in 1886. The association representing Ireland was called the Irish Football Association (IFA). The International Board's purpose was to standardize the rules of the game and agree on definitions (the nature of a 'throw-in', for example), but also to regulate the intricacies of relations within a United Kingdom and especially those involving: eligibility for international matches; and players signing for clubs based in associations other than their 'national' one.

Difficulties raised by both these issues related to the power of England at the centre of football matters, as well as economic and political affairs, and the peripheral position of the others. This was, and still is, well encapsulated in the official title of the English body being '*The* Football Association' (FA).

In 1895 all the associations came to an agreement that, 'In International Matches the qualification of players should be birth',[8] and, with a few amendments about the qualification of sons born on foreign soil to British fathers, this simple formula seemed to settle the matter.

In 1922 the political union of the Kingdom was broken and part of Ireland became a separate state. The minutes of the International Football Association Board record:

> An application was read from a new Football Association formed in Ireland for admission to Membership of the Board. It was unanimously decided that: 'Under the present constitution of the International Board, it is not competent for this Board to admit as Members the new FA of Ireland'. It was also unanimously decided that no Country could be represented by two Associations.[9]

This was the nub of the matter. How was a political division of a nation, created in strife and blood, to be reflected in sporting terms? If there already was an Irish Football Association how could there be a Football Association of Ireland, as the new body styled itself? The English FA initiated a conference in Liverpool in October 1923 to try to regularize matters at which the renamed FA of the Irish Free State (FAIFS) was recognized as a footballing authority with Dominion status within the British Empire. At first the newcomer had claimed jurisdiction over football throughout Ireland but soon claimed rights only over the geographical area controlled by its state, but it wrote to the FA in 1925 insisting that it was 'determined to secure that the use of the name "Ireland" shall not be monopolized in Football matters by the body in Northern Ireland.'[10]

However, this was not just a matter of a struggle for symbols but for players and 'nationality'. The Irish FA, based in Belfast, argued that on the sporting level the split could only be about organizing football within a particular area and that, in international matters, the original association had the name, the jurisdiction and the right to choose players from the whole area, north and south, of Ireland, and indeed, this did and still does happen in some sports, rugby for instance. This argument was not accepted for football. The FAIFS pursued its case through the Fédération Internationale de Football Association (FIFA) which was emerging as a rival to the International Board in the governance of world soccer and when in 1930 the IFA chose three players for an amateur international team who had been born in the south and played for a Dublin club, the FAIFS went to the High Court of Justice of the Free State for a judgement on the issues. Success there caused them to send a letter to the International Board declaring.

> That this Committee forbids any player or players who are present registered and playing under our jurisdiction and who were born within the area now known as the Irish Free State from playing in this or any other match arranged and controlled by the Irish Football Association Ltd.[11]

Counter letters were received from the IFA and the Scottish FA (SFA) and a vote was carried at the Board to take no action.

This led to the Football Association issuing a four page document which told much of the story in its grand title:

> Observations on the football situation in Ireland and the Defeat by the International Board on June 13th, 1931, at Gleneagles of the FA Proposal to add to the Agreement of June 1895: 'In International Matches the qualification of players should be birth', the words, 'within the area of the National Association'. The Scottish, Welsh and Irish Associations voted against the proposal, the FA. and the International federation in favour.[12]

The document reviewed the whole history of the dispute. In 1927 FIFA had designated the 'Irish FA' as 'Northern Ireland'. Only in the home internationals could its teams still play under the title of 'Ireland'. The FA had tried to effect an amalgamation or pooling of resources between the two associations to no avail. The 1931 decision had been to maintain the status quo, but for the English the problem was:

> What was the status quo? So far as The FA accepted it, it did not entitle the Irish FA to utilize the services of players born in the Free State. That was, at any rate, not in our minds, as we had always recognized the Free State as a National Body, politically separate from Northern Ireland; and in our view, while we were ready to accept a union of the two Associations in football to represent Ireland as a whole, we held that unless that was done, we were bound to admit the authority of the Free State within its own area.

In response the IFA reiterated its argument that the political division of Ireland did not alter its position as representing 'Ireland as a whole' for football. As Mr McBride of the IFA put it:

> North and South Wales, or North and South England might be politically separated, but the Welsh FA and the FA would still represent Wales and England internationally. What had happened to Ireland might happen to any country, and if the old-established Associations were pushed out it would be disastrous for the game.

The IFA also complained that since 1921 the phrase 'birth within the area of the National Association' had been inserted irregularly in the Rule Book of the FA *as if* this was part of the original decision of 1895. It was worried about what the FA might be up to behind the scenes, and revealed its anger that Imperial loyalty looked like being betrayed:

> The Irish FA had followed the lead of England for many years. When England asked them to join the FIFA they did so; and when England wanted them to come out they did so. Again they rejoined at England's request, and again withdrew; and they might be asked to rejoin for all they knew. They were getting suspicious of England. They did not know what was going on. Sir Frederick Wall was in communication with the Irish Free State and the FIFA and what was happening they did not know. It was time this sort of thing was stopped. England had abused her position, and he felt, deserved to be censured. The FA never made any objection when the Irish FA played men not born in their area, nor had it any right to do so.

Wall, the secretary of the FA, insisted that 'He had been punctiliously careful not to say a word that would be harmful to our Irish friends in their trouble with the Irish Free State'.

Speaking in opposition to the English view, the President of the SFA revealed how the 'nationality' of Irish players was negotiated through the filter of English League clubs with only migrants, likely to be amongst the best players of course, being selected:

> The proposal the FA puts forward today is quite unnecessary unless the Board is prepared to recognise the political position in Ireland. I have heard not a single argument in favour of that. Mr. Ferguson (Ireland) has pointed out that no other sporting body has recognized the political position. Why should we in football? ... They have selected players from players in English clubs, not from the Free State, who have been born in the Free State. Our English friends have never opposed that.

The issue ran on into the post-war years with the FA still trying, unsuccessfully, to add 'within the area of the National Association' to the agreement of 1895; the renamed FA of Ireland (FAI) pushing FIFA to action about the use of the term 'Ireland'; FIFA, involved in its own struggles for dominance with the International Board, chiding the continuing practice of what FIFA insisted on calling 'the Northern Ireland FA' of using players born in another political state; while in 1950 the IFA (i.e., Northern Ireland) asked a conference of the British associations to discuss 'the action of the FA of Ireland in requiring players to sign an undertaking with regard to playing in International matches as a condition for granting a clearance certificate for transfers to other national associations'.[13]

In effect, players who wanted to transfer from Eire to the more lucrative fields of the Scottish and, especially, English professional leagues had to agree they would only play in a team called 'Ireland' if it was selected by the FA of Ireland. The conference resolved that there should be no such restriction on the movement of players and passed the matter onto FIFA, which replied agreeing that such a rule was contrary to its regulations but adding: 'On the other hand, the Executive Committee consider it inadmissable to select players being citizens of Eire, for the representative teams of a country other than Eire'. The only exception allowed to this practice was in matches between the British Associations if no one objected. This provoked the Irish FA which sent a letter to all British Associations. It had been founded in 1883: 'The Irish FA functioned harmoniously until a political movement inspired by a religious element caused a re-adjustment of relations between Ireland and the British Government.'[14]

The breakaway section had had Dominion status within the Empire, then it had left and declared itself a Republic – Eire. So it was now plainly a foreign country and should be treated as such by the British Associations. It should only use the name Eire and had no claim at all to the term 'Ireland'. Football was not its national game and it did not have as many clubs playing football. The IFA asserted that, 'The position today is that the IFA remains the national association and indeed the only association entitled to use the title "Ireland". Its territory may be reduced in size but in every other respect it remains unaltered.'[15]

Meanwhile, in a letter (in three languages) to FIFA in July 1952, the FAI complained that the area it designated on an accompanying map as 'still held as part of the UK' was continuing to use the title 'Ireland' when the governments concerned had agreed its proper designation was 'Northern Ireland'; that it still was prohibiting cross-border sporting links in Ireland; and that it had used players in recent qualifying matches for the World Cup who had previously played in the *same tournament* for Eire.

This case study in the politics of football reveals some of the complexities surrounding matters of identity, nationality and sport in situations, not restricted to the United Kingdom of course, that can be designated as neo-colonialism. For example, in 1957 the International Board had cause to ruminate over the problems which would ensue if the Republic of Ireland *really* were treated just like any other 'foreign' country. In that case, players signed from there would require a two-year residential qualification before they could play for their English and Scottish clubs, a most inconvenient tap on the flow of talent.[16] This 'issue' seems to have been quietly dropped. Then the migration of talent, indeed, the migration of people more generally, sets up all kinds of resonances which disturb the foundations of any neat equivalence between geography and emotional attachment through sport. Often neither 'Irish' players nor spectators seem too clear where their allegiances lie precisely. Sugden and Bairner note just one aspect of this: 'During the 1980s, the red, white and blue scarves and Union Jacks were replaced on the terraces by green and white colours, which the team had always worn, and Northern Ireland flags.'[17]

They suggest that this is because the possibility of independence for Ulster grew during the course of the 'Troubles' and there was a move to stress the symbols of that, rather than those of the troubled Union. Conversely, the two great teams of Scotland have regular spectators and supporters clubs in both parts of Ireland, Irish flags wave at the games of Glasgow Celtic and those of Ulster at Rangers of the same city. It is regularly asserted, though on the basis of no adequate evidence, that many Scots of Irish origin are not very interested in the fortunes of the Scottish national team.[18]

However, as the letter quoted at the start of this essay indicates, those who organized football in the sovereign political state of Ireland eventually had to temper their assertiveness before the sheer weight of England in the sporting configuration of the British Isles. In a covering note to the IFA in Belfast, Mr Wickman set out the peculiar difficulties of the situation of football south of the border.[19] He alluded to an unsympathetic press, a school policy directed against the sport and the strong opposition of the Gaelic game. He had to acknowledge the power of English and Scottish football in the minds of his own spectators and ask for regular matches, a plea which was not granted. Small wonder, then, that a victory by the Republic of Ireland over England in the European Nations Finals of 1988 and a draw between the same sides in the World Cup Finals in 1990 were greeted with total delight, even if the Republic of Ireland's team manager and many of the players had indirect, distant, diffuse and tenuous connections with the country they represented; and many of the squad did not know the words of 'their' national anthem.[20] Nor, given the history sketched here, was it too surprising that a 'friendly' match between the two nations in Dublin in 1995, held at a time of a strong political effort to end the 25-year-long 'Troubles' In Northern Ireland, was the focus of a major riot. Some hundreds of English supporters chanted 'No surrender to the IRA!', gave Nazi salutes, called the Irish manager 'a Judas', and tore up seats and used them as missiles. The game was abandoned after only 28 minutes' play. The tensions Ireland provokes both for English nationalism and for a 'United' Kingdom still find expression and grounds for renewal on the football pitch.

Scotland

Scotland has always been the main counterweight to English domination of the 'United' Kingdom of football. Unlike Wales, the football authorities in Scotland struggled to keep their clubs out of English competitions, and one minor club, geographically in England, plays in the Scottish League. Unlike both parts of Ireland, Scotland has possessed a major professional league with clubs good enough, on occasion, to win European club competitions. Indeed, in recent years a group of Irish businessmen have made two attempts to persuade the *Scottish* League to accept a team from Dublin into its competition on the grounds that this was the only way the capital of Ireland would ever enter the top flight of European football, attempts treated with disdain by Scots. But the professional game in Scotland has not escaped the manifold tensions associated with uniting the Kingdom, and has been structured by four features of some relevance to matters of 'national identities'. Professional football in Scotland has:

1. had its professional competitions dominated by two clubs from one city – Rangers and Celtic of Glasgow;
2. clubs, especially the two just mentioned, linked to ethnic groupings and

antagonisms – 'Protestant', 'Catholic', 'Irish' – which exist in the wider society and which have other institutionalized forms;
3. been economically dependent upon transfers of players to the English League;
4. been surrounded by, and is a main force of expression of, a cultural dislike of 'England' and the 'English' which has been exhibited at the international level but has also structured club football.

This author has elaborated on these features elsewhere[21] and will not dwell on them here, but some consideration of the cultural ramifications of one taken-for-granted aspect of soccer – the transfer market for professional players – does reveal some of the ways particular kinds of 'nationality' are expressed through the routines of football.

Across the century, the English League and Scottish League have stood in a relation of buyer and seller. Thus one complex of cultural meanings surrounding Scottish football concerns the constant and, until very recently, largely unreciprocated movement of top players out of Scottish football, and indeed out of Scotland. This has had considerable effects, such as:

1. elevating the annual international match against England to the high point of the Scottish season;
2. doubts about the 'nationalism' of the 'Anglos' (broadly a pejorative term for Scots who play in England);
3. mingling the emotions of pride, sense of loss and fatalism, as over the century most of the best Scottish players have been sold to English clubs;
4. complaints about the quality of the Scottish League, since many of its professional clubs have, in effect, acted as feeders to talent to England;
5. accentuating the already over-determined significance of Rangers and Celtic as being the only clubs capable of matching the financial power and playing pretensions of the top English clubs.

'Anglos' were not picked for Scotland until the last years of the nineteenth century when, following a run of seven defeats by England, the selectors picked a team with five English-based players in 1896; and the non-English associations, the Scottish in particular, began worrying away on the International Board about being allowed to select players for international matches who were registered professionals with another, usually the English, association. In 1898 the Scots sought the 'right' to select such players but had to settle for a much less solid arrangement the following year: 'the International Board unanimously recommends that the respective Associations use their influence with clubs to ensure to other National Associations the services of players in International Matches'.[22]

The rumblings about the availability of players went on over the years and reached a high point in 1929 when representatives of the four countries held a special meeting to discuss the possibility of playing international matches on days other than Saturdays. Arsenal, a prominent English club, had sent a letter suggesting this to all the associations. Forty-six top clubs in England had declared in favour of the proposal. The problem was the number of players the English clubs had to provide for *all* the international sides. They estimated that they supplied all the players for England, Wales and Ireland, and a third of the Scots even though there was still a full League programme on international days. As one English delegate put it, disingenuously, 'I do not think it is the intention of the clubs that matches should not be played on Saturday subject to your not asking for their players. Of course, you can play on the Saturday, provided you do not select their players.'[23]

In effect the meeting was about the power of English League clubs in relation to the minor 'nations' of the United Kingdom. The discussion was a long one but the nub was nicely put in this exchange:

> Mr. Kingscott (England): There would be no difficulty if the various countries would select their registered players.
> Mr. Campbell (Scotland): Are we to understand that we are to substitute registration instead of birth as a qualification for International players? We could never agree to that.

It was another English delegate who alluded to the wider conflicts that lurked around the organization of football, which often made it necessary for all the countries to act as a truly United Kingdom:

> I'm also distressed to think we should be here this afternoon on this topic. I really am! I look upon International football as football of importance, more than that, I look upon our International relations as an organization of vital importance. We four British Nations have worked together, we have faced problems together and we have worked them out together. Together we joined the Federation, together we came out, and together, and only together, can we accomplish anything in the way of world or Imperial control of this game, which is coming in the future.

In other words, the submerged 'nations' of the United Kingdom preferred an imperial identity, albeit as lance corporals, to the possibility of extinction by unknown foreigners. For the way the British had organized and controlled football came under increasing threat through the course of the twentieth century.

The Rest of the World

When the International Board was established in 1886, rule seven stated that 'the Board shall discuss and decide proposed alterations in the laws of the game and generally any matters affecting Association football in its International relations'. But the 'international' relations of concern here were those between the 'countries' within the United Kingdom. The home associations took a lofty view of the place of the rest of the globe in the football world. A letter from the Dutch FA in the early twentieth century asking for some international matches and urging 'the founding of an international Association to promote football in Europe, arrange an International Championship, and to secure uniformity in the laws of the game for all countries',[24] was more or less ignored, as was a similar approach by the French FA to the Football Association in 1903.[25] FIFA was set up in 1904 by seven European nations. The English, without becoming members, did forge unofficial links with the new body and an Englishman soon became President of FIFA,[26] but the home associations continued to guard what they saw as their own ground. In 1911 the International Board noted that the congress of 'The International Federation of Association Football' had unanimously agreed to ask for powers to send a representative to the Board. One year later the Board considered such a request from the secretary of 'the Fédération Internationale de Football Association', but 'It was unanimously decided that the time was not ripe to invite a delegate to attend the Board meetings.'

However, in 1913, after lengthy discussions, a proposal by the FA to admit two representatives of the International Federation was accepted and Paris joined the likes of Portpatrick, Torquay and Llandudno as the Rest of the World's venue on the list of meeting places. However, part of the agreement for this change was that four-fifths of the members of the Board would need to vote in favour of change to effect any alteration to the laws, so the weight of the home associations was well safeguarded.

After the First World War a dispute arose within FIFA concerning the reluctance of some members to play matches against their former foes, the defeated European powers, and the home countries withdrew from the Federation. In 1920 a proposal by the Irish FA to exclude FIFA from the International Board was carried, and in 1923 a Conference was held between representatives of the International Federation and the national associations of the countries of the United Kingdom with two main themes: should the home counties re-join the Federation and how was an 'amateur' to be defined. Eventually, it was agreed that the home associations would consider rejoining FIFA if four conditions were accepted:

1. the articles of the International Federation should not affect the inter-relations of the associations of the UK;
2. the article of membership providing for a percentage of the receipts of all international matches to be paid to the Federation should not apply to the home internationals;
3. the reinstatement of the requirement for four-fifths of the International Board to be in favour of any change;
4. the Federation would not interfere with the rules of any association which related to its internal management.

These recommendations were accepted and representatives of FIFA again returned to the meetings of the International Board. Paris was the venue for the meeting in 1925. But any *entente* did not remain *cordiale* for very long. In September 1925 there was a meeting between representatives of the four home associations to discuss a resolution which had been agreed unanimously at a recent FIFA meeting in Prague which ran: 'The Congress of the FIFA declares that it considers the FIFA the highest authority on all football matters, and that it cannot accept the interference or guidance of anybody else in such matters'.

On the face of it, this looked like a direct challenge to the International Board, the control it exercised over the laws of the game, and to the countries of the United Kingdom. However, various elements in FIFA tried to smooth the feathers of the home associations. So the next meeting of the International Board was informed:

> Arising out of a resolution passed at the Annual Congress of La Fédération Internationale de Football Association at Prague in 1925, it was reported to the Board, that at the opening of the Annual Congress of La Fédération Internationale de Football Associations at Rome, in May, 1926, that Mr. Rimet, the President, made a statement to the effect that the Federation would never express its opposition to the authority of the International Board. Correspondence had been exchanged with the British football associations and there was no doubt, it was not the intention of the Federation to reduce the authority of the International Board as the highest authority in Association football. Mr. Rimet expressed satisfaction at being able to explain the misunderstanding.[27]

However, foreign presumption still rankled. In 1928 the home associations again withdrew from FIFA over the issue of 'broken time' payments to 'amateurs', which the British bodies viewed as a highly dubious practice. Their letter of resignation emphasized the underlying misgiving:

> The great majority of the Associations affiliated with La Fédération Internationale de Football Associations are of comparatively recent formation, and as a consequence cannot have the knowledge which only experience can bring.[28]

This led to a conference between the home associations and FIFA officials, including Jules Rimmet, who exclaimed through an interpreter, 'When he and the FIFA received the decision of the British Associations to withdraw from the Federation they were astounded. It came like a thunderbolt.'[29] The UK officials cited the two issues which had led to their resignation – 'broken time' payments and fear that FIFA would start to interfere in matters which were not its concern. However, the men from FIFA were not convinced that these really were the matters that had precipitated the withdrawal and insisted on being given all the reasons. Eventually, one of the English representatives referred to the Prague resolution. One of the FIFA officials replied that there had been a misunderstanding, the resolution had been a defensive reaction by FIFA against the International Olympic Committee which had been trying to tell it how to organize football at the Olympic Games. Another FIFA man, Seeldrayers of Belgium, sketched the regard of the rest of the world in the most flattering terms:

> In our Rules there has always been a special position for the British Associations and Dominions. All our Associations affiliated by the Federation are on the same footing. They must all be ruled by the same Rules, but taking into account what the British Associations have done for football they have an exceptional position. We might have deleted the Rule that gave special position to the British Associations. Even if you left us for good, we would in consideration for the past maintain that you were the men who were making the Rules. We know that they are the best Rules for the Game. Is it not a sign of good will on our part that we are content to accept the Laws of the Game?

While another FIFA official argued, 'I think the four British Associations should not lose their position with regard to football. They should continue to be our leaders and our advisers.' The men of the United Kingdom regarded such foreign blandishments with suspicion. A Welsh official said, 'The harm that was done in 1925 by that Resolution has never been wiped out.' While another from Ireland recalled a previous meeting, 'I have no doubt that Mr Seeldrayers said distinctly "if you do not come back we will make Laws of our own".'

Eventually, the representatives of the UK football authorities did draw up some 'heads of agreement' which would have allowed their associations to rejoin FIFA, including one that stated that any dispute should be referred to the International Board, but in 1930 FIFA deemed these unacceptable. Interchanges dragged on with, basically, FIFA wanting a joint meeting between the two groupings, while the UK bodies argued that the International Board was the place to resolve difficulties. FIFA's response was that the Board was a forum in which to resolve 'technical' but not 'political' problems. In 1931 the home associations agreed that they would work with FIFA by agreement but would not again become members,[30] and it was not until after the Second World War that England, Northern Ireland, Scotland and Wales rejoined FIFA and began taking part in World Cup competitions. Rous, then secretary of the FA, indicates how he attended a FIFA executive meeting in November 1945 to see if re-entry might be negotiable. It was, but one of the conditions was that the British Associations should always be entitled to nominate one Vice-President of FIFA, a right shared only with Russia, also joining in the post-war period, who insisted on having similar privileges to the United Kingdom as a condition of entry.[31] Certainly, the tone of the secretary of the Scottish FA writing in 1947, suggests that, even at this date, the British stance remained essentially condescending:

> One of the chief functions of the FIFA is to see that the Laws of the Game are applied in each country as issued by the International Board. Thus, these Laws translated into French, Spanish, German, are sent all over the world along with the English version, and this ensures uniformity as far as possible in the playing of the game. True it is that some things are allowed in continental tactics which are alien to our British game, but, in the main, these variations are caused by temperament and may in the course of time disappear as a result of more frequent contacts with British teams and British style of play and standards of sportsmanship.[32]

Conclusion

Through the first half of the century, led by England, the associations of the 'United' Kingdom battled with the fledgling FIFA about who was to be the ultimate authority in world football. That battle was eventually lost, but, for example, the home associations still fill half the places on the International Board which continues to be the authority for interpreting and changing the rules of the game. The continuing privileged position of the 'one state but several countries' in the power structures of football is a testament to that struggle, and to the compromises the four 'nations' extracted even as they were deposed from prime position. So what Nairn calls the 'internationalization of duality' of national identities among the non-English British[33] is, at least in some measure, just an accurate reflection of the joint action they usually take in the sporting structures in which they are represented.

But united imperial endeavour is only part of the story. For throughout the twentieth century the 'United' Kingdom has been engaged in a process of building and redefining what the 'nation' it refers to is exactly. This study of the politics of soccer has revealed some of the tensions that this has created. However, more is involved than simply treating sport as an inviting window through which to view more important issues. Rather, given that sport is an activity with great cultural significance, football can enter into these political and economic relations, especially at the level of popular perceptions. If nations are 'imagined communities'[34] then celebrations, events and incidents are needed to feed imaginations, especially those of the vast majority who are not university intellectuals. The place soccer has played in the exact kinds of 'nationalism' the subordinate countries of the Kingdom have exhibited has varied, but what the regularities of the sport have done is to drive home the diversity of conditions within the 'United' Kingdom and to highlight the unthinking arrogance of rule from England. Occasionally the smaller 'nations' within the union have stood out firmly against England whenever they have felt that its negotiations with other bodies might threaten their own interests. In parts of the Kingdom sport has been a means through which a definite nationalist project could be broadcast. In other parts the sport has become a complex ethnic marker, an institution invested with great emotional power, both defining antagonistic groupings within the population (Catholics and Protestants) *and* reproducing a strong cultural nationalism. Neither of these social divisions, of course, has that much to do with class identities.

Within Britain sport has been one of the main strands to which the submerged nations have clung in order to assert their distinctiveness, but this cultural nationalism has lacked a sustained political drive. The deputy leader of the Scottish National Party, deposed as a Member of Parliament at the General Election in 1992, castigated his country people as 'ninety minute patriots', whose nationalist outpourings were evident only at sporting occasions and who lacked the strength of character to demand self-government. It seemed doubtful to him that this kind of nationalism could ever be translated into the political form, and it is rather the continuance of the cultural nationalism which is now under threat.

The occasional threat to the over-representation of the four countries in world football, now usually coming from the Third World, is regarded with head-shaking disbelief in the submerged 'nations', evidence that, for their own ends, many foreigners prefer to feign ignorance of the importance of the special 'national' mix of the United Kingdom. But the fight with foreigners is not over, and as they grow ever more numerous the weight of the home associations has declined. In recent years the assurance of England's touch has waned, and it is not sensible, at least in football terms, to be seen to be too close. The Welsh FA has recently established its own League so as to be able to make a more substantial claim to a place as a full football 'nation'.[36] Scotland likes to picture itself as like other European 'nations', the potential victim of endemic English thuggery. Scotland versus England, for a century and more, *the* pivotal game on the tartan calendar, has been abandoned as a regular event, and most Scots are not overly keen to reinstate it. Now, as Europe fractures into more and more real nation-states all seeking their own football status to emphasize their separateness; as bureaucratic definitions and legal rules become more important aspects of legitimacy than tradition; as economic and televisual imperatives drive major clubs towards a European League which could well threaten the well-being of many national associations and the place of international competition at the apex of football; as multi-nationalism, in all its forms – economic, political and cultural – steadily dissolves traditional ties, 'communities', and old allegiances; it may well be that the strange case of 'one state, several countries' will come under increasing scrutiny. It seems unlikely that the process of building a 'United' Kingdom – in football or political terms – has ended yet.

NOTES

1. National Library of Scotland, Edinburgh, Minutes of the Meetings of the International Football Association Board, lodged by the Scottish Football Association (hereafter MIFAB) 20 June 1959.
2. A. Williams, *Life in a Railway Factory* (1915, reprinted Devon, 1969), p.287.
3. See, for example, J. Clarke and C. Critcher, 1966 And All That, in A. Tomlinson and G.Whannel (eds.), *Off The Ball* (London, 1986), pp.112–26.
4. H.F.Moorhouse '"We're Off To Wembley!"', in D. McCrone and S. Kendrick (eds.), *The Making of Scotland: Nation, Culture and Change* (Edinburgh, 1989) pp.207–27.
5. B.Anderson, *Imagined Communities* (London, 1991), p.2.
6. R.Holt, *Sport and the British* (Oxford,1989), p.237.
7. M. Hechter, *Internal Colonialism: The Celtic Fringe in British National Development 1536–1966* (London, 1975).
8. MIFAB, 17 June 1895.
9. MIFAB, 10 June 1922.
10. MIFAB, 11 March 1925.
11. MIFAB, 13 June 1931.
12. MIFAB, no date.
13. MIFAB, 29 November 1950.
14. This is not a dead issue. Consider the ambiguous title of M. Brodie, *100 Years of Irish*

Football (Belfast, 1980) 'Published by authority of the Irish FA'. Moreover, in this history, this minute is recorded on page 15 as part of a memorandum sent from the IFA to a FIFA Congress in 1954, but the phrase 'inspired by a religious element' is omitted.

15. MIFAB, 30 January 1952.
16. MIFAB, 15 June 1957.
17. J.Sugden and A. Bairner, *Sport, Sectarianism and Society in a Divided Ulster* (Leicester, 1993), pp.78–9.
18. B.Murray, *The Old Firm:Sectarianism, Sport and Society in Scotland* (Edinburgh, 1984) p.231. G.P.T. Finn (1991), 'Racism, Religion and Social Prejudice: Irish Catholic Clubs, Soccer and Scottish Society', parts I and II, *International Journal of the History of Sport*, 8 (1991), pp.392–3. J. M. Bradley, 'Football in Scotland: A History of Political and Ethnic Identity', *International Journal of the History of Sport*, 12, 1 (April 1995), p.91. Those eager to stress the ethnic significance of football in Scotland tend to seek only confirming evidence, and often deploy contradictory arguments. Thus, though it is often asserted that Scottish Catholics do not support the national side, when the national stadium was being refurbished and some Scottish international matches were played at Ibrox, the home of Rangers FC., poor attendances led some to argue that many supporters of the Scottish team would never enter Ibrox because of its 'sectarian' associations. Other, rather more plausible, reasons for the lack of interest were overlooked.
19. MIFAB, 20 June 1959.
20. The Irish manager is a former England international player. Many of the current Irish squad were born in England or Scotland and qualify to play for Ireland by having one parent or one grandparent who was born in Ireland. Irish use of the FIFA 'grandparent' rule to widen the pool of players was sneered at by the Scots, but in 1994 they announced that they would be applying the same regulation to define possible 'Scots' in the future. It should be noted that the Scots have no 'national' anthem – a fact which causes much debate and merriment in Scotland about just what popular song should be played at the start of international matches. J. Sugden and A. Bairner, 'Sectarianism and Football Hooliganism in Northern Ireland', in T.Reilly *et al.* (eds.), *Science and Football* (London, 1988), pp.572–8, indicate how International matches against England in Ulster sometimes developed an anti-English tone among 'loyalist' supporters following the 'Anglo-Irish agreement' at the political level.
21. H.F.Moorhouse 'Professional Football and Working Class Culture: English Theories and Scottish Evidence', *Sociological Review*, 32 (1984), pp.285–315. H.F.Moorhouse 'Repressed Nationalism and Professional Football: Scotland versus England', in J.Mangan and R.Small (eds.) *Sport, Culture, Society* (London, 1986), pp.52–9. H.F.Moorhouse 'It's Goals that Count? Football Finance and Football Subcultures', *Sociology of Sport Journal*, 3 (1986), pp.245–60. H.F.Moorhouse, 'Scotland against England: Football and Popular Culture', *International Journal of the History of Sport*, 4 (1987), 189–202. H.F.Moorhouse, 'We're off to Wembley!', in D. McCrone and S. Kendrick (eds.), *The Making of Scotland: Nation, Culture and Change* (Edinburgh, 1989), pp.207–27. H.F.Moorhouse 'Shooting Stars: Footballers and Working Class Culture in Twentieth Century Scotland', in R.Holt (ed.), *Sport and the Working Class in Modern Britain* (Manchester, 1990), pp.179–97. H.F.Moorhouse, 'Blue Bonnets over the Border: Scotland and the Migration of Footballers', in J. Bale and J.Maguire (eds.), *The Global Sports Arena: Athletic Talent Migration in an Interdependent World* (London 1994), pp.78–96. H.F.Moorhouse, 'From Zines like These? Fanzines, Tradition and Identity in Scottish Football', in G. Jarvie and G. Walker (eds.), *Scottish Sport in the Making of the Nation* (Leicester, 1994), pp.9–26.
22. MIFAB, 19 June 1899.
23. MIFAB, 18 Nov. 1929.
24. MIFAB, 16 June 1902.
25. S. Rous, *Football Worlds; A Lifetime in Sport* (London, 1978) p.91.
26. Ibid.
27. MIFAB, 12 June 1926.
28. MIFAB, Conference of Representatives of UK Associations, 17 Feb. 1928.
29. MIFAB, Notes of Observations on the International Conference, 19 Nov. 1928.

30. S. Rous, *Football Worlds*, p.92.
31. Ibid.
32. G. Graham, *Scottish Football Through the Years* (Glasgow, 1947), p.21.
33. Quoted in A. Bairner, 'Football and the idea of Scotland', in G. Jarvie and G. Walker (eds.), *Scottish Sport in the Making of the Nation*, p.11.
34. B.Anderson, *Imagined Communities*.
35. *The Herald* (Glasgow), 21 May 1992.
36. Though the big professional clubs based in Wales are not in it, some of the smaller clubs, who have been playing in semi-professional English leagues, are threatening to take the Welsh FA to court because they do not want to be forced to play in the league of 'their' country.

Forging a French Fighting Spirit: The Nation, Sport, Violence and War

JEAN-MICHEL FAURE
(translated by Peter Snowdon)

Is it possible to explain how an English pastime called 'sport' should have come to serve as the model for types of competition that are recognized, accepted and practised throughout the world? This question, raised by N. Elias,[1] and the theory he has constructed in an attempt to answer it cannot be ignored. Together they form an essential problem for the historian.

Elias sketches the outline of a particular structure in which political institutions, relationships of interdependency between social groups and specific types of economy are all bound up together. This structure has a coherence and a meaning, but to discover them it is necessary to establish the relationship between each of its characteristics and the emergence of the nation-state. It is this historical event that constitutes the theoretical cornerstone of Elias' intellectual edifice. It is only when the State comes to hold the monopoly of legitimate violence that political confrontations can be channelled into the form of the peaceful, rule-governed competitions which control power relationships in democratic societies.

According to this theory, parliamentary democracy and sport are parts of a single historical structure. The rules of sport replicate in a different field those which govern political structures based on universal suffrage and on the sovereignty of free and equal individuals. They exclude any recourse to violence which might put the individual in physical danger, and thus they require the individual to control his or her behaviour and restrain aggressive instincts while taking part in an organized confrontation. Sport may therefore be defined as a form of combat which offers all the pleasures of a real battle while largely removing the risk of injury and death which is inherent in military conflict. It belongs to the great process of the progressive civilizing of behaviour characteristic of Western societies.

The approach taken by Elias is certainly attractive, but it entails the acceptance of certain presuppositions which are not entirely unambiguous. If the peaceful coexistence of men depends upon the existence of the State, the absence of the State will necessarily lead to permanent and universal conflict. Thus, in order to halt this anarchy men must institute a common power which commands the respect of all, and so binds them to a society. Societies without such a government exist only on the margins of socialized humanity, and according to one theory of biological determinism invoked here by Elias such societies are destined to be in a state of war. This theory claims that aggression and the taste for violence are rooted in man's nature: the plasticity of these instincts will allow them to be codified, ritualized and reduced, but they can never be eliminated.

Every society is confronted by this general problem, which it must resolve if it is not to be destroyed: how to channel and control an aggressive instinct which is inherent in the species? Nevertheless, the various forms of social and institutional control adopted can only themselves become sources of social tension, for their purpose is to shape and even remove a powerful source of pleasure: the excitement produced by aggressive confrontation. Organized forms of competition use the simulation of violence to relieve and reduce the aggressive instincts that have survived the repression of their original forms. As a cultural form which can be dated historically, sport belongs to the domain of the mimetic: it is intended to free the human soul from the passions that weigh it down. In the modern world, it fulfils the principal function assigned by Aristotle to classical tragedy: 'a representation which by acting out pity (*eleos*) and fear (*phobos*) produces the purification (*katharsis*) of this sort of emotion'. Sport is the euphemistic representation of the latent violence of the Western mind.

For Elias, any weakening of the regulatory institutions which preserve the state monopoly of violence leads directly to a regression, a degradation of the process of civilization, and ultimately returns men to a state of nature. But how, by this logic, are we to understand the resurgence of violence that has so often accompanied the reinforcement of state structures throughout the history of modern societies? This phenomenon can be imputed 'to the absence of any effective monopoly and of any effective regulation of physical violence in relations between States',[2] or it may appear as a perversion foreign to the aims of the various institutions which have been developed to protect life and to keep the peace within society.

The great merit of Elias' study is to have clearly demonstrated the existence of a strong correlation in the history of nation-states between sport and power; but the weakness of his analysis lies in the hypothesis he advances in order to explain this correlation. By restricting himself to a positive definition of the State as an authority whose purpose is to regulate the life of its people, to protect their social well-being, and to keep the peace, he overlooks an essential detail. The State's influence over life is matched by an awesome power to cause death: the two are complementary. World wars, colonial conflicts, countless local confrontations, and many more recent events all bear witness to this fact. 'Never,' writes M. Foucault, 'have wars been so bloody as they have been since the nineteenth century, and never, even allowing for differences of scale, have governments imposed such massive holocausts upon their own populations ... War is made in the name of the survival of all; entire peoples are pitted one against another, to kill each other in the name of their need to live. Killing has become a vital necessity.'[3] Modern societies bring together in a single institutional reality the power to control life, to increase it and to protect it, and the power to condemn entire peoples to death. A high level of civilization and a strong commitment to the prosecution of war go hand in glove and for this reason it is necessary to redefine the parameters of Elias' hypothesis.

Sport is a legitimate method of socialization only to the extent that it may help to resolve one of the major problems facing all democratic societies: how can one create an autonomous, non-violent individual, who is nevertheless adapted to a form of society constructed on competition and conflict, an individual who has the permanent status of a fighter, locked into individual agonistic relationships with others, but available at any moment to be mobilized for the highest form of collective social confrontation of war? The educational and political strategies developed in the field of sport since the beginning of the century have had two aims: to discipline and correct individual behaviour; and to mobilize, bring together and shape what have commonly been called the masses. These two goals are determined by two different perceptions of sport: that of the competitor and that of the spectator. They thus involve two very different modes of intervention. In the first case, the aim is to produce legitimate forms of individualization through the training of the body; in the second case, to produce through the highly ritualized presentation of the body's performance, the consciousness of an identity and the sense of belonging to a national community. Historically, sport has indeed been organized to this dual purpose, but the practical side of the scheme has always been dominant. The effective mobilization of the crowd must depend upon the effective disciplining of the individual body. The two operations correlate and depend upon a single social mechanism.

Starting from an analysis of this mechanism, this essay will attempt to verify two hypotheses: that the manner in which the mechanism operates determines the specific relationships between sport, violence and war; and that the structure of this mechanism is in turn determined by power relationships and class structure.

The Age of the Stadium

In early twentieth-century France[4] the practice of physical exercise was popularized according to two models. The first, gymnastics, adopted both the paramilitary methods of organization and the nationalistic rhetoric that F.L. Jahn had developed in Prussia. There was only a slight difference of emphasis: whereas the *Turnkunst* had been designed to promote German unity, after 1780 the French were using the same device to prepare themselves for a war of revenge. Gymnastics associations proliferated, and their names are eloquent testimony to the patriotic mission with which they were charged: *La Française, La Patriote, Le Drapeau, La Sentinelle, La Vaillante.* Sport was a later import, which made its way to France from England, in the guise of an agreeable pastime which was reserved for the privileged classes. The differences between the two activities, however, should be seen in context, for they share certain common assumptions and aims: whatever form it takes, physical exercise develops the taste for self-exertion and arguably strengthens the character, teaches the art of self-discipline and stimulates the competitive instinct. The only truly noteworthy difference is between the groups at which the two types of activity were directed. Gymnastics was for the masses, and was meant to encourage devotion to national causes. It aimed to create an autonomous individual who would freely employ his strength in the service of the state: a citizen who was at the same time a soldier. Sport was aimed at the ruling elites, for whom the pleasure of competition would legitimize the idea of confrontation. It sought to produce an individual who would be capable, in the admirable phrase of Richard Holt, 'of governing himself so as to be able to govern others':[5] a citizen who would be ready to assume the responsibilities and battles of his class.

The Gymnastics of the Republic

Gymnastics and sport were not to enjoy the same destiny, and each followed a different chronological pattern. In the early years of the century, gymnastics associations were part and parcel of a society at war, simple appendages to the military institution, helping to ensure continuity between civilian and military life, 'between the nation that works and the nation that will fight'.[6] Their manner of operation did not however depend upon training techniques that were forcibly imposed; but rather, with the aim of increasing physical skill and strength, they concentrated first and foremost on the inculcation of moral virtue. In his fine book, A. Ehrenberg[7] has shown how the army changed after the Revolution in order to provide the Republic with the sort of man it required: 'An individual who knew how to deport himself in battle without the guidance of a commanding officer ... A man who, in combat, knew in himself that he could count upon his own strength', a self-reliant and docile individual who was prepared to put his initiative at the service of collective goals. The gymnast and the soldier are similar in character: a controlled fighting spirit, voluntarily prepared and always available 'for the struggle for existence, as for the struggle between peoples'. This 'fighting spirit' is a legitimate form of social behaviour and an aid to correct social conduct, and is thus the exact opposite of violence. Violence is an instinct and its excesses are characteristic of the behaviour of asocial types, agitators and trouble-makers, whose actions were stigmatized in official discourse. These were the people whom the political powers saw at the heart of the crowd, 'that barbaric, atavistic collectivity ... sign of social degeneration'. Gymnastic exercise and physical games were good ways for soldiers to protect themselves against the threat of such excesses. By submitting to the rules of the sport and to the codified constraints of the game, the soldier learned of his own will to discipline himself: he became the antitype of the violent man. Organized competition was well suited to the task of shaping his social behaviour. These new processes for training the individual changed the traditional hierarchy of disciplines without totally eliminating them. The army had taken charge of the collective strength of the nation with the aim of increasing it, and for this reason military commanders remained hostile to competitive sport, which singled out individuals and classified their achievement, thus potentially endangering the cohesion of the group. Military regulations therefore advised that 'physical exercises should be chosen to suit the strength of the weakest men'. The army encouraged physical education and was wary of sport for that reason. In order to carry out this great project of fusing the nation into a single mass of properly-trained citizens, the army relied upon the gymnastics associations, which applied the same precepts and stood by the same principles. As a member of the congress of the *Ligue de l'enseignement* put it: 'Through gymnastics, the army penetrates into the nation, just as the nation takes possession of the army: gymnastics and military exercise are the moral education of a democracy'.[8] Gymnastics places the citizen on a war footing, and mobilizes the soldier in times of peace.

Rule Britannia

Gymnastics societies began to disappear after 1920 and were rapidly replaced by a network of sports clubs and societies. Fashioned in the public schools of 'Her Gracious Majesty' and disseminated in France by distinguished anglophiles, sport operated outside the ambit of the military establishment, although its purpose was similar: to 'coordinate discipline and mobilization'. But the practice of sport did not simply borrow modes of socialization previously elaborated in a military context: it proceeded in its own particular way and according to different principles. Competition is the true end of sporting activity, being to the conduct of sport what battle is to the conduct of war. Only through competition can the qualities of the competitor, his capacities and moral resources be measured accurately. The purpose of the sporting confrontation is to reveal those virtues which are required to exercise power: daring, courage, determination, the will to win and respect for the rules. Through sport the bourgeoisie created for itself a 'class corps', characterized by health, cleanliness, and skill in competition. Sport was a way of developing the fighting spirit which had been originated by the ruling classes. 'We must certainly admit,' writes Michel Foucault, 'that one of the primordial forms of class consciousness is the affirmation of the body'.[9] This process of 'valorization' takes place largely on the sports field, but its scope cannot be restricted to the skills of those who have been trained to participate. The fighting spirit is not a mode of behaviour, but a manner of practising virtue; it is an ethos, a general disposition which can be transposed into every domain of social activity: business, the administration of men and of war. It should be the prerogative of the elites, of all those responsible for the government of the nation. Enamoured of excellence and of progress, those who promoted sport certainly sought to spread the practice, but with various qualifications. The participants must be educated, so that they come to see the benefits of competition: one must not lower oneself to their level in order to seduce them. 'We must be suspicious of the weak man,' wrote P. de Coubertin. 'Only yesterday he was master of civilization; one would have thought he was the most interesting of all characters, and that sport was to be brought down to his level along with everything else.'[10] The necessity for progress established an order of permanent confrontation. Life belongs to those who fight.

Ludus Pro Patria

The opposition between gymnastics and sport was first expressed in terms of their goals: the former emphasizes posture and self-discipline; the latter stresses the body's performance as the outer and visible sign of an inner, personal excellence. But this difference was not as clearcut as it might appear. Initially, as G. Vigarello has shown,[11] sport followed the established patterns of gymnastics, merely adding to them new standards of perfectibility and an obsessive concern for training. In this way it substituted methods of individualization for training procedures that had been directed towards the 'multitude'. Yet the orchestration of these differences, the specific way in which each of these practices conceived and achieved its aim to mobilize the crowd, pointed to the emergence of a more radical divergence. If the body was still the focus for a disciplinary method, the structures that controlled it were now based on different strategies. As E. Weber has pointed out, gymnastics associations were part of a vast movement whose aim was to mobilize and nationalize the masses. Their significance was thus not limited to providing battle training and physical education for several thousand adherents. Their gymnasts were intended to communicate the virtues that they embodied to others, helping to influence the thinking of those who had to be governed. Festivals, competitions, parades and marches were tried and tested means, efficient instruments for propagating ideas and moralizing behaviour. The festivals of the gymnastics societies were the high points of a national programme which strove to bring together the masses in order to educate and enlighten them. 'It was in these festivals that there grew up that mutual understanding and communication which fired their hearts; it was there that faith in the mother country and love of liberty were renewed.'[12] There is but a short step from bringing a crowd together to converting it. Gymnastic displays functioned as magical operations in which like grew from like. The presentation of the symbols of the Republic was in itself sufficient to encourage people in their patriotism: 'heroism and willpower are contagious'. In her book on the revolutionary festivals, M. Ozouf[13] notes the educational function which political authority attached to these great collective gatherings. At the beginning of the twentieth century, legislators shared the same convictions, and placed an absolute faith in the power of images. What could be seen at the festivals, the spectacles and the way in which they were presented would have the power to impress men and to change them. Gymnastic performances were ordered like a liturgy: they were one element in the celebration of the high mass of the Republic. No symbol was lacking: patriotic hymns, flags, uniforms, and arms drills accompanied the demonstrations of the gymnasts. Celebrating the civic virtue of the performers, political discourse revealed the reality of a community that, though at peace, might be mobilized at any moment for unavoidable wars. 'Youth feels the need to act,' wrote Dr Philippe Tissié, 'patriotic games draw the young into gymnasiums... Let us give them strength, for only strength will never fail. The power of words depends upon the power of actions ... Let us prepare them for the struggles that are to come'.[14]

In addition to their open hostility to the discipline of the barrack room, the partisans of sport rapidly became disillusioned with the real effects of such spectacles on their spectators. Despite all the efforts that were being made, these great competitive ceremonies rarely led to a more athletic society. Faced with the excesses of the 'rabble', a widespread problem in the stadiums of that period, critics spoke out more harshly, and their words looked forward to significant changes of strategy.

> We have acquired the habit of judging the success of a festival according to the number of people who were present at it; as long as they keep turning out, as the peasants say, as long as they're happy...

and this is a grave error. Too many spectators, the majority of whom are not themselves sportsmen, are dangerous for sport... If sport is to found a realm of tranquillity, and if it is to take place in the calm atmosphere that is indispensable, we must get rid of the impatient element, and the crowd, the two vampires of our present civilization.[15]

These crowds that gathered at festivals were still crowds, hideous, ugly both in form and in character: living images of sedition and disorder, they were a threat which had to be excluded and controlled. The promoters of sport no longer had much faith in the virtue which springs spontaneously from spectating. They placed instead an absolute trust in the effects of practical participation: only active involvement would educate, inculcate values and form the new man which civilization required. The spectator who was merely a voyeur was no longer an acceptable figure: to be re-admitted into the community, he had to begin practising sport himself.

> The ideal spectator for sport is the sportsman at rest, who has interrupted his own activity to watch the actions of a fellow sportsman who is more able or better trained ... We should like to see the creation of a sports centre where entry would be limited to those who participate in at least a few exercises ... Such a place would be the temple of our regeneration. It would serve as an example; gradually its rules would be copied and people would praise the benefits of its draconian regime.[16]

Successful mobilization relied on the participants; on this firm ground its work was carried out, acting on the body and penetrating the mind. It brought together individuals, transformed them, increased their strength and prepared them for their duties as citizens. In this way, practising a sport was able to create the feeling of belonging to a national community. 'Coubertin has shown us,' writes one of his disciples,

> the young sportsman who, having arrived at the age of maturity, rediscovers in the struggles of life all the emotions, all the drama that he has known, all the victories that he has won on the green fields that were the theatre of his youthful escapades. As then, so now, the scrum of interests gathers around some ball which he must grasp firmly so that he can take it from the reach of his opponents' desire!... Whether we like it or not, the law of national solidarity will make us dependent upon our fellow citizens, who make up the great national team of which we are obliged to be members.[17]

Outside the context of such lapidary pronouncements, the spectator remained an awkward character. The increasing number of places that were designed to accommodate him bears witness to the interest he aroused. Stadiums were, to begin with, spaces primarily designed to offer maximum visibility. The crowds which gathered around the 'gardens of bravery and the swimming pools of struggle'[18] would be united by the spectacle of excellence and so converted. The spectator, educated and illuminated, was a potential sportsman. But alas, this pedagogical initiative failed, for the masses who thronged to these splendid competitions confused them with the entertainments of the circus. So barriers were erected to contain them and fence them off, to select and separate the different groups who entered there, the better to control them.

Security measures became necessary.[19] The problem was no longer how to integrate the crowds into the society created around sport, but how to control them and prevent them from getting out of hand. It would be a mistake to interpret this as an admission of impotence or as a first gesture of despair: as the fatal acceptance of the 'fact' that the crowd could not be educated nor its passions governed. Rather it was an emergency measure, designed to create a breathing space, during which a long-term strategy could be devised. The ultimate aim was still to bring together the spectator and the sportsman. As P. Rosanvallon has stressed, in a democracy the purpose of the State is to create the nation: 'to influence everything which has a significant bearing upon the social fabric, so as to create in men's imagination a sense of participation which is no longer directly symbolized by any social structure'.[20] Sport is one of the most important elements in this democratic project.

The National Order

Generation after generation, sport has tightened its grip on physical culture: taking over traditional games, incorporating new forms of physical exercise, assimilating older forms that originated in other civilizations and in foreign cultures. In 1967 the old distinction between sport and physical education was finally discarded and the doctrine of sport established once and for all the predominance of the competitive ethos. Until this moment, school children had still been subjected to the rigid discipline of group exercises, that poor cousin of gymnastics. Henceforth, physical education was responsible for contributing to the development of the sporting activities by which it had been annexed. However this reform cannot be considered as a departure point, but rather as the ratification of an already existing state of affairs. Sport now underwent a rapid development: the scale of this expansion can be traced through the decades that follow. In 1967, 40 per cent of French people claimed never to have practised a sport: by 1987 this number will have halved. This growing enthusiasm for sport cannot be attributed to raising the school leaving age, with which it is contemporaneous. In 1967 less than 10 per cent of young people aged between 14 and 27 said that they did not practise a sport, so the growth among this age group has been relatively limited. On the other hand, the increase is especially marked among the adult population, and reaches quite spectacular proportions among those aged over 30. Although the way in which sport is practised varies between different social classes, sport today is an activity common to the whole of society. The French are playing more sport, more often, and they spend more years within the structure of sports institutions, whatever form these may take. Another important observation is that their performance is continuously improving, and that this improvement is not restricted to an elite, but is shared by all those who engage in these activities.

   This phenomenon, with its seemingly infinite capacity for expansion, owes nothing to verbal exhortation, and cannot be explained merely by the alchemy of the spectacle. All the words spent on encouraging people to take up sport would have borne little fruit without the patient and thorough organization of the campaign by the ruling classes. The coherence of such a design can be seen in the prominence that it has been accorded. In France, sport is an affair of state. No sports association can exist outside the regulations laid down by the government. The activities of each federation must be sanctioned by the supervising ministry, and the extent of this dependency on the authority of the state can be altered at will. At the moment this power belongs to the Department of Education and to the Secretary of State for Youth and Sports, whereas formerly the prerogative was held by the Ministry of Defence. But these changes in administrative location serve only to obscure the presence of a permanent strategy: the aim is still to bind the individual to the state and to enroll him in society; however, the sort of identity the nation requires of him may change with historical circumstances. To impose their choices on society, government institutions can apply powerful forms of pressure. They alone have the right to authorize competitions. They supervise the provision of facilities and equipment to sports bodies. They determine the nature of the teaching certificates required by sports instructors and control by law the recruitment of instructors and technical assistants. And finally, through various institutional channels, they supply most of the resources required by the various bodies.[21] This description, however, defines only the general framework of centralization, the conditions under which the system exists, and not the manner in which it actually operates, which is a much more pragmatic affair worked out through practical experience. Work on the ground is performed, even its obscurest details, meticulously, painstakingly, and efficiently. It is in the care of a militant proselytizing spirit which gauges its own success by its actions, and through which the bourgeoisie demonstrates its practical sense, its stubbornness and its particular attitudes to the art of managing and administering the life of the collectivity.[22]

The Art of Managing Behaviour

In his work *France 1848–1945*, Theodore Zeldin repeatedly points out the involvement of the ruling classes in the organization of sport. Everywhere, at the head of clubs and societies, the same men were to be found. Doubtless they were eager for official honours and decorations, but they were also devoted to the public cause. This state of affairs during the period between the two wars admitted of no exceptions, and can be seen as constituting a structural feature of French society. Now, as then, the management of those who play sport is a class prerogative. This proposition is generally true, but in order to make this analysis more plausible, this study will concentrate on one example, that of the French rugby federation.

Players are recruited from many different social groups and in each team members of the privileged strata of society can be found alongside manual labourers and lowly employees.[23] This melting pot of classes and cultures is in complete contrast to the composition of the administrative committees of the same clubs. In the committee room, a monopoly of power replaces the socially integrated world of the rugby pitch. Management of the club brings together captains of industry, large and small businessmen, members of the liberal professions (barristers, doctors, architects, solicitors) and local politicians (mayors, deputies, senators); while it excludes altogether, or reduces to the smallest of the groups involved, the representatives of the workers and employees. All these influential men who are in charge of the club's activities act out of a sense of duty and conviction, rather than from a desire for glory. Their carefully deliberated decisions do nothing to increase their own wealth and very little to augment their personal influence. Their methodical action bears witness to a keen sense of organization and a pronounced taste for the government of individuals. 'To govern,' writes Foucault, 'is to structure the space in which other people will act.'[24] A coherent set of procedures and measures sustain a project whose explicit objectives are simply to define, prescribe and impose forms of behaviour.

This strategy first of all aims to ensure strict control over the disposition of space: there is no village or town, small or large, that does not have its sports grounds, its clubs and teams. These clubs and teams form part of a pyramid of individualization. On each level of the pyramid are grouped those players who have the same level of competence and the same degree of talent. This careful allocation of positions is not essentially designed to guarantee opponents a more or less equal footing, but to preserve a real sense of confrontation. The opposition of equals both keeps the struggle going and legitimates the universal principle of inevitable inequality, which is immediately translated into a system of classification. The championship, with its end-of-season assessments and its system of promotions and relegations, provides for perennial competition, for the results obtained are always only provisional, and the positions held are never definitively occupied. Thus, at all levels of regional organization, the performance of local village clubs and of national league teams are likewise inscribed within a system of rigid hierarchies. If in the space of a few years and the cycles of success and failure can see the most prestigious teams reduced to competing in obscurity against non-league clubs, these collective adventures do not immutably fix the destiny of the individual. The logic of the system is to produce ceaseless changes and displacements, and to generate previously unseen trajectories. The place of each participant, their point and level of departure, are determined only by their own abilities, their determination and their inspiration. The match represents the moment of truth, the decisive hour in which all is at stake, in which the skills acquired in training are assessed and the efforts that have been made are justly rewarded. Actions are measured by the standards of the fight, precisely judged, rewarded or punished so that the truth of each individual is revealed to all. This recognition of personal value ratifies the criteria of a society entirely constructed around relations of competition and confrontation. Through the valorization of such performances, competition is endowed with a regular, differential, hierarchical structure, so that it will continue to produce without resort to constraint the sorts of individuality which are appropriate to the social order. Foucault has reminded us of this: 'The individual is doubtless the atomic fiction of an ideological representation of society; but he is also a reality created by that specific technology of power which we call discipline.'[25]

The efficiency of this discipline is proved in the context of the match, but the conditions under which the competitive test takes place are constantly increasing and reinforcing the results achieved. The social organization of each sport makes its own contribution to the overall order which holds together the different specific practices. Rugby is still constrained by the imposed regulation of amateur status, and only the laws of chance and of the labour market should govern the distribution of players between the various clubs. But the reality is quite different, for if there is a labour market, the goods that are sought through it are not the professional abilities of those employed, but their qualities as sportsmen. The great migrations that structure their careers are not in the least haphazard, for the superiority of the best clubs relies entirely upon a controlled programme of recruitment. An analysis of the club origins of national league players demonstrates this, for in 1981 less than one-fifth of them were still with their original club. Such population movements are particularly visible at the time of the year when transfers are arranged, when more than one player in four will seek a new future with a new team.[26] There is bitter rivalry among the different clubs, and control of the market-place falls to those clubs who have the most resources at their disposal. In these affairs, the aim of the patrons and local worthies is clear and unambiguous: they want to build the best possible team by obtaining the services of the best players. Businessmen, financiers, industrialists and politicians all join together to capture the talented players and find them a niche in local society. Thus they offer them not only many forms of paid employment, but also the management of businesses, interest-free loans, and many opportunities to establish themselves in self-employed jobs. Housing bought by the club for its players, offers of free lodging, bonuses, financial compensation for what is discreetly referred to as 'loss of earnings', and disguised remuneration[27] complete the panoply of different devices whose range depends upon the power of the clubs, which is to say, in the last analysis, upon the power of their board of directors.[28]

Each player thus finds himself bound by specific ties of allegiance to the club that has recruited him, and in return for the advantages, he must devote himself 'body and soul' to improving the reputation of his team. A serious approach to training, self-abnegation, courage, self-sacrifice, and a sense of effort and self-discipline are the ethical obligations that are laid upon him. The results obtained are the practical manifestation of the way each member has accomplished his duty. Poor performance, a casual attitude and repeated failures constitute faults which lead to stigmatization and punishment by the managers.[29] The aims of these administrative geniuses are clear: the practice of sport requires everyone to accept an extensive and regular use of their time. Membership of a club and a team demands an exclusive solidarity built around the shared values of agonistic competition. Only an individual's performance determines his place in the hierarchy, establishes his integration into the group and dictates the nature of his social bonds. Competition, competence, fighting spirit, records, these are the key words in a system that appears to be transparently lacking in any equivocation and which nevertheless defines a specific form of organized social life. The order of sport continually attempts to break down forms of community based upon neighbourhoods, local solidarity and social struggles in order to replace them with more ambiguous forms of identity: the club or the team; and with forms of solipsistic individualization centred around the search for physical excellence. These explicit yet limited tactics contribute by their specific operation to the generaliztion of the system: once we move outside the context of the department[30] we find that the same logic dictates the arrangements governing the sport. And yet there is no one who might have conceived such a plan: 'the *implicit* character of great anonymous strategies, which, almost silently, coordinate the loquacious tactics whose inventors and operators are lacking in any such hypocrisy'.[31]

Sport as Public Celebration

As a means of measuring fighting spirit, competitions justify themselves by mobilizing the crowd with ritual representations of confrontation. The purpose of these public meetings is not to offer mere entertainment, a spectacle whose effects are exhausted in the pleasures of the moment, but rather to bring people together in order to educate them. This purpose has a long history, going back to the eighteenth century, when the elite first began to denounce those spectacles which 'numbed' the spirit of the people, and encouraged passivity in the crowd, a crowd which was already perceived as 'lazy, ignorant and sentimental'. The pedagogy of sport has become more ambitious, and belongs quite naturally to the interventionist tradition of popular festivities which characterized Jacobin democracy. Like the revolutionary festival, the sports festival looks to the future.

> When the festival is over, men must go home from it happier and more enlightened: which is, after all, the same thing. One might even say that the festival has no beginning and no end: not because it is anticipated and remembered; but through the continuity of the discipline it creates, the moral habits it inculcates and the system of rewards and punishments which it popularizes.[32]

Competitions combine in a single educational project to achieve discipline and mobilization, and to control individual behaviour and transform the composite plural crowd into a single people. Sporting events are frequent, regular and carefully arranged, and not a Sunday goes by without the collectivity being called on to assemble at the stadium, in the gymnasium or around the swimming pool. These innocent pastimes are far from anodyne: beyond the pleasures and the conviviality they invoke, they serve as an initiation which prepares society for great national gatherings. On this level, sporting events reveal another aspect of their nature, for they possess all those properties which we would associate with religious and political rituals: interrupting the banality of daily life and vernacular culture with their repetitive and encoded patterns of behaviour, their symbolic resonance and their expression of community membership.[33] Each year, great occasions bring the people together, first of all to celebrate the champions of the nation, and then to be united as a community through the exploits and struggles of their representatives in international competitions. As the legitimate representatives not only of the institutions of sport, but of the French state itself in its relations with other states, the members of this elite explicitly embody in their acts all that a society likes to consider to be the intrinsic qualities and virtues of the nation, or even of the race. The symbolic trappings of their performances (tricolours, patriotic hymns, and the obligatory presence of political dignitaries) bear witness to the function of such grandiose ceremonies in promoting social cohesion. At such privileged moments, as Durkheim, the zealous propagandist of national consensus, has written, 'society becomes conscious of itself, positions itself, and individual destinies are regulated by collective criteria'. The possibilities for identification afforded and encouraged by such representations contribute to the formation of a community which discovers itself in the image of the institution which establishes its unity: the State.[34] This mobilization of the masses is made possible by the methodical organization of the practice of sport. Thanks to this organization, the champion no longer appears an exceptional being, his performances simply place him in a differential position within a hierarchy which unites and allows interaction between all those who play the given sport. Identification is made possible because in each sport the best athletes are bound by ties of proximity and collaboration to the mass of those who participate. The French champion is a talented individual to whom all other athletes can compare themselves, he belongs to the same sporting culture and his activities are part of a collective imagination and exemplify qualities which are specifically French. The national styles that are created in sport are less to do with the way in which men play or live, and more to do with the particular way in which they take pleasure in recounting their activities and their collective existence, and in recognizing themselves in their discourse.[35] Sport is thus involved in the construction of a popular national consciousness, without which the power of the State would have no legitimacy. It effectively mobilizes the community, prepared by practical participation, around patriotic values.[36] The practice of sport itself generates a form of combative socialization, and produces individuals who can be mobilized for any form of confrontation. Sport represents the utopia of ceaseless and merciless struggle in a society that has been completely pacified.

Conclusion

Despite the many metaphors[37] which describe sport in terms of war, the two forms of confrontation do not coincide. Sport is a codified test of strength the goal of which is not to destroy the adversary but to dominate him. Thus it admits of no definitive victory: the struggle is never finished. The aim of competition is to prolong itself. It creates a sort of individual whose logic is close to that of the primitive warrior:

> On every feat of arms which he performs, both the warrior and society pronounce the same judgment: I did well, but I can do better, win even more glory, says the warrior. You did well, but you must do better, win recognition from us of an even greater prestige, says society ... The warrior exists only in war, as such he is doomed to a continual activity.[38]

Each individual existence becomes a personal adventure which can only be forged through struggle and confrontation. The enactment of conflict stimulates and energizes social relations, it is the true crucible in which bourgeois society is formed.[39] As a major factor in socialization, sport creates agonistic personalities on which the mechanisms of mobilization can get a grip. Sport is not a substitute for war and it does not generate a pacific alternative to the range of arms and the explosion of aggression. It does not create the conditions for war, but it does maintain the possibility of those conditions, and adds its own efficiency to the other forces which produce a social order in which trials of strength are seen as part of the natural course of things. As George Orwell has said: 'It is not important whether a state of war really has been declared, and since no decisive victory is possible, it is not important to be victorious. All that is necessary, is that the state of war should exist.'[40]

NOTES

1. N. Elias, *Quest for Excitement* (London: Basil Blackwell, 1987).
2. N. Elias, 'Le sport, l'Etat et la violence', *Actes de la recherche en sciences sociales*, 6 (Paris, 1976).
3. M. Foucault, *Histoire de la sexualité. La volonté de savoir* (Paris: Gallimard, 1976).
4. E. Weber, 'Gymnastique et sport en France à la fin du 19ème siècle: Opium des Classes?' in *Aimez-vouz les stades?*, *Recherches* (avril 1980).
5. R. Holt, *Aspects of the Social History of Sport in France 1870–1914* (London: Macmillan, 1980).
6. Pierre Chambat, 'Les muscles de Marianne', in *Aimez-vous les stades?*, 139–85.
7. A. Ehrenberg, *Le corps militaire* (Paris: Aubiè, 1983).
8. Cited in Chambat, op. cit., pp.166–7.
9. M. Foucault, *Histoire de la sexualité*, pp.162–8.
10. P. de Coubertin, cited in Ehrenberg, p.146.
11. G. Vigarello, *Le corps redressé* (Paris: J.P. Delarge, 1968).
12. P. Bert, *De l'éducation civique* (Paris: Picard Bernheim), p.18.
13. M. Ozouf, *La fête révolutionnaire* (Paris: Gallimard, 1976).

14. Ph. Tissié, *La fatigue et l'entraînement physique* (Paris, 1894), pp.84–5.
15. *Revue Olympique* (février 1910), 27–8.
16. *Revue Olympique*, 'Pour que le sport puisse enrayer la névrose universelle' (octobre 1910), 154–5.
17. E. Seillière, *Un artisan de l'énergie français* (Paris: Pierre de Coubertin, 1917), pp.22–3.
18. G. Rozet, *La défense et l'illustration de la race française* (Paris: Alcan, 1911).
19. Faure-Dujarric, *L'organisation matérielle d'une société sportive* (Paris: Encyclopédie des sports, 1924), pp.180–5.
20. Pierre Rosanvallon, *L'Etat en France de 1789 à nos jours* (Paris: Le Seuil, 1990).
21. Professional football clubs may serve as a good example of the scale of the economic resources made available to sports organizations through the various channels of the civil service and the government. The 18 first-division clubs, which remain non-profit-making organizations, like the smallest of village clubs, receive enormous subsidies each year. In 1989, the 400 million francs handed over for this purpose did not prevent those clubs from recording a record deficit of a thousand million francs. The gravity of this crisis and the prospect of a single status for all European clubs may well lead to profound alterations in the management of French football, but it seems doubtful whether the State would give up all of its prerogatives.
22. For the theoretical definition of the concept of social class, the remarks of E.P. Thompson admirably define a position which coincides exactly with my own: 'When we speak of a class, we are thinking of a category of the population which is very vaguely defined, of people who share the same set of interests, of social experiences, of traditions and the same system of values, who have a tendency to behave as a class, to define themselves in their actions and their consciousness in relation to other groups in germs of class. But a class is not in itself a thing. It has to be brought into being.' *La formation de la classe ouvrière anglaise* (Paris: Gallimard, 1988), p.771.
23. For the studies on which these claims are based, see J-M. Faure, 'Sport, Cultures et Classes sociales,' Université de Nantes, thesis for the doctorat d'Etat, 1987. Workers and employees represent 41.4% of rugby players: they are thus as significant a proportion as business and industrial leaders, members of the liberal professions and managerial staff, which is a very different situation from that prevalent in other sports such as tennis, skiing, mountaineering, sailing and road racing, which are still socially very exclusive. But it must be observed that even in rugby, statistics show that a member of the liberal professions is ten times more likely to take part in this sport than a mere worker.
24. H. Dreyfus and P. Rabinow, *M. Foucault, Un parcours philosophique*, p.308.
25. M. Foucault, *Surveiller et punir* (Paris: Gallimard, 1975), p.196.
26. At the time of our investigation in 1981, the French rugby football federation reported slightly less than 80,000 registered players. At the end of the year, the transfer committee dealt with 26,231 requests, of which six out of ten were from national league clubs, and three out of ten from local league clubs. This shows that the local leagues and the very small clubs which play in them belong to a very different social reality.
27. A simple, effective and risk-free procedure. An interest free loan is accorded to a player to allow him to set up house for himself. Each month the player must pay off one of the loan bills deposited with the club's solicitor in order to repay his debt. Unless the player should unexpectedly disappoint his managers, at the end of each month the loan bills are held to have been paid off but the player is excused from having to hand over the relevant sum of money.
28. The board of managers of C.A. Bègles, a national league club in the Bordeaux region, is made up of seven industrialists, three prominent merchants, two tax inspectors, two doctors, and a magistrate. The honorary committee includes several deputies, one of whom is J. Chaban Delmas, many regional councillors, the prefect of Acquitaine, three generals, the managing director of the newspaper *Sud-Ouest* and a pleiad of businessmen.
29. Managers repeatedly proclaim their own virtue and denounce the negligence of the players. The following words of a club president, recorded on the occasion of his team's elimination from the national league championship, may be considered representative: 'We have a team of managers who give everything they've got. I mean, who take part in the life of the club

by opening their wallets as wide as they can. We do everything we can. We help our players as much as we can, we find work for them and for their wives. We use all our connections. And what do they give us in return? Nothing, absolutely nothing. No gratitude once their belly's full. No heart, no desire to get out there and fight. It's appalling and it's very discouraging.' J.M. Faure, op. cit., p.625.

30. J-M. Faure, *L'ordre des stades, les désordres des rues* (Paris: Ed. Lieu commun, 1992). Small clubs and associations that are not known outside their immediate area tend to have a very strong working-class recruitment. The practice of sport among the working classes is defined by its place in local life; villages, towns, cities and their *quartiers*. Through their combination of competition, fair play and high performance, they continually mark their distance from the standard norms. Working-class sport reaffirms forms of social membership and solidarity which go against the logic of the institution of sport. Many networks of relationship – family, relations, friends, workmates – interfere with those created by sport and demolish the authority of physical skill and excellence. The institution of sport is thus subordinated in its operation to forms of social integration which are expressed and asserted through community rituals, often celebratory in nature, and which are foreign to the ethic of sport and to the ascetic standards of competition. Surveys have given empirical evidence of this organization: as a team progresses up the hierarchy, the constraints and obligations deriving from the institution of sport increase in number, its recruitment is socially more broadly based and more complex, and the number of workers diminishes. Skill in the sport comes to be the only criterion for membership of the association.

31. M. Foucault, *Histoire de la sexualité*, p.125.

32. M. Ozouf, *La fête révolutionnaire*, pp.326. The essence of these ideas, and in particular the claim that the sports competition is not a pure form of entertainment, were put forward by A. Ehrenberg in a remarkable article, 'Des jardins de bravoure et des piscines roboratrices', published in *Le Temps modernes* (février, 1979).

33. The ethnological review *Terrain, Carnets du patrimoine* devoted a special edition to the analysis of *Contemporary Rituals* (Paris, 1982), All these approaches derive explicitly from Emile Durkheim. 'Rituals,' Durkheim wrote, 'are above all the means by which the social group can periodically reaffirm itself ... What is essential, is that the individuals should be gathered together, that common feelings should be felt, and these feelings expressed through common acts.' E. Durkheim, *Les formes élémentaires de la vie religieuse* (Paris: La Découverte, 1988).

34. E. Balibar and I. Wallerstein, *Race, Nation, Classe. Les identités ambiguës* (Paris: La Découverte, 1988).

35. Ch. Bromberger, 'Pour une ethnologie du spectacle sportif: Les matchs de football à Marseille, Turin et Naples', *Terrain*, 8 (avril 1987).

36. Field work on this question has shown very clearly that the great majority of spectators to be found at sporting events are people who have practised sport. This is true of football, the preferred activity of the working classes, and of tennis, the most popular activity with the higher social classes. In response to surveys that asked them to cite the ten greatest French champions, eight out of ten gave priority to champions of the sport they had themselves played. But while the working classes followed this rule closely and mentioned only footballers and cyclists, after their first choices, the higher social classes diversified their answers, and tended to choose players who had won international awards. Thus they did not forget G. Carpentier and N. Cerdan, world boxing champions, rarely mentioned by workers who preferred to name R. Poulidor and R. Vietto, two cyclists who have never succeeded in winning the Tour de France. J-M. Faure, op. cit.

37. Such usages are frequently to be found throughout the century. Before the Great War, young men of good family could be found in Agathon declaring that 'sport has given them the taste for blood ... and that war is not stupid, cruel and detestable. It is simply sport, played for real.' E. Weber, op. cit., p.210. And, more recently, during the Gulf War, R. Domenech, trainer of the professional team of Lyon, declared that: 'I told my players that they must be more aggressive in order to defend their territory. They must not accept the superiority of the enemy. To say that you like your opponent is complete hypocrisy. They are your enemies... you must hate them to be able to dominate them.' *Libération*, 4 Feb. 1991.

38. P. Clastres, *Recherches en anthropologie politique; Malheur du guerrier sauvage* (Paris: Le Seuil, 1980), p.231.
39. The political and educational strategies at work in sport operate upon society as a whole. Nevertheless, their aims of moralization and mobilization provoke resistance and opposition which can be deciphered in the antagonistic relationship between the working classes and the sporting establishment. The masses are not the infinitely malleable product of the various operations of the political powers. The lower classes introduce disorder into the harmony of the stadium. J-M. Faure, op. cit.
40. G. Orwell, *1984* (Paris: Gallimard, 1980).

The Dual Meaning of 'Fatherland' and Catholic Gymnasts in Belgium, 1892–1914

JAN TOLLENEER

When we write about the relationship between sport and physical exercise on the one hand and nationalism on the other, especially around the turn of this century, we are confronted by two kinds of problem. First, if we define nationalism as an active expression of group consciousness – a consciousness which tends to be defined by an awareness of what is external or 'foreign' – we have to be very clear about the precise groups we are dealing with. When Belgium was created as an independent kingdom in 1830 it was composed of two distinct regions. Flanders lies in the north and is linguistically linked to the Netherlands, which between 1815 and 1830 controlled both parts of what was to become Belgium. To the south lies Wallonia, the French-speaking region, which has been culturally close to France; it was the French who took over the lands that were later to become Belgium from the Austrians in 1794 and ruled them until after the battle of Waterloo in 1815. After 1830 a growing sense of a new Belgian nationality was evident and this was cultivated by politicians, industrialists and the leaders of the powerful Catholic Church – all of them French-speaking, even those in the northern parts. The new monarchy acted as a unifying national force and promoted the idea of Belgium as a nation-state, with a strongly centralized government in the capital, Brussels. However, historical reality was rather more complicated than those who tried to forge the new state properly understood. The economic and cultural neglect of the Flemish-speaking population gave rise to a growing sense of popular Flemish nationalism. There was a grassroots national consciousness in Flanders which was not present to the same extent in Wallonia, where there was no linguistic conflict of interest between Belgian identity and regional identity. Without wishing to renounce their identity as Belgians, the Flemish made increasingly strident demands for equal language rights. Although in practice state-led nationalism from above (that of 'Belgium') and this popular linguistic nationalism from below (especially in Flanders) were not in direct opposition, it is essential to make a clear distinction between them.

Secondly, we need to clarify the differences between the social groups involved in the various forms of sport and physical education that developed around the turn of the century. In studying in particular the world of voluntary associations which grew up independent of state control it is important to distinguish between different kinds of club. Apart from the traditional culture of play, which in Flanders continued to have a symbolic role in defining ethnic identity,[1] there were also gymnastics societies and sports clubs. The modern sports clubs, which were in the hands of the French-speaking bourgeoisie, had little or no contact with the Flemish struggle for emancipation before 1918. However, gymnastics was unlike sport in this respect. The social and pedagogical function of gymnastics in the internal life of Belgium has already received some attention[2] and this essay will expand on some of this research. Gymnastics played a different role to that of modern sport, especially in terms of its international contacts. Some of the differences between sport and gymnastics have been touched upon by P. Arnaud in his stimulating survey of nationalism in France[3] and by R. Holt in his comparison of Britain and France published in this volume.[4] From France and Britain (on the other side of the Channel) as well as from Germany (in the East) there were strong and contrasting influences on Belgium. In fact, it could be said that Belgium was a cultural meeting place or crossroads, and this applied to the domain of sport and exercise as much as it applied to other aspects of Belgian life.[5] This essay deals with a certain form of gymnastics (*turnen*) which was imported from Germany in 1839.[6] The intention here is to focus on the nature of the Catholic Gymnastics Federation of Belgium (hereafter CGFB) which was founded in 1892. However, before doing this, we need to spend some time looking at the gymnastic activity which preceded the formation of the CGFB.

Origins

A quarter of a century after the introduction of German gymnastics into Belgium, the Belgian Gymnastics Federation was founded in 1865 (hereafter BGF). The city of Antwerp, where the gymnastic milieu was bourgeois and French-speaking as it was elsewhere in Belgium at that time, was the home of N.J. Cupérus (1842–1928). In considering the role of state-led and popular nationalism in gymnastics, his enormous influence cannot be ignored. The progressive liberal politician Cupérus became President of the BGF in 1873 and remained in that position for fifty years until 1923. This federation linked gymnastics to patriotism in a very explicit way. In a similar way to Germany and France the preparation of youth for military service was one of the most important objects of the so-called gymnastic and rifle societies. G. De Meyer[7] has written about the similarities between Cupérus and the German 'Turnvater', F.L. Jahn (1778–1852). However, Jahn's extreme nationalistic motives were not present in Cupérus, whose activities pointed in a quite different direction; take, for example, his attendance at the first meeting of the International Working Men's Association in London in 1864, and his role as a founder member and later as President of the Fédération Européenne de Gymnastique (FEG), subsequently re-named the Fédération Internationale de Gymnastique (FIG); in addition, one can point to his involvement in the Franco-Prussian War of 1870–71 as a volunteer medical orderly as an indication of the importance of both his wider international interests and his humanitarian concerns.

Yet Jahn and Cupérus did share common values and enthusiasms, notably the will to preserve and develop their own language, and the social and cultural customs associated with their linguistic communities. Just like M. Tyrs, the leader of the Bohemian Sokol Movement,[8] Cupérus was convinced of the value of gymnastics for the emancipation of ethnic and linguistic groups. Moreover, Pierre Arnaud has linked Cupérus with the leaders of the Union des Sociétés de Gymnastique de France (USGF) and mentioned the way in which they shared ideals derived from the French Revolution.[9] The beliefs of Cupérus were put into practice through the formation in Antwerp of the Gymnastische Volkskring in 1868 and by the publication of the Flemish gymnastics journal, *Volksheil*, from 1873 to 1895. Gymnastics acted as an early and important instrument in the slow emancipation of the lower classes and of the Flemish-speaking population in general.[10] However, the fact that there was still some resistance to popular linguistic nationalism to be overcome within gymnastic circles is revealed by the following extract from *De Turner*, the successor to *Volksheil*:[11]

> In Flanders, Flemish! ... Time and again we have stressed the need for gymnastics leaders in the Flemish regions to use their own language. On the occasion of the French national gymnastics federation at St. Etienne the leader of the Vriendschap [a gymnastic society from Ghent] gave instructions to his men in good Flemish and, far from being abused as 'Prussians', the spectators warmly applauded them with three double shouts of 'Vive Gand' [Long Live Ghent!]. Why then should not others do the same? Why do most of the people renounce their own roots? If you want to be respected, first respect yourself![12]

Catholic Patriotism

When the Catholic Gymnastics Federation of Belgium was set up alongside the Belgian Gymnastics Federation of Cupérus it was not as a result of a linguistic conflict nor was it because of technical differences of gymnastic technique. Rather it was the product of the conflict between clerics and anti-clerics that coloured the whole political scene in Belgium.[13] This division is directly comparable to the one in France. Alongside the Union des Sociétés de Gymnastique de France (USFG), there was a movement which resulted in the foundation in 1903 of the Fédération Gymnastique et Sportive des Patronages de France (FGSPF). For the Catholics this new network of gymnastics and sports societies became a weapon in the struggle against anti-clericalism. In discussing this Arnaud refers to what he calls the 'divine patriotism' and the 'muscular Catholicism' of the FGSPF.[14] In Belgium there was a similar development despite the fact that unlike France it was the Catholics rather than the anti-clericals who controlled the political system without a break from 1884 to 1914. There was a further difference in terms of the physical activities undertaken. In France within the Catholic clubs gymnastics and modern sports were enjoyed side by side, but in Belgium this was not the case. There was from the beginning a strongly purist element in Belgian gymnastics which led to the creation of separate Catholic federations for sport and for gymnastics – a profound division and distinctive feature which has survived right up to the present day.[15]

The full name of the Catholic Gymnastics Federation of Belgium (CGFB), which also undertook a certain amount of rifle training, is significant in this context: Nationalen Bond der Katholieke Turnen Wapenmaatschappijen van België/Fédération Nationale des Sociétés Catholiques de Gymnastique et d'Armes de Belgique. The pre-war Presidents of the CGFB, P. Poullet (1892–93), E. de Lalieux (1893–1909) and P. de Dieudonné (1909–19), all of them Catholic politicians, gave the CGFB the impression of an organization prepared to fight in two respects: as far as internal politics were concerned, the CGFB was willing to respond to the activities of the anti-clerics; on the other hand, in terms of external threats the CGFB actively promoted the physical health of the fatherland and the preparation of youth to serve it.

This second dimension of national defence touches closely upon the central issue of this essay. How nationalistic was the CGFB in this period and what did the term 'fatherland' precisely mean to the gymnasts? 'It is with pride that I greet the flag of the fatherland, which was planted gloriously by the Belgians in 1830 as a symbol of those freedoms we won for ourselves. We shall hold dear this symbol of fatherland, religion and kingdom and in the hour of danger we shall unite to defend it with obstinacy and devotion.'[16] Such were the words of President de Lalieux in 1897 to the Catholic gymnasts on the occasion of the national gymnastic festival. These festivals had a central significance in the yearly programme of the Federation. They were designed to reveal the flourishing state of the Federation and the able-bodiedness of the Catholics; these events brimmed with symbols of the fatherland; apart from the show of flags, there was always the playing of the 'Brabançonne', the national anthem. We can read in the instructions for the national festival held in Bruges in 1898 the following: 'At the seventh command all pyramids must be complete ... exactly at the moment that the federation's flag flaps at the top of the central pyramid, the musicians play the national anthem (Brabançonne) and at that moment the flags of the societies as well as the gymnasts themselves salute.'[17] Flags were also placed near statues of Jan Breydel and Pieter de Koninck, who embodied the struggle for emancipation of the Flemish people and especially the victory of the Flemish footsoldiers over the French cavalry in the Guldensporenslag (Battle of the Golden Spurs) on 11 July 1302 – a date which to this day remains the Flemish commemorative national holiday. The Vlaamse Leeuw (the Flemish Lion) is the title of the Flemish national anthem which refers to the victory of 1302. This may explain why in the above-mentioned set of instructions for the national gymnastic festival it was necessary to specify which national anthem was to be sung – i.e. not the Vlaamse Leeuw but the Brabançonne.

Order and discipline were important values, as was shown by the choice of exercises and the marching style of the gymnasts. From the very beginning attention was paid to the weapons exercise of the gymnasts. How strong this militaristic attitude was and how it evolved in a concrete way has been examined elsewhere.[18] Analysis of the primary source material shows that these technical developments were closely related to changes in legislation concerning conscription. The traditional system of drawing lots for military service was replaced in 1909 by the 'Law on Limited Personal Military Service' and in 1913 there was a further refinement laid down in the 'Law on Personal Military Service'. Military affairs in general were the subject of long-drawn-out political arguments. All Belgian political parties defended the neutral status of Belgium in international military relations. In conservative and military circles a stronger army was preferred, precisely to defend this neutrality. Socialists and Christian democrats, however, thought that one should have confidence in the surrounding Great Powers, which after all had granted the status of a neutral power to Belgium in 1839.[19] The gymnastics federations, in fact, had a number of anti-militarists in their ranks. This was one of the reasons why full military training was not given. Activities were restricted to general forms of physical cum moral training, for which the gymnastics federations claimed a monopoly within the world of physical exercise and youth work.

The Catholic Gymnastics Federation of Belgium was in 1910 one of the founding members of the Association des Fédérations Belges d'Exercices Physiques pour la Préparation Militaire (AFBEPPM), of which N.J. Cupérus and the Belgian Gymnastics Federation had been the most important instigators. The AFBEPPM was an umbrella organization for the existing sports and gymnastics federations. The fact that in 1912 the largely anti-militarist Fédération Nationale des Cercles Socialistes de Gymnastique et des Groupes d'Enfants du Peuple affiliated to this wider body was a clear sign of the times as international tension and nationalist rhetoric reached new heights throughout Europe.

What had previously been a fairly moderate kind of patriotism evolved within the Catholic Gymnastics Federation of Belgium into more outspoken forms of nationalism. The influence of army weapons instructors increased not only in the local societies but also on the national level. In terms of rhetoric speeches moved from a more generalized and mild patriotism to more specific issues of military preparedness. The way in which President de Dieudonné spoke at the annual council of the Federation and the manner in which he lauded the efforts of his predecessor, de Lalieux, were symptomatic of this changed attitude:

> to teach the soldier never to be afraid of the enemy, and particularly to teach him never to deny his beliefs and to behave with honour, this, Gentlemen, in a few words is our task ... I turn now to my friend de Lalieux ... Please accept, dear friend, this small *objet d'art*. Our societies offer you a Joan of Arc, symbol of piety, of bravery and of determination. Like Joan of Arc at the head of her troops, you will not retreat in the face of any difficulty in order to make sure of the victory of our good cause, and like Joan of Arc once did you will take as your device : 'For God and King !'[20]

According to Arnaud, Joan of Arc played a role in the Fédération de Gymnastique et Sportive des Patronages de France as a symbol of French unity. The Belgian Catholic gymnasts were inspired by the militant language of their French neighbours. The French Federation's President, P. Michaux, often set the tone as far as the ideological foundation of Catholic gymnastics was concerned. On several occasions the text of his speeches were published in the Belgian federation journal, which significantly took the name *Belgica* in order to stress the importance of national unity. Michaux's themes were the influence of gymnastics on the improvement of the race and the reinforcement of religion and fatherland.[21] From 1913 onwards the programme of the Belgian national Catholic gymnastic festival included military exercises, practical and theoretical.[22] A side effect, incidentally, of this growth of nationalism was a better understanding between the Belgian Gymnastics Federation of Cupérus, which had 210 societies and 21,000 members in 1911, and the Catholics of the CGFB, which was rather smaller with 130 clubs and 12,000 members.[23]

International Orientation

International co-operation was deeply ingrained in Belgian gymnastics but there were still differences in this respect between the Belgian Gymnastics Federation and the Catholic one. As a counterbalance to the Fédération Européenne de Gymnastique of Cupérus, the Union Internationale des Oeuvres Catholiques d'Education Physique was created, which is in fact still in existence under the name Fédération Internationale Catholique d'Education Physique (FICEP).[24] How did this come into being and what role did the Belgians play in it ? Could it be that the international dimension arose as a kind of antithesis to the rising tide of nationalism?

As the number of Catholic gymnasts in Belgium grew, so too did the range of contacts between them and the outside world. For example, on the occasion of the tenth anniversary of the gymnastic society of Eintracht in Eupen – in an area that had been added to Prussia in 1815 and only went back to Belgium after the First World War[25] – the journal *Belgica* explicitly advised the gymnasts to take part.[26] This illustrates the commitment to keeping contact with the wider family of Catholic gymnasts, especially those who were closely linked to the historic territories from which Belgium was created. As further evidence of cross-border co-operation amongst Catholic gymnasts one could cite the regional festival of Liège–Limbourg in 1909 where there were, besides 44 Belgian societies, 4 from Germany, 5 from the Netherlands and no less than 10 from France:

> The courage of societies from the Netherlands, who have attended despite the ban with the international bureau of the so-called 'neutral' Fédérations Européennes placed upon them, is most admirable. Bravo for the men from Holland for this fine gesture of pride and independence! As for our German neighbours, the public much appreciated their military discipline and their energetic marching to the sound of the pipes and drums.[27]

In the previous year, 1908, at the regional festival in Halle, near Brussels, there were representatives from France, and it may be that the French were more open to such initiatives from Belgium after the separation of the Church and State in 1905 had made French Catholics more vulnerable. Belgian Catholic gymnasts expressed their solidarity with their French counterparts who were being 'put to the test' in the words of the Mayor of Halle, the President of the regional association.[28]

The Belgians participated in the great Catholic festival in Rome in 1908 on the occasion of the fiftieth anniversary of the ordination of Pius X into the Catholic Church. There was quite remarkable grassroots enthusiasm amongst Catholic Belgian gymnasts for this event, an enthusiasm which resulted not only in a large delegation (17 Belgian societies as against, for instance, 15 French ones) but also in very good results in the competitions.[29] The gymnasts of Ganda Gent were received as 'world champions' when they returned from Rome; this began a series of victories for the gymnasts which made them famous and turned them into gymnastic ambassadors for the Catholic Church in Belgium.[30] The style in which their activities were reported was reminiscent of that of modern sports, notably the great successes of their neighbours in Ghent, the Sport Nautique, a rowing club which had an international reputation at that time.[31] The great Catholic festival of 1908 in Rome was held in a true spirit of fraternity, where solidarity was more important than results. Within the Belgian delegation in Rome there was Baron de Dieudonné, future president of the Federation, who held the honorary title of 'Chamberlain' to the Pope. In his address an emotional Pius X talked about a spirit of moderate competition and particularly about the defence of religion in the context of 'an independent patriotism and sincere sense of charity'.[32] After the festival the council of the Belgian federation urged strongly that these bonds of friendship should be institutionalized through a real international organization.[33] When this organization was founded in 1911 it was the Belgians who proposed that it should be named the Union Internationale des Œuvres Catholiques d'Education Physique (UIOCEP), and it was de Dieudonné who became one of its vice-presidents along with Dr Michaux of France.

Back in Belgium the CGFB continued its efforts to promote international contacts between Catholics, and the federation played a dominant part as host for a series of congresses, meetings and festivals. For example, in Diest in 1911 visitors were greeted with a special song of welcome[34] and the following year the city of Spa acted as the venue for a major festival whilst Brussels acted as host for the Third UIOCEP congress, for which Pope Pius X himself sent a handwritten letter of encouragement. However, there was no escaping the reality of national identity.[35] In the Festival at Ghent in 1913 the national anthems of the Netherlands and the Marseillaise of France were played along with the Brabançonne of Belgium. In a situation of growing international tension, especially the fear of a war with Germany, the President of the Belgian gymnasts, in handing over the flag for the coming year to the people of Ghent, spoke ominously of the need to 'keep the flag high during 1913/14 and to defend if necessary this symbol of the Fatherland'.[36] Despite its international orientation, the tone of the Federation's pronouncements became more and more explicitly nationalistic without going beyond a fairly defensive or moderate approach. Thus, the leaders of the Belgian Catholic gymnasts tried to walk a difficult line between encouraging internationalism on the one hand and accepting the need for vigorous national defence on the other.

State Nationalism and Popular Nationalism

In the eyes of the outside world the Catholic Gymnastics Federation of Belgium (CGFB), like the state of Belgium itself, appeared to be well integrated with few problems between the Flemish and the French-speaking Walloons. Was this in fact correct and what were relations between the two groups actually like? At the moment when the CGFB was founded in 1892 a close link already existed between the gymnastics movement and the Flemish movement. It was in the period 1860–80 that the Flemish consciousness began to be translated in more concrete terms and that Cupérus began his gymnastic initiatives, which have already been mentioned. In the city of Antwerp there was a concentration of Flemish democrats, which created a unique political situation. There the 'Meetingpartij', which was an anti-militaristic collaborative venture between Catholics and progressive liberals until the liberals left in 1879, was extremely successful. It was in these circles that important stimulus was given to the foundation of the CGFB. The Berchemse Turnkring, based in a suburb of Antwerp, was founded in 1887 and played a central role in setting up the CGFB. Frans van Hombeek, the mayor of Berchem and a prominent member of the Meetingpartij, became the honorary president of the new Catholic Federation. Another progressive political figure, Prosper Poullet from Leuven, was the first president of the CGFB. He was a Christian democrat who became prime minister of Belgium for a short time after the First World War. It was the city and province of Antwerp which set the tone in the new CGFB; they were the first to create a regional association: the Katholieke Antwerpse Turngouw (1896).[37] Another important initiative was the journal of the Federation, *Belgica*, which from its inception in 1895 appeared in both languages. This made the CGFB quite different from the 'Belgium-minded' and bourgeois world of modern sports. Members of the Flemish movement and Christian democrats were both suspicious of modern sports, which according to the celebrated historian K. Van Isacker tended to blunt the cutting edge of Flemish emancipation.[38] It may well be that the aversion to modern sports within the CGFB was related to the defence of Flemish ideas. However, this hypothesis awaits further research (certainly the powerful Cardinal Mercier [1851–1926], an opponent of the Flemish movement, took relatively little interest in gymnastics and favoured greater Catholic participation in modern sports).[39]

Within the CGFB could it be said that the relationship between the two languages was harmonious? An article which appeared in the *Gazet van Antwerpen* in 1898 suggests that it was not:

> The Federation is made up of Flemings and Walloons; the former are the architects and instigators and they still form the majority.

Well, what do we see taking place. If our facts are correct, then the Walloons have the majority in the administration of the Federation. French has always enjoyed the privileged place and the affiliated Flemish societies are left with only a poor translation ... The meetings of the Federation are even worse; there, everything or almost everything takes place in French.[40]

This writer did not get all of his facts correct but the Federation was unable to deny some of his criticisms. Not only were the published Flemish translations sometimes abominable, but speeches were also in French, as happened in the 15th national festival in Aalst in 1907; the societies participating were three-quarters Flemish, but 'everything, everything was in French'.[41] President de Lalieux and secretary J. van Elderen were able only to speak French.[42] In 1909 de Lalieux gave up his presidency, in his own words, 'to give it to a younger colleague who was able to speak both national languages and to lead our noble Federation to great things'. Van Elderen was replaced by a secretary for Flanders and one for Wallonia. However, he did return later to take up a co-ordination function as a general secretary/treasurer.[43]

The bilingual nature of *Belgica* has in this context to be seen as an early success for the Flemish. According to the content analysis of van Haver,[44] for the period 1895–1914 a half, sometimes even more, of the space in *Belgica* was given over to articles in Flemish. However, contributions to *Belgica* concerning the Flemish movement were rare; much rarer, for instance, than in Cupérus's *Volksheil*. *Volksheil* ran articles on the 'Willemsfonds',[45] a liberal, social and cultural society founded in 1851 which became a central part of the Flemish Movement and was named after J.F. Willems, a Flemish pioneer. On the other hand, *Belgica* paid no attention to the Davidsfonds, the Catholic counterpart of the Willemsfonds, and named after J.B. Davids. The editorial policy of *Belgica* was reflected in the person of Karel van Assche, the editor, a bilingual Fleming from Boom; he was a latent supporter of Flemish emancipation but a more militant Belgian nationalist.[46]

Within the Belgian Gymnastics Federation of Cupérus there were clear tendencies towards a more popular cultural nationalism, a good example of which was the marked sympathy for the Sokol Movement in Bohemia in its nationalist struggle with the Austro-Hungarian Empire. The Bohemian struggle was explicitly compared on some occasions to the battle for Flemish emancipation.[47] The Orel Movement, the Catholic counterpart to the Sokols, however, was very infrequently mentioned in *Belgica* in the period before 1914.[48] It seems from this that Flemish popular nationalism was less evident amongst the Catholic gymnasts than amongst the non-

Catholics. For the Catholics their Flemish identity was always linked to the question of Belgian identity as a whole, as is revealed in the following remarkable piece of rhetoric from a priest from Ninove in 1908: 'you have to struggle as a Catholic to love your homeland and to defend your beautiful Flemish language; to be, in one word, a real Belgian, a defender of God and Fatherland'.[49] In Belgium, love for the fatherland was inextricably linked to religion. However, in contrast with most countries, the concept of 'fatherland' had a dual meaning. In the northern part this concept could mean Flanders on the one side and Belgium on the other; the Flemish Catholic 'people' found a safe home in Belgium; and Belgium after all worked well as a 'state', especially at that time when the movement towards equal rights appeared to be making some progress.

Conclusion

In the period before 1914 the Flemish movement was characterized by cultural nationalism rather than political nationalism, in the sense that political self-determination was not yet a goal.[50] In the cultural emancipation struggle of the Flemish the Catholics did not always play the major part. The role of the Flemish militants within the Catholic Gymnastics Federation of Belgium (CGFB) was certainly less significant than within the liberal ranks of the Belgian Gymnastics Federation (BGF). Church leaders curbed those Catholic gymnasts who tried to emulate elements of the popular nationalism of people like Cupérus. The Church in general was one of the most important preservers of the idea of the Belgian state and of the use of the French language. Cardinal Mercier, for instance, was against the introduction of Flemish into the school system. The basilica of Koekelberg in Brussels, a huge church constructed in 1905, came to be seen as the symbol in stone of Belgian nationalism.[51] When, in 1908, Cardinal Mercier promoted British sports in Catholic schools,[52] the Catholic gymnasts reacted critically. They argued that gymnastics offered the only guarantee of physical and moral improvement for youth and said that 'school champions' should be turned into 'conquering soldiers for the good cause'.[53] The fact that Cardinal Mercier met the gymnasts and along with King Albert offered an official prize for the 17th CGFB national festival was sign of the times. Everyone began to place greater value on gymnastics as a form of military preparation in the immediate pre-war years when international tension was running high. Unlike Great Britain, where sports – as part of the typical British educational system – played an important role in the development of the Empire,[54] in Belgium, gymnastics had no apparent impact upon colonial activities in the Belgian Congo (now Zaïre). Nor was there the kind of chauvinism which was present in the gymnastics movements of Germany and France.[55] Aggression and 'revanchism' were absent from this small, neutral country. At most, one could identify a kind of defensive nationalism which balanced both militaristic and anti-militaristic tendencies. The moderate patriotism of the late nineteenth century evolved into the Belgian state nationalism of the pre-war period. Moreover, as war approached, clerical versus anti-clerical divisions began to dissolve. Discussions over the joint implementation of military preparation between Catholic gymnasts and liberals (like Cupérus) began in 1910 and even the Socialist Federation had joined in by 1912. This can be seen as symptomatic of the growing sense of co-operation between the socio-political groups in Belgium, a co-operation which was strongly promoted by King Albert and which led to the political 'union sacrée'[56] of the First World War.

In concluding, we cannot restrict ourselves simply to questions of popular and state nationalism. The history of European gymnastics and sports has shown that these years also saw the emergence of new forms of internationalism. For the Catholics naturally the Church of Rome provided a common focus and the important gymnastic gatherings of Catholics in Rome and elsewhere can be seen as a kind of latterday 'ultramontanism' where national differences were submerged in a common religious solidarity. This led to the foundation in 1911 of the Union Internationale des Œuvres Catholiques d'Education Physique (UIOCEP) in which the Belgians played so prominent a part.

Leaving aside the religious–ideological dimension, it remains the case that the French used German gymnastics techniques. So that when the Belgian Catholics modelled their gymnastics on France they too were basically adopting German methods and purposes. The concept of the improvement of the race was developed in those countries where national consciousness was sharply focused. In this respect Belgium showed a certain reluctance to go too far down the extreme nationalist road. Although at first the government had shown more interest in sports and horse-racing, as the international crisis deepened so the momentum of the gymnastic movement and the support of the government for it increased. The question of physical preparedness, which for so long had been a matter of internal clerical and anti-clerical politics, now gradually came to be clearly linked to the defence of the borders of the Belgian state.

NOTES

The author wishes to thank R. Holt, R. Renson, B. Vanreusel and J. De Maeyer.

1. R. Renson and T. Vanleeuwe, 'Sport en de Vlaamse beweging aan de Leuvense Universiteit (1835–1914)', *Onze Alma Mater*, XXXVII (1983), 283–306.

2. J. Tolleneer, 'The Reception of Modern Sports by Belgian Catholic Gymnasts (1895–1914)', in R. Renson, M. Lämmer J. Riordan and D. Chasiotis (eds.), *The Olympic Games through the Ages. Greek Antiquity and Its Impact on Modern Sports*, International HISPA Congress 13, Athens–Olympia; (1991), pp.217–27. J. Tolleneer, 'Gymnastics and Religion in Belgium (1892–1914)', *International Journal of the History of Sport*, VII (1990), 335–47.

3. P. Arnaud, 'Diviser et unir: sociétés sportives et nationalismes en France (1870–1914)', *Sport histoire: revue internationale des sports et des jeux*, IV (1989), 31–47.

4. R. Holt, 'Contrasting Nationalisms: Sport, Militarism and the Unitary State in Britain and France before 1914' (see pp.39–54 in this volume).

5. W. Laporte, 'Ontwikkelingen in de lichamelijke opvoeding in België, in K. Rijsdorp *et al.* (eds.), *Handboek lichamelijke opvoeding en sportbegeleiding* (Deventer, 1983), pp.1:I.3.Lap.1–17.

6. H. Smulders and R. Renson, 'A Social Analysis of the Introduction of Jahn's Gymnastics in Belgium: Its Propagators and Opponents', *Stadion*, IV (1978), 309–23.

7. G. De Meyer, *Nicolaas Jan Cupérus (1842–1928) en de ontwikkeling van de turnbeweging* (Rapporten van de Onderzoekseenheid Sociaalculturele Kinantropologie 6) (Leuven, 1986), p.268.

8. De Meyer, op.cit., pp.121–2.

9. Arnaud, op.cit., p.35.

10. L. Wils, Letters to R. Renson and G. De Meyer January 14th, (Leuven, 1983), p.2

11. F. Van Haver, 'Het turnen en de Vlaamse beweging 1830–1914: een analyse van de bondstijdschriften' (Leuven, dissertation, 1985).

12. Pol, In Vlaanderen Vlaamsch, *De Turner*, III (1898), 5: 79.

13. Tolleneer (1990), op.cit.

14. Arnaud, op.cit. He also refers to M. Lagree, *Les origines de la F.G.S.P.F. du Catholicisme social au mouvement de jeunesse* (Nanterre, 1969) and B. Dubrueil, 'La fédération catholique et la gymnastique', in P.Arnaud (ed.), *Les athlètes de la République: gymnastique, sport et idéologie républicaine 1870–1914* (Toulouse, 1987).

15. Tolleneer (1991), op.cit.

16. *Belgica*, 3, 5 (15 July 1897), 69.

17. *Belgica*, 4, 5 (15 July 1898), 73. See also P.Carson, *The Fair Face of Flanders* (1977).

18. J. Tolleneer, 'Education for war and education for life: the case of the National Federation of Catholic Gymnastics and Weapons Societies of Belgium (1892–1914)', (International Society for the History of Physical Education and Sport; First Congress; Sport and Contest; Las Palmas; 1991).

19. E. Witte and J. Craeybeckx, *Politieke geschiedenis van België sinds 1830: spanningen in een burgerlijke democratie* (Antwerp, 1985), pp.156–7. T. Luyckx and M. Platel, *Politieke geschiedenis van België 1: van 1789 tot 1944* (Antwerp, 1985), p.235.

20. *Belgica*, 16, 9 (Nov. 1910), 92.

21. *Belgica*, 17, 9 (Nov. 1911), 95–7.

22. Tolleneer (1991), op.cit.; *Belgica*, Vol.19, No.5 (May 1913), 87.

23. *Belgica*, 17, 6 (Aug. 1911), 63–5.

24. J. Tolleneer, 'De Fédération Internationale Catholique d'Education Physique (F.I.C.E.P.) en de turnbeweging in Oost- en West–Europa (1911–1989)', *Hermes*, XXI (1990), 2–3: 651–67.

25. Witte and Craeybeckx, op.cit., p.188.

26. *Belgica*, 8, 2–3 (April–May 1902), 26–9.

27. *Belgica*, 15, 6 (Aug. 1909), 61–4. For the rise of the Catholic gymnastics and sports movement in the Netherlands, see M. Derks, '"Wij zetten Roomsche vanen om voetbalvelden heen": een geschiedenis van de katholieke sportbeweging in Nederland 1910–1940' (Nijmegen, dissertation, 1988).

28. *Belgica*, 14, 6 (Aug. 1908), 70–71.

29. *Belgica*, 14, 8–9 (Oct.–Nov., 1908), 93–102.

30. *Belgica*, 19, 10 (Oct. 1913), 169–170.

31. E. De Sloovere, 'Geschiedenis van de roeisport in België: bijdrage tot het Archief voor de

Moderne Sport (MOSAR)' (Leuven, dissertation, 1988).

32. *Belgica*, 14, 10 (Dec. 1908), 111–16.
33. *Belgica*, 15, 10 (Dec. 1909), 123.
34. *Belgica*, 17, 7 (Sept. 1991), 79.
35. *Belgica*, 18, 99–120, 128–33.
36. *Belgica*, 19, 8 (Aug. 1913), 130.
37. C. Meeusen, 'Ontstaan en evolutie van de Koninklijke Katholieke Antwerse Turngouw (1896–1990)', *Hermes*, XXII(2), 141–53.
38. K. Van Isacker, *Mijn land in de kering 1830–1980 1: een ouderwetse wereld 1830–1914*, (Antwerp, 1983), p.212.
39. E. Pittoors, 'Koninklijke Katholieke Sportfederatie van België' (Leuven, paper, 1990–91).
40. *Belgica*, 4, 10 (15 Dec. 1898), 150–52.
41. *Belgica*, 13, 5 (July–Aug. 1907), 50.
42. Van Haver, op.cit., p.54; *Belgica*, 10 (15 Dec. 1898), 150–2.
43. *Belgica*, 15, 10 (Dec. 1909), 124–5; 12 (Feb. 1911), 125.
44. Van Haver, op.cit., p.83–7.
45. Van Haver, op.cit., p.77.
46. *Belgica*, 9, 5 (July 1903), 77. See also J. Tolleneer, 'Karel Van Assche (1874–1945): een boom van een turnleider', *Salto* (Brussels), X, 1–5.
47. De Meyer, op.cit., p.121–2.
48. Tolleneer (1990), op.cit.
49. *Belgica*, 14, 7 (Sept. 1908), 89.
50. H.J. Elias, *Geschiedenis van de Vlaamse gedachte 4: taalbeweging en cultuurflamingantisme, de groei van het Vlaamse bewustzijn 1883–1914* (Antwerp, 1971), p.374.
51. Witte and Craeybeckx, op.cit., p.144.
52. W. Uten, 'Voorgeschiedenis en ontstaan van het Nationaal Sportverbond van het Vrij Onderwijs (N.S.V.O.): 1908–1949: bijdrage tot het Archief voor de Moderne Sport (MOSAR)' (Leuven, dissertation, 1986).
53. *Belgica*, 14, 1 (March 1908), 1–2.
54. Holt, op.cit.
55. Arnaud, op.cit.
56. Witte and Craeybeckx, op.cit., p.157–8.

Body Culture and Democratic Nationalism: 'Popular Gymnastics' in Nineteenth-Century Denmark

HENNING EICHBERG

'The largest sports meeting in the world' is not the Olympic Games. If we can believe the Danish press, the Olympics are outranked by an event that took place in Horsens (Jutland) where the Danish federations of gymnastics, sports, rifle and youth held their traditional summer festival in June–July 1990. It attracted 23,000 men and women, among them many foreign participants. Activities and displays of Sukuma people from Tanzania, Poles, Saami, Greenlanders and others attracted special attention. The Danish gymnastic festival, which is held every five years, has established its own tradition for nearly a century. It is a highlight of what is called in Danish the *folkelig idræt*, popular sport.[1]

Folkelig idræt, however, could also be translated as 'national sport' or even as 'nationalist sport', being related to the national romantic terms *folk* (people) and *folkelighed* (the untranslatable spiritual dimension of the people), that is, to the Danish people and their sense of nationality. How does this nationalist aspect accord with the internationalism of 'popular sport' in Denmark, where *folkelighed* in particular is applied to international activities, such as the sports and gymnastics exchanges with Tanzania, Nicaragua, Poland and Britain?

Furthermore, there is a tradition in Denmark of juxtaposing gymnastics, which is regarded as a Nordic *folkelig* and national form of body culture, with sport, which is considered an essentially English import. How could this contradiction arise? And how do these two parts of body culture dovetail in practice in festivals and in the Danish sport federations in general?

These questions lead to a third. Denmark is the only country in Europe where gymnastics of the Swedish Lingian type have become popular and a broad cultural movement based on voluntary grassroot associations has developed. How could this have happened? And there is a further question to be asked – what is the relation between this essentially Danish form of body culture dating from the nineteenth century and the 'popular sport' of the 1990 Horsens festival?

Answers to these questions and an explanation of Danish individuality must be sought in the interrelations of body culture and national identity, cultural revolution, and class conflict in the nineteenth century. The decisive period was the 1880s and thereafter, and it was preceded by three preparatory phases.

'Non-Popular' Gymnastics

Philanthropic Innovation, 1780–1820

Industrial culture in Denmark started with the socio-economic liberation of the farmers, heralding the capitalistic transformation of the agrarian economy. The farmers made up the majority of the population, and, liberated in 1788 from feudal–military bonds, acquired freedom of movement and could become wage earners. Because of the redistribution of their land they often settled outside villages. Thus, not only was the repressive mechanism of local power challenged, but so too was the traditional solidarity of village life and collective self-organization.

In the atmosphere of reform, gymnastics as a new type of physical education was introduced in its philanthropic–pedagogical form by reform-oriented noblemen from 1780 onwards, that is, shortly before the social liberation act.[2] Gymnastics reached the Danish people geographically from Germany and socially 'from above'. Both of these origins hindered rather than helped gymnastics to become really 'popular' on account of a growing awareness of Danish national identity fuelled during the nineteenth century by opposition to the German Reich to the south and the aristocracy – often of German origin – at the top of the Danish state hierarchy.

The founder of Danish gymnastics was Franz Nachtegall (1777–1847), who established in 1804 and 1808 respectively a military and a civil gymnastic institute following the gymnastic model of J.C.F. Gutsmuths.[3] In 1814 an educational law made school gymnastics obligatory, and Denmark became the first country in history to introduce compulsory gymnastics – in theory. (The practice trailed far behind until the end of the century.)

Military Gymnastics and Spiritual Revival, 1820–60

The philanthropic impetus of gymnastics soon took a more military direction. Only Nachtegall's military gymnastic institute survived after 1816 and gained control of all physical education in the country, against a background of increasing conflict between the farmers and the ruling absolutist system. This is why the democratic movement, which surfaced during the 1848 revolution, turned against gymnastics as being unnatural and useless. In 1858, parliament, with its left wing majority, voted for the abolition of school gymnastics, but the right wing, the nobility and the bourgeoisie, which dominated the second chamber, annulled this decision.[4] The farming population was, however, not only reactive but also proactive. From the 1820s 'divine revivals' expressed the population's autonomous needs in pietistic, sometimes ecstatic forms. The revivals are regarded as the first popular (*folkelig*) movement in Denmark and created a special spiritual atmosphere which later on marked both Danish folk nationalism and Danish folk gymnastics.

New Gymnastic Milieux, 1860–1900

From 1860 onwards new institutional frameworks developed which later would connect gymnastics and the socio–cultural, spiritual and nationalist movement. Of particular significance were the *folkehøjskoler*, folk academies, which were established from 1844 onwards, based on ideas of the poet N.F.S. Grundtvig (1783–1872). They were a specific result of religious revival.[5] At the same time, private gymnastic institutes for women were, from 1859, established in Copenhagen as a part of urban bourgeois culture. Rifle associations started in 1861, with national defence in mind, but later on the clash between the left and the right wing in Danish politics created internal divisions. Assembly halls were established in the villages after 1870, becoming the backbone of new communal and social life in the countryside.[6] Eventually, from 1872, gymnastic clubs began to spring up in the towns against the background of urbanization, industrialization and the formation of a working class and bourgeoisie.

The 'Folkelig' Breakthrough, 1884–1901

In 1884, at the folk academy of Vallekilde (Sealand), an event took place which is regarded as a decisive stage in Danish body culture. On 25 February a new gymnastic hall was opened at this *folkehøjskole*, and the inauguration ceremony included a demonstration of Swedish Lingian gymnastics. A new form of exercise entered Denmark, and it soon became the preferred way of expressing national identity through physical culture. The significance of the new 'popular gymnastics' lay in its cultural integration. It was founded upon the exercises which Per Henrik Ling (1776–1839) had developed from about 1800 within the framework of national romantic Nordic Gothicism.[7] But later, Ling's gymnastics – in Sweden as well as internationally – developed more physiologically, anatomically and 'rationally' and came to be regarded as a set of pedagogical, medical, military and æsthetic exercises.

In Denmark, Lingian gymnastics was then practised in the spatial frame of the Vallekilde gymnasium – a representative architectural monument of

Nordic national neo-romanticism. Above the entrance of the magnificent wooden hall hung a painting from Nordic mythology: Thor, the courageous god of war, puts his hand into the mouth of the Fenris wolf in order to chain the dangerous beast, thus sacrificing a part of his body for the common good of the Ase gods. The architect of the gymnasium, Martin Nyrop, later became a leading Danish architect as a result of his work on the Copenhagen industrial exhibition of 1888 and the Copenhagen town hall (1901). His gymnasium was the model for a new generation of halls erected all over the country, though in less elaborate national-romantic and more functionally reduced forms.

At the inauguration of the Vallekilde gymnasium, 700 participants heard a speech made by the principal Ernst Trier. It became a sort of ideological manifesto of the new gymnastics, treating 'the whole human being' in the spiritual perspective of Grundtvigianism. The poet Jens Christian Hostrup wrote the song 'In hard times, we are not sad, we are not bowed' for the occasion. It became a battle song of the *folkelig* gymnastic movement. Thus, the 'triple sound' of the Grundtvigian national cultural movement was established: lecture, song and gymnastics. Body culture had entered the Danish spiritual movement.[8]

The cultural significance of the gymnastic event in Vallekilde was possible because it coincided with political tension on national and social levels. As a nationalist event, the inauguration at Vallekilde must be seen against the background of the lost war of 1864, when Prussia annexed not only the predominantly German Holstein and Schleswig, but also the whole of South Jutland. Large areas inhabited by the Danish population were now under foreign rule – a source of national frustration and permanent national mourning. In this context Nordic gymnastics was a demonstration of 'Nordic' against 'German', an affirmation of Danish identity against the powerful empire in the south.

This body-cultural manifestation of nationalism did not, however, lead to a militarization of gymnastics, as in some other countries at that time, for example in Slavic Sokol gymnastics and German *Turnen*. The reasons are found in political tensions in Denmark, in particular the social–political conflict between *Højre* (the right wing) and *Venstre* (the left wing). The democratic constitution of 1848 had not been successful in breaking the real power of the Danish oligarchy. The landed gentry held on to government, overruling the majority in parliament. In the elections of 1884, *Højre* obtained only 19 deputies, whilst *Venstre* scored 83 without being able to overthrow the *de facto* dictatorship of the right-wing prime minister Estrup. (The 'shift of system' did not occur until 1901.)

The political imbalance could have led to civil war. But the democratic majority chose – voluntarily or not – another way, that of social and cultural self-organization. What happened has sometimes been called the Grundtvigian cultural revolution. Its institutional pillars were the folk academies, the assembly halls, the rifle associations and the co-operative societies of production. The new type of Nordic gymnastics proved capable of linking these different institutions together. Thus it became not only national – against 'Germanization', but also social – a part of the class struggle of the majority against the ruling minority.

The result of this conflict can be measured by the change in gymnastic practice in the 1890s, particularly in the rifle associations and school education. From 1861 the rifle associations were the first to emulate the folk academies and change from 'Danish' (German) to 'Nordic' (Swedish) gymnastics in spite of violent protest from officers of the political right wing. In some regions Lingian gymnastics prevailed soon after the Vallekilde event, as for example in Ribe district in 1887. At the national level, in the mid-1890s the division was:

	Danish gymnastics		Swedish gymnastics	
	districts	gymnasts	districts	gymnasts
1893	191	3745	156	3468
1899	184	4480	239	6106

Eventually, at the 6th national festival of the rifle and gymnastic associations in Copenhagen, in 1901, there was only a small minority of – mostly urban – teams demonstrating Danish gymnastics. The large majority – and nearly all the teams from the countryside – demonstrated Swedish gymnastics.[9]

The state school system soon followed the trend, accompanied by serious political struggles and moreover by many pedagogical and personal controversies.[10] From 1856 the authoritative teaching manual had been largely made up of military exercises, whilst in 1883 apparatus work – trapeze, rings, parallel bars – appeared, after the model of German *Turnen* gymnastics. A commission, established in 1887 in order to review physical education in elementary schools, inclined towards Swedish gymnastics. In 1889 a second commission, the so-called large gymnastic commission, recommended detailed school exercises. This commission's work resulted finally, in 1899, in an authoritative manual of school gymnastics, based wholly on the Swedish Lingian system. The book's second part, concerned with ball games and other games and sports, was entitled 'Applied Gymnastics'.

Thus, 'left wing' gymnastics with its nationalist appeal – but supported at the same time by 'scientific' and hygienic arguments – had prevailed over 'right wing' gymnastics both outside the schools – in the influential folk academies and rifle associations – and within state school physical education. This was all the more remarkable because it preceded by some years the shift in the balance of power which occurred in the state itself. In 1901 the *Venstre* took political power from the *Højre*, thus continuing the change which had already become visible in physical education.

Three Configurations

The Danish case of national 'popular sport' raises questions concerning relations between nationalism and body culture. What was the 'language' of the body movement in *folkelig* nationalization? Other Nordic countries have favoured other body-cultural manifestations of national identity. Sweden and Finland, for example, have preferred to affirm their national identity by emphasizing success in sports competition. In Greenland, by contrast, it is the traditional drum dance which is regarded as an expression of Inuit cultural identity.

In these and other nations certain configurations of body-cultural identity recur, forming a tripolar pattern, or what Danish sociology of sports has called the trialectics of body culture.[11] Identity can be effected by:

- success in competition and records
- social discipline
- dialogical body language.

One typical example of 'sporting nationalism' is what could be called *production-orientation*. High achievement in sport produces results – in centimetres, grams, seconds and points – that can serve as symbols of identity. 'We must win the football tournament', expresses a classical model of product-oriented identification. The collective 'we' is linked to a result, which can be measured exactly or put into a hierarchical system. The Football World Cups and Olympic medal competitions with their ranking lists are typical formal celebrations of this model. All attempts to de-nationalize the Olympic rankings have hitherto failed.

Another configuration focuses on the *disciplining* of the participants' bodies. In this case, national identity is affirmed by masses marching in rank and file, dressed in military uniforms and showing collective discipline by moving on command in the 'right' way. Social values such as self-discipline, social integration and community spirit are often mixed with biological images of muscular Darwinian strength. Uniforms make the conformity of movements more visible. The highlights of this enthusiasm are national celebrations in the form of *Turnen* festivals, Spartakiads, Sokol mass meetings and sport festivals in some Third World countries. 'We' are demonstrating 'ourselves' by the exactness of 'our' common rhythm, by the precision of 'our' straight lines, by the radiation of 'our' healthy bodies. The 'we' manifests itself by collective fitness.

There is, however, a third configuration – or type of configuration – where the identity of the individual is affirmed neither by results nor by the process of discipline. The Inuit drum dance creates a dialogue between actors and public, a bodily experience producing laughter. In this case, 'our own' movements are those which are just not comparable to those of others – neither 'quicker, higher, stronger' nor more disciplined, but unique. In folk dancing, a shared rhythm unites the participants, sometimes raising them to states of collective trance or drunkenness (in contrast to the organized folkloric dances of the nineteenth century with their formal movements). Experience of 'our own' nature, 'our own' landscape is part of the body-culture movement, and is sometimes directly incorporated into games: water in Danish joust games, earth in Aosta casting sports, trees in Basque trunk competitions. Thus, a wide range of social experience constitutes the sensuality of folk identity, forming a sort of *social body language* or *bodily dialogue* by rhythm and game, ecological experience and meditation, expressivity and festivity, ecstasy and silence, trance and laughter. The particular patterns can be and often are sanctioned by repetition and tradition, but – and this is most often overlooked – they are also open to creative experimentation.

Reality as Contradiction and Conflict

The trialectical differentiation of body culture in general, and of its identity-related dimensions in particular, should be understood as a means of analysis and comparison. It is not meant to assert ontological patterns or to classify and reduce the cultural phenomena. Every phenomenon is in principle both composed and contradictory. Therefore a detailed analysis of its configuration with reference to its internal dynamics, contradictions and hegemonies is required.

This is specially true in the case of Danish 'popular gymnastics'. At first sight it looks – in its classical form of 1884 – like a typical example of disciplinary exercise. Seen in the context of Swedish military gymnastics, German *Turnen* and Slavic Sokol, it shows all the purposeful elements of social integration and national hygienics:

- The exercises follow a fixed time pattern and a measure of *drill*, structured by the leader.
- They celebrate the *straight line* of body and bodies: the straight spine, symmetry of movement, geometrical position.

- Their space is the *hall*, the disciplinary indoor environment.
- The bodies are in *uniform*.
- Their movements consists of *static* positions in order to be controllable and predictable, exposed to scrutiny.
- The exercises are *synthetically constructed*, following a pedagogically logical scheme.
- The leader is in *command*, and there is no gymnastics without an instructor.
- The superstructure of the movements consists of a system claiming for itself *scientific* truth, derived from anatomy and physiology.
- The relationship between practical activities and values – health, pedagogics, patriotism – is one of *instrumentality*: the body serving as instrument for external purposes.

Considering only these features, however, it is hard to understand why Lingian gymnastics became so much more popular in Denmark than German military gymnastics. Surprisingly, the *folkelig gymnastik* emerged from the conflict as non-disciplinary or even anti-disciplinary. What is the explanation?

Political interests might be one of the reasons. The success of *folkelig gymnastik* from 1884 up to its official recognition as *the* system of gymnastics in Danish schools (1899) was achieved despite great opposition from military spokesmen who advocated the older Danish–German model. In 1887, 46 army officers signed a declaration, published in the review *Vort Forsvar* (Our Defence):

> The undersigned officers from the garrisons in Fredericia, Nyborg, Odense, Århus, Viborg, Ålborg, Randers, Horsens and Copenhagen hereby declare that we strongly object that rifle associations in our country have introduced Swedish gymnastics into the rifle districts and educated for this purpose teachers in the named gymnastics in certain folk academies while Danish military gymnastics, once widespread in Denmark as in no other country, is now displaced in some districts of the rifle federation. We consider it to the advantage of these associations to return to the sort of gymnastics most suitable for riflemen as future soldiers.[12]

The initiator of this appeal, Captain Edvard Nielsen, a right-wing member of the rifle federation board, commented that he would resign his membership in an association which included 'people under the influence of the folk academies, because the spirit of some of these academies is so radical and detrimental to society that it would be better to get rid of them. It seems to me impossible to cooperate with them because of their whole view of life.'[13]

The political antagonism between military interests and the farmers' cultural revolution can explain, to an extent, why the Lingian gymnastics, in spite of its disciplinary character, did not become a militarist exercise with revanchist goals in Denmark. This remains, however, an explanation at the level of the ideological–political superstructure.

The other side of the antagonism – and, thus, of the possible explanation – was the farmers' class, their everyday life and their social image of the body. Here, the social historian is surprised. The farmer and his body culture are normally automatically associated with quite different patterns of movement, related to his work: rough competitions of strength (being in some respect forerunners of modern sports), grotesque games, folk dances – heavy motion and individualism. The rank and file exercises of Lingian gymnastics seem to be diametrically opposed to this way of movement. The Danish case consequently questions this stereotype, that occupation determines movement culture. The historian has to accept that, under special conditions, in the context of social conflict and nationalist aspiration, gymnastic discipline was an appropriate pattern through which to express farmers' social identity.

It should also be noted that Grundtvigian ideology connected *folkelig* gymnastics and the folk academies with the religious revivals of the 1820s, and it deserves to be analysed in depth: what were the body-cultural conditions and expressions of the 'divine revivals', and how did they influence the genesis of popular gymnastics?

In describing the dynamics of Danish Nordic gymnastics imprecise metaphors such as 'spirit', 'emotion', 'energy', 'rhythm' or 'common vibration' were often used. This terminology must be taken seriously, as referring to an atmosphere connecting the pietistic sentiments of a spiritual community with the emotions of gymnastic sociability. Sentimental autobiographic statements can be read as an expression of this. A multitude of songs and psalms contributed to the creation of this peculiar atmosphere. The community of rhythm, created by the integration of gymnastics and national songs, constituted the body-cultural part of a class history, linking the farmers' uprising of 1820–48 with the farmers taking on an hegemonic national role in 1884–1901.

Gymnastic Politics of Gender

Besides the farmers (as practitioners of the new gymnastics) on the left wing and the officers (as opposition) on the right wing, a further group merits attention: women. Their participation in gymnastics illustrates some special aspects of the development of body culture in Denmark and of the politics of gender.

As in other countries, in late eighteenth-century Denmark the inclusion of girls demonstrated a philanthropic aspect to gymnastics, but gymnastics was developed by men and for boys. Later militarization confirmed the imbalance in male participation. On the fringes, however, special gymnastics institutes for women or girls were founded in the mid-nineteenth century, but they remained restricted to the urban bourgeoisie. They followed German, Swedish and French systems of exercise. The most successful among them, founded in 1878 by Paul Petersen in Copenhagen and still in existence, combined the different models in a pragmatic, pedagogic way.[14]

This gender relation – women as late newcomers – was changed by the development of Nordic gymnastics in 1884 when the Swedish gymnastic instructor Sally Högström was called to the Vallekilde Folk Academy to instruct the girls of the school during their summer course in Lingian gymnastics.[15] She also trained a smaller group of girls to become gymnastic instructors themselves. Among these were Ingeborg Schrøder, Ingeborg Trier and Charlotte Bonnevie, who developed women's gymnastics at Danish folk academies.

Sally Högström continued teaching gymnastics at the academies of Vallekilde and Askov and through her gymnastics demonstrations also became involved in the troubled political life of Denmark. With her short hair and reform dress she symbolized a new age. After her gymnastics demonstration in Kolding a few years later, the leader of the Danish left-wing party, C. Berg, stated that if Swedish gymnastics succeeded, then women's suffrage would follow. It was indeed achieved in 1915.

The atmosphere of early gymnastics, from the perspective of a woman in the process of emancipation, was described by Ingeborg Schrøder (later Appel) in her autobiography (1940):

> For the young girls of today it will certainly be impossible to imagine the wonderful pleasure of putting on a gymnastics costume in which one could move freely, though the sleeves were long and the frock went down below the knees. This dress was still regarded as improper, and many years were to pass before we could do our exercises in the open air. But how beautiful it was to feel one's strength growing from arm exercises on the horizontal bar, from climbing the rope and from those many wonderful vaults which required courage and agility.[16]

From the 1880s onwards, gymnastics for men and for women developed in tandem. Later Elli Björkstén (1870–1947), a Swedish Finnish gymnastics teacher, provided a new stimulus. She made the rather static Lingian gymnastics more rhythmic and more dynamic. The older drill-like exercise configuration became transformed into a flow of movement. At the same time she placed gymnastics in a green outdoor environment and emphasized the rhythmic dynamics of the new women's gymnastics with songs and music. The demonstration of Björkstén gymnastics during the Olympic Games in Stockholm 1912 brought her international attention.[17]

In Denmark, Elli Björkstén's influence took two different directions. Women gymnasts in Denmark, where she had taught since 1906, welcomed Björkstén's movement model as a 'gymnastic revolution against the wooden dolls' and inspired Jørgine Abildgaard and Anna Krogh to found a gymnastic academy in Snoghøj in 1925. This school, in the tradition of the Danish folk academies, became for 30 years the centre of Danish women's gymnastics.

In men's gymnastics, the gymnastic teacher Niels Bukh (1880–1950) was also fascinated by Björkstén's new style, discovering it at the 1912 Olympics. He combined it with the French gymnastics of Georges Hébert and formed a new style which he called 'Primitive Gymnastics'. In 1920 he founded the first Danish folk academy specializing in body culture, the Ollerup Gymnastic Academy, which became predominant in the education of gymnastics instructors – male and female – in the inter-war years.[18]

The competitive relationship between the Snoghøj and the Ollerup models was also significant in the development of nationalism in Denmark in the age of Fascism. Travelling with his gymnastic teams around the world, Niels Bukh found especially positive responses in Japan, in Fascist Italy and in Nazi Germany, and he reacted sympathetically to German body culture after 1933, as is documented in the autobiography of his assistant Krogshede.[19] Bukh's participation in the Berlin Olympics of 1936 with a team from Ollerup aroused great interest in Germany and was followed by an invitation to the Nazi Parteitag in Nuremberg. After the German occupation of Denmark in 1940–45, these and other facts made him unpopular as a 'collaborator', though he was never an ideological Fascist or Nazi.

In contrast, the academy of Snoghøj was engaged in criticism of and struggle against the nazification of Denmark. A prominent speaker for Nordic and democratic values was the literary critic Jørgen Bukdahl, who became the regular orator in the annual Snoghøj summer festivals. Referring to Herder and Grundtvig, he advocated a *folkelig* national alternative to German–Italian Fascism. His speeches became a source of inspiration to the Danish resistance during the years of occupation.[20]

The antagonism between the two gymnastic schools, both based on the national democratic and romantic tradition of the Grundtvigian folk academies and both inspired by Elli Björkstén's gymnastic reform, was not only ideological: conservative Danish nationalism (Bukh) versus *folkelig* democratic Nordic nationalism (Bukdahl), but arose also from the conflicting gymnastic models. Ollerup gymnastics favoured a discipline in straight lines, in ranks corresponding to the right angles of Ollerup architecture, very masculine in appearance, even when women were participating, under the command of a leader positioned on a high podium. In contrast, Snoghøj gymnastics was performed in circles, in swinging groups or lines in the open air, using musical accompaniment and demonstrating its Nordic roots with beech twigs. From a feminist perspective, the different body images were described as being 'Egyptian' in Ollerup – the chin drawn in and the poise strained, a fortified body – in contrast to the 'Nordic' image of Snoghøj, the forehead raised to the sky and the movement rhythmic, free and relaxed.[21] From a trialectic point of view, Ollerup gymnastics was nearer to the social hygienic model, whilst the Snoghøj configuration demonstrated a greater affinity to the dialogical movement culture of *folkelig* sociality.

Both music and relaxation, which played an important role in Snoghøj, became – after the Second World War and under changed circumstances – important characteristics of the new gymnastics in general. Female gymnastics reflected yet again changes in Danish gymnastics history. Women, too, became much more strongly represented in the organization and leadership structure of the Danish Federation of Gymnastic and Youth Associations (DDGU) than in other sport federations inside and outside the country. All in all, the complex gender relation in Danish gymnastics with its impact on national ideological orientations seems so significant as to make one wonder about hidden 'matriarchal' traits in daily Danish culture.[22]

Movement Culture and Cooperative Economy

The specific combination of gymnastics and *folkelig* nationalism in Denmark also became an important factor of what could be called the Danish economic model in the age of agrarian industrialization. The organized form of this exceptional economy were the farmers' cooperatives of production. Whilst the capitalist transformation of the agrarian economy in the twentieth century led – in nearly all European countries – to a marginalization of farmers to the advantage of the urban bourgeoisie, Danish farmers could enter into capitalist competition through their cooperative organization and survive, raise their productivity and contribute to the national identity of their country.

The new social economic organizations started with the first dairy cooperatives in 1882. In 1890 there were 679, in 1900, 1029. Butchers cooperatives followed soon, 26 between 1887 and 1900. Energy production was also built up in cooperative and decentralized forms; one hundred electric works were producing by 1908, one third of them based on wind power. Cooperative shops spread over the country, about 500 by 1890.

Export cooperatives, foodstuff associations, cooperative banks, cooperative cement factories, fertilizer and seed purchase associations completed the picture of farmers' self-help.[23] With the help of these new organizations of economic democracy and solidarity, the farmers managed to master the market crisis during the years of depression between 1876–77 and 1900 and to maintain their decentralized ownership structure in spite of pressure from the great capital.

Observers from other countries have repeatedly reflected on this exceptional case. Lenin, for example, was interested in the experiment, but he could not concede it any economic chance under capitalist conditions. History did not confirm his negative view. An English economic historian, who studied the comparative politics of energy in different European countries, concluded by contrasting two main strategies: centralization of electrification (or the 'Napoleon model'), as realized in France, England and Sweden; and decentralization, based on municipalities and farming cooperatives (or the 'Grundtvig model'), as realized in Denmark.[24]

This classification could be understood as rather idealistic, basing the changes in production on ideas and personalities. But understood in another, more 'materialistic' way, it demonstrates the importance of social psychological conditions in production. What was the concrete connection between the Danish economic model on the one hand and the popular patterns of solidarity and cooperation, established by the *folkelig* movements of religious revival, folk academies and Grundtvigianism on the other? It is here that gymnastics enters the picture. *Folkelig* gymnastics in the villages of the 1880s was a sort of bodily link between the farmers' ideas and their practical economic cooperation. When the (mostly young) farmers trained their bodies in ranks to the accompaniment of sentimental national romantic songs and refrained from individual competition – as represented by the older Danish German gymnastics as well as by urban bourgeois sports – so this expressed a peculiar social language. It contributed to their collectivity and enabled them to compete in the capitalist market.[25]

The direct connection between cooperative and technological development on the one hand and gymnastics on the other can also be illustrated by the life and work of one individual, Poul la Cour (1846–1908). Poul la Cour was an eminent inventor and meteorologist with a promising career at the University of Copenhagen, but for personal reasons he decided to become a teacher at the Folk Academy in Askov. There he developed a new historical perspective of science, published as *Historisk Mathematik* (1881) and *Historisk Fysik* (1896–1901). His view was deeply influenced by the romantic sentiment of Grundtvig and the *folkelig* movements. During his lectures he often burst into tears, weeping about the beauty of the universe – and also about the anti-Danish politics of Bismarck. These emotions made a strong impression on his young students. At the same time he continued his technological work of experiments in wind power. His experimental windmill in Askov became recognized as a state centre of technological innovation; he was appointed titular professor and called by the press 'Denmark's Edison'. In 1903 he started the 'Danish Society for Wind Electricity', hiring consultant engineers to advise on the erection of electricity works all over the country.[26]

At the same time, Poul la Cour was a fervent promoter of the new Nordic gymnastics. He had been present at the first demonstration in Vallekilde in 1884 and immediately took the initiative of organizing a course of Swedish gymnastics for Danish teachers, held in Lund in 1885. Twelve Danes joined him, and together they trained for seven weeks under the Swedish captain C.H. Norlander.[27] From 1885 to 1905 la Cour was a member of the board of the rifle federation and contributed actively to its change from the 'Danish' to the Swedish Lingian gymnastic system.

The outstanding feature of Danish physical culture in the nineteeth century was thus a form of gymnastics which balanced the patterns of social hygienics and social body experience, and provided a counterbalance to result-oriented sport. It was related to a specific superstructure of *folkelig* nationalism, to gender politics and to Danish cooperative economy.

Nationalism Is Not Just One

The analysis of body culture under the headings of plurality and contradiction leads also to a revision of the unitary term of nationalism. Evidently there are different models of nationalization and national identification which correspond to body cultural configurations. The sport model of achievement–orientation suggests a *nationalism of production* and an identification with economic success, growth and expansion. The 'citius, altius, fortius' of Olympism describes a pride in results, present in sports as well as in economic and social fields. In an historical–cultural perspective, this type of nationalism seems to be represented especially by the Anglo-American tradition.

Different in some respects is the *nationalism of integration*, based on egality and national–pedagogical formation. National gymnastics, with its focus on uniform appearance and linear movement, fits this model. This national hygienic pattern seems to be hegemonic both in French Jacobin nationalism and in the Prussian model of discipline.

As a third configuration, *national–popular identification* is determined by neither economic nor integrative power, but instead by factors more distant from power formation in general: by language and everyday life. Dance, festivities, games and plays contribute to this form of interdependence, to popular (folk) reciprocity. There seems to exist an affinity between this pattern and the processes of nationalism in some minor countries, among Nordic peoples, in Balkan countries and in Celtic nations. The Danish case is interesting, because it shows the links between the model of nationalism, a specific history of class relations and a special form of body culture. This is true also in the late twentieth century, the time of the Horsens festival and its 'folk sport'. The activities of the new *folkelig* festivals are borne by popular grassroot initiatives, associations and folk academies, working strictly locally, cooperatively and voluntarily, but at the same time under the influence of social pedagogical and hygienic tendencies in the public sector. The cultural innovations of the new middle classes are mingling with some traditions of the Social Democratic workers, and of *folkelig* farmers and make up the socio-cultural profile. The result is a democratic nationalism noted for its reservations towards the new 'Empire' of the capitalist European Community. This nationalism is very different from the production-oriented model; and it is not a nationalism of integration and discipline, though clearly influenced by the Scandinavian welfare system with its corporative–integrative tendencies. Hegemonically, it is a third type of national identification, stressing democratic and grassroot values.

Nationalism is, therefore, as pluralistic as sport. Likewise, models of national identification do not exclude each other, but overlap in reality. Their dynamic in relation to class and power still remains to be examined properly.[28]

If the relationship between nationalism and sport is understood in this way, it does not mean the creation of another field of academic specialization, another adjectival historiography. The study of sport and body culture may add something new to the already established literature on society and nationalism, following the psychological theory that collective identities are created by common rituals. Rituals can be of very different character; likewise, identities.

NOTES

1. *Ungdom og Idræt*, XCIII (1990), nos. 26–27/28.
2. Ove Korsgaard, *Kampen om kroppen* (Copenhagen 1982), pp.21–37. J.C.F. Gutsmuths, *Kort Anvisning til Legemsøvelser*. V.K. Hjort (ed.), *Et Udtog af Gutsmuths Gymnastik* (Copenhagen, 1799), a shortened version of the German edition from 1793. Peter Villaume, *Om Legemets Dannelse med Hensyn til Menneskets Fuldkommenhed og Lyksaglighed, eller den psykiske Opdragelse i Særdeleshed* (Copenhagen, 1802; German edition 1787). Peter Hans Mönster, *Om Gymnastikkens Anvendelse paa Ungdommens Opdragelse* (Copenhagen, 1804). Jens Krogslund, *Gymnastik-historiske kilder* (Odder, 1982–87), vols. 1–2.
3. Franz Nachtegall, *Instruction i Gymnastikken for de Lærere, som er ansatte ved Kavalleriets og Infanteriets Underofficer- og Exercerskoler* (Copenhagen, 1805). Franz Nachtegall, *Lærebog for Almue- og Borger-Skolerne i Danmark* (Copenhagen, 1928), (German:

Lehrbuch der Gymnastik, Tondern, 1837). Franz Nachtegall, *Gymnastikkens Fremgang i Danmark fra dens Indgørelse i Aaret 1799 indtil Udgangen af Aaret 1830* (Copenhagen, 1831, reprint 1976). H.P. Langkilde, 'Franz Nachtegall' *Dansk Biografisk Leksikon* (Copenhagen, 1939), Vol. 16, pp.500–3.

4. *Rigsdagstidende*, Forhandlingerne paa Folketingets tiende Session (Copenhagen, 1858).
5. Kaj Thaning, *N.F.S. Grundtvig* (Copenhagen, 1972). Thomas Rørdam, *The Danish Folk High Schools* (Copenhagen, 2nd rev. ed., 1980). Jørn Falk, '*Et jævnt og muntert virksomt Liv paa Jord': Vor uforbrugte kulturarv fra det 19. århundrede*, Kultursociologiske skrifter, 12 (Copenhagen, 1980). Steven Borish, *The Land of the Living: The Danish Folk High School and Denmark's Non-Violent Path to Modernization* (Nevada City, 1991).
6. *Forsamlingshuse på landet*, ed. Ministry of Culture (Copenhagen, 1979). See also Niels Clemmensen, *Associationer og foreningsdannelse i Danmark 1780–1880* (Øvre Ervik, 1987).
7. Pehr Henrik Ling, *Schriften über Leibesübungen*, transl. H.F. Massmann (Magdeburg, 1847). Kristen Lange, *Den Lingske Gymnastik i Danmark 1884–1909* (Copenhagen, 1909). P.C. McIntosh, 'Therapeutic Exercise in Scandinavia', in John Gretton Dixon *et al.*, *Landmarks in the History of Physical Education* (London, 1957), pp.81–106.
8. Korsgaard, *Kampen om kroppen*, pp.82–4. See also Preben Breds *et al.* (eds.), *Gymnastik–historie*, Idrætshistorisk Årbog, 3 (Aabybro 1987). Else Trangbæk and Preben Breds, *Dansk gymnastik – folkelig kultur: Fra folkeopdragelse til motion* (Copenhagen, 1988), pp.46–66. Henning Eichberg, '"Folkelig gymnastik": Über den dänischen Sonderweg in der Körperkultur', in Klaus-Jürgen Gutsche and Hand Jochen Medau (eds.), *Gymnastik: Ein Beitrag zur Bewegungskultur unserer Gesellschaft* (Schorndorf, 1989), pp.52–95.
9. Ole Jørgensen Daneved, 'En sund sjæl i et sundt legeme: Gymnastik– og skyttesagen i Danmark 1884–1905', *Den jyske historiker* (1981) no. 19/20, pp.89–138, her p.118. Ove Korsgaard, *Krop og kultur: Andelsbøndernes gymnastik mellem almuens leg og borgerskabets sport* (Odense, 1986), p.58.
10. Else Trangbæk, *Mellem leg og disciplin: Gymnastikken i Danmark i 1800–tallet* (Aabybro 1987), pp.134–96.
11. Henning Eichberg, 'Body Culture as Paradigm: The Danish Sociology of Sport', *International Review for the Sociology of Sport*, XXIV (1989), 43–63.
12.. Korsgaard, *Krop og kultur*, pp.57–8.
13. Ibid. p.58.
14. Poul Petersen, *Den danske Kvindegymnastik* (Copenhagen, 1909). Else Trangbæk, 'Den danske kvindegymnastiks fader – Poul Petersen', *Idrætshistorisk Årbog*, V (1989), pp.46–66.
15. Ove Korsgaard, *Kredsgang* (Copenhagen, 1986), pp.63–6.
16. Korsgaard, *Krop og kultur*, p.64.
17. Elli Björkstén, *Kvindegymnastik* (Copenhagen, 1933). Gertrud Wichmann, *Elli Björkstén* (Helsinki, 1965). Magdalynne Solomon Lewis, *A Philosophy of Finnish Women's Physical Education as Represented in Selected Writings of Elin Kallio, Elli Björkstén, and Hilma Jalkanen* (London, 1980).
18. Niels Bukh, *Gymnastik im Bild* (Oldenburg, 1926). Niels Bukh, *Dansk Gymnastik (primitiv)* (Ollerup, 3rd ed., 1935), (German: *Grundgymnastik*, Leipzig, 7th ed., 1927).
19. Kristian Krogshede, *Minder fra Ollerup og Gerlev: En bondedrengs livseventyr* (Copenhagen, 1980).
20. Poul Engberg, *Jørgen Bukdahl: Den folkelige stridsmand* (Mikkelberg, 1991).
21. Korsgaard, *Kampen om kroppen*, pp.235–41.
22. Henning Eichberg, 'Matriarkalske undertoner', in Tone Saugstad Gabrielsen and Marie-Alice Séférian (eds.), *Hvor danske er danskerne* (Copenhagen, 1991), pp.124–43.
23. Martin Zerlang, *Bøndernes klassekamp i Danmark: Agrarsmåborgerskabets sociale og ideologiske udvikling fra landboreformernes tid til systemskiftet* (Copenhagen, 1976), pp.84–96. Also Borish, op.cit.
24. N.J.D. Lucas, cited by H.C. Hansen, 'Poul la Cour – en grundtvigsk naturvidenskabsmand', in Per Warming (ed.), *Fremtidens videnskab* (Copenhagen, 1983), pp.93–114, here pp.110–11.
25. Korsgaard, *Krop og kultur*, p.56. Also Borish, op.cit.
26. Hansen, op.cit.

27. C.H. Norlander, *Kort Redegørelse for den svenske Gymnastik* (Kolding, 1885).
28. Henning Eichberg (ed.), *Nordic Sports, History and Identity* (Helsinki, 1989).

Phases and Functions of Nationalism: Norway's Utilization of International Sport in the Late Nineteenth and Early Twentieth Centuries

MATTI GOKSØYR

Ban the sports fever which from abroad is about to invade us.
It brings us no good.[1]

We will always remember that the nation is behind us.
We promise: Everything for the fatherland![2]

Introduction: Methodological Problems

Nationalism in sport can be considered from various angles. Since research on this topic is in its infancy in Norway, the purpose of this study is to suggest questions and hypotheses rather than to reach firm conclusions. The approach will be twofold: first, to outline the various phases in the relationship between sport and nationalism from the middle of the last century until 1912. This will be the basis for the second topic: the functions of nationalism in sport through various phases and configurations. One fundamental question will be: how did the internationalization of sport influence the national content and identity of Norwegian sport?

Nationalism, perhaps more than other fields of history, requires *international comparisons* to permit theoretical generalizations. However, the accurate empirical evidence needed for this purpose can be difficult to acquire. Questions of nationalism are complicated. The methodological problems associated with the questions are substantial: the social-psychological intricacies involved in measuring what is genuine national emotion is one, trying to isolate and evaluate the effects of nationalistic expression through sport is another. There is also the question of the level at which to carry out the analysis. Most historians, like Eric Hobsbawm, attribute the rise of nationalism to the emerging middle classes of the nineteenth century.[3] However, it remains relevant to pose the question: whose 'national sentiments' are we to study? This is an important question, because in the concept of nationalism there is a strong component of *popular* consensus. Most historians and social scientists in this area have stressed the element of *community* as a key ingredient in nationalism. Ernest Renan's statement of 1882, 'A nation is a daily plebiscite ...', has been quoted from time to time in the last century.[4] Modern historians have elaborated on this, but still emphasize the *unifying* forces lying within the sentiment of national identity.[5] This means that if nationalism was able to have influence as a motive force in history, popular support was a necessary condition. Lacking 'genuine popular resonance' nationalism would be little more than playing with words.[6]

It is therefore of some importance to find out *who* are defining and formulating nationalism in sport. Is it an official, state affair? Would it be more rewarding to investigate the sports officials, the sports federations and their leaders? Or is it, in the end, the people themselves – at least the sports interested part of the 'nation' – who are the true keepers of genuine national sentiments? If the last assumption is true, one fundamental question arises: who are the spokesmen expressing the people's real nationalism?

Finding historical evidence of popular attitudes is a general problem of history. Sources available from the last century mainly derive from the first two levels of would-be opinion-makers. It was the middle- and upper-classes who were capable of having their attitudes and ideologies recorded for the future. It would, of course, be a drastic misinterpretation to say, for want of sources, that 'the common man' was without any national consciousness at all. We can, however, in certain cases, obtain data about grassroots attitudes and possible national sentiments. Files of sports clubs with a socially, broad recruitment and official archives concerning public law and order, give direct information. Literature and pictorial materials, can provide useful evidence. This study will therefore try to touch upon aspects of nationalism in sport as they were expressed at all three levels.

The essay will focus, not on political doctrines or philosophical interpretations,[7] but on nationality and nationalism as historical realities and motive forces that were sometimes decisive factors in international historical development. The purpose is not to explain the rise of nationalism, but to investigate and discuss how this new phenomenon functioned in connection with sport.

Nationalism

Terminology associated with the term nationalism is dogged with pitfalls. Here the concepts, nation, nationality and nationalism, will be applied in a way that is related to the historical development of the nineteenth century, according to the view that 'nations' first obtained their political significance at this time.[8]

This statement is not uncontroversial. A. D. Smith[9] uses the concept of nationalism on a broader scale, including pre-modern variants. E. Gellner and others connect the rise of nationalism to modernization and industrialization.[10] What both views have in common is the acknowledgement that something new, or at least a new phase of nationalism, occurred from the end of the eighteenth century in Europe. We shall focus upon this epoch of nationalism. Eric Hobsbawm states that the phenomenon of nations is a relatively 'recent historical innovation'.[11] Recent as they may be, these nations frequently used history as a legitimator and a unifying force. This created a search for 'cultural community', and it is here that we should examine the relationship between sport and nationalism.

The French Revolution of 1789 has been a common reference point for European nationalism, and historians stressing economic and social factors tend to cite industrialization and modernization as the catalysts. In western Europe nationalism started to emerge as a force to be reckoned with in the nineteenth century. In the Scandinavian countries, and in Norway particularly, this development became evident during the first half of the nineteenth century. How did nationalism manifest itself? The principle of *self-determination*, with its roots in 1789 and in the American Declaration of Independence, can be summed up in the idea that political and national unity should be one and the same.[12] In Europe during the nineteenth century this conviction contained both a constitutional element and a principle of independence.[13] The idea of the nation-state also implied cultural unity. National romanticism in Germany in the nineteenth century added this cultural element of the liberal patriotism growing out of the French Revolution. The creation of national identity became an almost universal, legitimizing task for political authorities in most new nation-states. A compulsory educational system is often considered as the key mechanism in such a cultural socialization.[14] It should be kept in mind, though, that the development of national schooling systems often lagged behind actual national sentiments. Local versions of Eugen Weber's now classic *Peasants into Frenchmen* have been and should be applied to investigate the emerging consciousness of nationality. It is relevant, too, to question if, and when, peasants evolved into industrial workers and industrial workers became Norwegians.[15] When did the various social classes cross the line to nationally defined social membership? That nations had a right to their own states and, subsequently, the creation of states, were convictions that spread rapidly in Europe during the nineteenth century. The development of Norwegian nationalism in such a perspective has been, and still is, a matter of considerable discussion among historians.[16]

For the purpose of this study, however, Miroslav Hroch's thesis of a three-step evolution of national movements seems to be useful, even though he has been heavily criticized for his comments on Norway before 1814.[17] Hroch's view of the emergence of Norwegian nationalism is that the years before 1814 can be counted as an initial phase, consisting of a non-political and mostly cultural, literary and folkloristic interest in the 'national', expressed by a narrow intellectual 'elite'. However inadequate this may appear to some, as Lunden has pointed out, Hroch's other phases seem more convincing. According to Hroch a second phase of Norwegian nationalism building, characterized by patriotic agitation, dominated the years from 1814 to 1840. This period was succeeded by a third stage in the last half of the century where expressive nationalism revealed by popular movements came to the fore. We shall return to the evidence behind these arguments shortly, after one additional remark.

Hroch does not discuss a possible fourth phase of particular relevance to this study. Early in the twentieth century Norway was an example of an established nation. Was there a need to promote nationalism in such a situation? This is a pertinent question. For this reason the nature of nationalism is not static. Its meanings and implications change in history. This is why the questions of *who* is formulating the content of the concept, as well as who is putting it into practical operation, are questions of some importance. The Norwegian example raises inevitable questions about phases and functions of nationalism. The varying phases that the sports–nationalism relationship in Norway have gone through illustrate how the role of sport changes as the meaning of nationality alters and nations develop, constantly introducing new international relations.

The First Phase of Nationalism: The National 'Revival' in the Nineteenth Century

The nineteenth century led to important changes in most spheres of Norwegian society. After 400 years under the Danish kings, the year 1814 had given Norway an independent and radical constitution inspired by the ideas of the French Revolution. Although Danish rule had been replaced, after the Kiel Convention, by a more formal union with Sweden, the constitution gave both a foundation and a symbol on which to build a national consciousness.

The Norwegian constitution soon had to be protected from attacks from the Swedish king, and Constitution Day, 17 May, became a day for mobilizing support. The celebration of the day evolved in a way which might also be of some relevance for our larger topic. In the decades after 1814, meetings to celebrate the Constitution were mostly organized in private. The public celebrations, which became popular in mostly large towns in Norway from the 1830s onwards, can be regarded as the successful mobilization of the whole middle class in defence of the Constitution.[18] And as we shall see, sport became an important means of increasing public participation in these national festivals.

Industrialization and urbanization changed the country's socio-economic structure, especially in the latter half of the nineteenth century. From being a poor nation on the fringes of Europe, living off the sea and the woods at the start of the century, Norway developed into a relatively prosperous state with strong industrial growth, a mechanized agriculture and a powerful merchant fleet.[19] Radical political and national ideas were primarily expressed by individuals from the upper middle class, especially from intellectual and commercial groups, and were only reluctantly supported by the ruling class of government officials and the mass of voting farmers.[20] A narrow patriotic liberal group developed, from around the middle of the century, into a broad national movement also influenced by German romanticism. This development was perhaps most prominent in the cultural field where national romanticism became an influential force in literature, painting, music and theatre. In the sciences as well, national revival dominated the scene; one result was a growing demand for a national, written language, distinct from the Danish taught at schools and used by all officials in State and Church bureaucracies.

The historical and national nature of the environment was discovered in this period and the formerly wild and inhospitable mountains became a national image.[21] From around the middle of the century there were references to the 'mountain-home' as the Norwegian's native environment, creating a 'national iconography'.[22]

Patriotic Pastimes?

Where did sport stand in this national revival? Until around 1860 most sports had been performed in a relatively private or popular and informal way. From the 1860s a 'modern' sports movement started to develop, mostly characterized by the growth of organizations and a more 'rational' view of sports and especially sports competitions.[23]

In this development towards more rational sport, the festivities of Constitution Day played a vital role.[24] This day can be seen as a symbol of a new development in several ways. Formerly festive days had been local and linked to religious occasions and the rhythms of a pre-industrial economy, like Shrovetide ballgames and ski competitions at winter fairs. Constitution Day, this product of the nineteenth-century national revival, introduced a new type of popular celebration day and new forms of sport. The day was soon to become the most important of all popular festivals. It differed from the others in at least three respects: it was secular; it was political; and most important of all, it was a national, not a local, event.

Constitution Day brought sport and nationalism together.[25] An important part of the festivities were sporting contests. Climbing, wrestling, running, gymnastics and sailing were all ingredients of the celebrations at some point. Rowing, a traditional activity, was the dominant athletic event. The rowing contests are worth mentioning for more than one reason. National celebrations gave various sports, but principally rowing, an opportunity to develop from loosely organized contests for popular amusement into sports competitions with rules, time-keeping and referees. National celebrations thereby played a part in the promotion of modern sport in Norway.

While before the 1860s the 17 May sports activities had no specifically national features, they were a means of attracting the common man to the national celebrations. The working classes did not take an active part in the general celebrations in the first half of the century, with one major exception: the sports competitions. Sport was used as a deliberate instrument for extending the popular basis of the celebrations. The contests were meant to be 'popular amusements', but they were also to a much larger degree than the rest of the celebrations meant to be open to active participation from broad sections of the public. This strategy for the social propagation of nationalist ideas met with considerable success. Most of the rowers in the city of Bergen came from the pre-industrial working classes complemented to a considerable degree by surrounding rural crofters and fishermen.[26]

Sport also played a part in the geographic diffusion of nationalism. The rifle clubs, for example, growing out of rising tension in the union with Sweden around 1860, linked much of their celebratory symbols to national symbols (17 May and Constitution). And in the countryside especially the rifle clubs' celebrations of the Day introduced the population to the national festivities. From the 1860s onwards there was a new stage in the development of the relationship between nationalism and sport. Conflicts over the union with Sweden sharpened. After a period of minor decline in the 1870s, the national question blossomed again in the 1880s and the 1890s, when the organized sports movement made great strides.

The Second Phase of Nationalism: Struggle for Parliamentarism and Independence

The period from about 1880 to the collapse of the union with Sweden in 1905 was a turbulent phase, introducing a new political and social structure in Norway. Growing industrialization and urbanization were accompanied by the new influential social classes – the entrepreneurial middle classes and the industrial working class. It was a time of political upheaval. Struggles over a parliamentary system of government, the union and for universal suffrage paved the way for the foundation of political parties and altered the social constellations of power. Nationalism entered a new era. The oldest political party in Norway, 'Venstre' (meaning Left), was founded by 1884 by a broad popular movement made up of farmers and liberals. One of the pillars of the 'left movement' was a growing feeling of nationalism, implying both self-determination as a constitutional, democratic principle and independence based on a unique identity as 'Norwegians'. The movement spread over most of the country, and was particularly strong in what could be described as periphery Norway,[27] namely rural and coastal areas geographically and culturally distanced from the capital Kristiania (today's Oslo). This political awakening resulted in the introduction of a parliamentary system of government in 1884 and eventually ended in 1905 with the break up of the union with Sweden, which had lasted for more than ninety years. From the 1880s it was a matter of gradual separation, with the Norwegians as instigators. For radical nationalist forces in Norway from the 1890s it was not a question of *if* the union was to break up, but *when*.[28]

Growing political and cultural awareness also led to temporary internal political divisions in various elements of society, including sport.

National Sports

The sports movement that developed in Norway in the latter half of the nineteenth century, was in itself an international phenomenon. Impulses from abroad shaped much of Norwegian modern sport. German 'Turnen' came to Norway in the 1850s, soon followed and rivalled by Swedish (Ling) gymnastics, while British sport started to make its impact on the development of sport in Norway in the late 1870s. Throughout this whole period, however, traditional local sports were performed and developed, primarily as popular activities with differing degrees of competitiveness and became 'idræt'. Thus four different athletic 'impulses' were introduced or developed at various moments in the century, and existed in more or less peaceful co-existence with other other. Roughly speaking, adherents of the three older physical cultural streams merged to form something like a national sports ideology, opposed to what were regarded as the negative effects of British sporting impulses. The national sports ideology had an organizational stronghold in the Central Association for the Spread of Physical Exercise and the Practice of Arms.[29]

This national sports ideology was developed and consolidated to confront some of the perceived consequences of British sport. Its main idea was that sport should be more than a pastime. It ought to serve greater purposes, such as strengthening the fatherland and its defence by making better soldiers and improving public health. The main ingredients of British sport were seen as contradicting these ideals. The Norwegian interpretation of British sport was clear. Above all, it was accused of being sport for sport's sake, while the Norwegian parallel term 'idræt' meant much more. These different concepts of the role of sport in 1902 gave Frithjof Nansen a chance to proclaim 'Practise *idraet* and detest *sport* and record-breaking', while a more liberal character like Laurentius Urdahl ten years earlier had called for a ban on 'the sports-fever which from abroad is about to invade us. It brings us no good'.[30]

In the late 1880s the notion 'national' was applied to sport.[31] In Bergen it is possible to date when this association came about. For some years the rowing club Njørd (f.1880) had practised traditional rowing, i.e. in local boats. Only in 1888 did the middle-class rowers of Njørd apply the ideological term 'national rowing' to their activity. The transformation from local to national sport was mostly an ideological one. It was, in other words, a development in the superstructure not based on changes in the practice of rowing. Hereafter the British way of rowing, conceived as less 'rational' from a utilitarian view, involving crafts only suited to shallow waters and competition, was doomed: 'Outrigger-rowing has its adherents and ... will perhaps become the most fashionable, but I dare to say, that this *imported* sport, here on the West coast will not gain any firm foothold – as our "frætrings"[32] are too much adapted to the *people's* and *nature's* practical requirements.'[33] The 'national' view met with some success. Of the six rowing clubs in operation in Bergen around the turn of the century, only one practised rowing the international 'English' way. However, this club also had a section for 'national' rowing.

The concept of 'national sport' was a response to a corresponding general political and cultural development. To form a coherent sports culture that was considered Norwegian, the sports organizations resorted both to foreign impulses like German 'Turnen' and Swedish gymnastics as well as to domestic sporting traditions such as skiing, skating, rowing and sailing. These influences had been introduced so many years before that they were considered part of Norwegian traditional culture. The foundation and development of a Norwegian identity among the dominant social classes had been established long before the actual break up of the union in 1905. From 1850 to the 1890s a Norwegian cultural identity became widespread, building a foundation not only for an independent state, but for a nation.

Sport and especially the traditional, national activity of skiing were essential parts of this. One example might be mentioned. Fridtjof Nansen, scientist, sportsman, explorer and humanist, was a pioneer of what were to become important spheres of Norwegian national assertion. His career as explorer and skier had a considerable impact on skiing internationally.[34] Nansen's book on his first major expedition across Greenland on skis in 1888–89 was published in English and German in the same year as the Norwegian original in 1890.[35]

In this book Nansen, as a pioneer in the field, describes the history of skiing in an unprecedented and unparalleled way. Typically for both historians and social scientists of the time, he connects activity to nationality and to nature:

> Skiing is the most national of all Norwegian sports,[36] and a thrilling sport it is...
> Nothing strengthens the muscles, renders the body so strong and elastic, teaches the qualities of dexterity and resourcefulness, calls for decision and resolution, and gives the same vigour and exhilaration to mind and body alike, like skiing.
> Can there be a healthier and purer delight than on a brilliant winter's day to put on one's skis and set out into the forest?
> Can there be anything more beautiful and noble than the northern winter landscape, when the snow lies foot-deep, like a soft white mantle over wood and hill?[37]

Fascination with an environment formerly viewed as wild and inhospitable as well as cultivation of national heroes in the field of polar exploration helped establish a national identity. It should be noted though that not only in Norway were polar and other explorations an integral part of national assertion at the time. From Sweden, Nordenskiöld and Andree set out on more or less successful operations. Both Englishmen, Americans and Continental Europeans undertook similar ventures.[38] However, in a new nation struggle for independence, this played a vital role as an identity-creating activity. The achievements of men like Fridtjof Nansen, Roald Amundsen (first to reach the South Pole in 1911), Otto Sverdrup, Hjalmar Johansen and others meant much to a Norwegian self-image of an enduring, daring and healthy nation surviving in spite of a sometimes inhospitable environment.[39]

As tension with Sweden increased in the 1890s sport became more closely linked to national symbols: the use of a Norwegian national flag, not recognized by union authorities, as club standards were common,[40] and the practice of combining the celebration of Constitution Day (17 May) with club celebrations. Furthermore, clubs founded in the 1890s very often had names with direct political import.[41] Titles such as 'Viking', 'Norrøna', 'Valhalla', 'Nornen', 'Ull', 'Sverre' and 'Tjalve', 'Mjølner' were typical, recalling a glorious independent past in Norwegian history; the Middle Ages and its mythology.[42] The activities in themselves were, however, only rarely performed in a specifically national way. It was the symbols surrounding sports, their cultural contexts, and the political and ideological ambitions of the time that decided how the various activities were to be interpreted.

Another distinct feature of nationalism and sport of this period was their close association with domestic political battles. Nineteenth-century sports nationalism was for internal use. Competitions were local or national, and the identity created by the mere activity in national sports like skiing, skating, rowing, sailing and hiking was the essential outcome. To be successful in contests with foreigners was very seldom on the agenda in the nineteenth century.[43]

The Third Phase of Nationalism: National Independence and Internationalization of Sport

The international sports competitions developing around the turn of the century provided sports and thereby nationalism with a new arena in the Nordic countries. The breakup of the union between Norway and Sweden in 1905 correspondingly stimulated a new development in the relationship between nationalism and sport.

One of the new competitive sports events in Scandinavia in the early twentieth century was the Nordic Winter Games, first held from 1901. The history of this event illustrates how international sports competitions with a swift change of direction can function along a whole scale from brotherly friendship to national assertion. The Nordic Games was an event meant to promote fraternity between the Swedish and Norwegian peoples. Originally the idea was launched among Swedish sports leaders, and backed by a bilateral organization, 'For the Benefit of the Brotherpeoples', from 1903.[44] The event was clearly designed to reduce prevailing clashes of interest in the union. As the Swedish sports leader Victor Balck stated, 'Sport is *the* safe line that connects us...'[45]

Two meetings, in 1901 and 1903, in Stockholm and Kristiania (today's Oslo) respectively, proved relatively successful, and Scandinavism on the sports fields was something of a reality for a couple of years. But this was short lived. A crises in the union, based on a conflict over the two nations' foreign representation, was brewing. This led to a tense situation in 1905, with mounting dissatisfaction on the Norwegian side of the border. The Nordic Games that year were to take place in Stockholm. For the Norwegians, participation was normally considered unpolitical and uncontroversial, but the 1905 situation was not normal. On 26 January the Norwegian Committee for the Games, with Fridtjof Nansen, the closest one could come to a national hero in Norway, as spokesman, declared that

Norwegians did not intend to participate. The reason was 'depression of the most serious kind' created by Swedish attitudes to Norwegian demands in the escalating political conflict.[46] Support from the Norwegian community, especially sportsmen and skiers, was uniform. An influential newspaper like the conservative and not very sports orientated *Morgenbladet* stated that sport could not be regarded as unimportant: '... every citizen feels the honour of the nation as his own'.[47] The sports magazine *Norsk Sportsblad* claimed that under 'normal conditions' sport and politics had nothing in common. But, in the prevailing circumstances, 'it is natural that no sportsman could be so unpatriotic as to be present at sportsmeeting held by a people, which enjoys stamping on our rights, and regards and treats us like a vassal state'. The superior goal for a sportsman was to protect his fatherland: 'To this he devotes his forces and abilities'.[48]

A measure of the strength of Norwegian feeling was the fact that the Norwegian parliament, the 'Stortinget', in March 1905 voted an extraordinary grant of 500 kr. toward preparations for the Nordic Games, while turning down applications for less controversial financial support to sport.[49] The first Norwegian political boycott of an international sports event had been carried through. The boycott was, however, only part of a general trend in the union conflict. Mounting tension led to the declaration of 7 June 1905 by the Norwegian parliament claiming that the Swedes accepted an almost unanimous referendum. The plebiscite showed a massive majority for sovereignty. Only 184 Norwegians voted against separation from Sweden in the summer of 1905.[50]

Swedish attitudes in general were negative and the response to the sports boycott, in particular, was one of indignation and offence. All Swedish invitations to Norwegian sportsmen were withdrawn. Colonel Victor Balck was in the frontline keeping watch against tendencies to melt the icefront.[51] Fridtjof Nansen was expelled as an honorary member of the semi-official Swedish ski organization 'Föreningen för skidlöpningens främjande i Sverige' in 1905.[52] No Norwegians were officially invited to compete in Sweden before the Olympics in 1912, with the one exception of skaters in the World Championship in 1909, a situation which led to fierce controversy about raising the Norwegian flag. One of the outcomes of independence in 1905 was an intentional breakdown of Scandinavian sports competition. The reason given, in the voice of an official, was that Swedish sport already had reached a 'high-ranking international position outstripping that of Norway and Denmark'. Scandinavian championships would accordingly 'largely mean a repetition of the Swedish events'.[53] It should be noted, however, that segregation was not true of all sports. Encounters occasionally took place outside Sweden from 1907 in some summer sports, for example in track and field athletics.[54] But winter sports, and skiing especially, were activities with national connotations in both countries, and as such were better suited to national battlefields.

Normal relations at the official level were established before the Olympic Games in Stockholm in 1912. Long before 1912 political tension between the two nations had lessened. On the sports scene, however, tension grew into rivalry, and continued.

The Olympic Games as Arena: Assertion Promoted by the State?

Competition on the Scandinavian sports scene led to a new arena of conflict: the Olympic Games. Norway's participation in the Olympics before independence was limited. Two athletes and a team of six marksmen Paris 1900, had been the only Norwegian representatives in Paris 1900.[55] After full independence had been achieved in 1905, however, such international events assumed greater importance. This is why the extra-Olympics in Athens in 1906, which are not recognized by the International Olympic Committee, have a central place in early Norwegian Olympic history and took on the mythological title of 'the Athenian expedition'.[56] The importance of the event was not based primarily on achievements in sport, although the first Norwegian 'Olympic' victories were achieved in Athens, but on the act of participation. Official and public opinion was clear and congruent; it was important to appear on the international scene as an independent nation. A partly private committee joined by sports officials urged for support to enable a visible Norwegian representation. The main reasons for the importance of this in 1906 were clearly political. It was vital for Norway as a new nation to appear among equals. The reports that Sweden and Denmark were going to Athens with substantial teams added to the importance of this. A private fundraising campaign was a success, and for the first time the state gave financial support, although modest, for Olympic participation.[57]

The thirty-two athletes of the 'Athenian expedition' were joined in Berlin by Danish and German participants, while the Swedes travelled by themselves. Tension between the two 'brotherpeoples' were visible in 1906. The sports magazine *Norsk Idrætsblad*, on several occasions, did not try to hide allegations that the programme in Athens was 'openly designed along Swedish lines' by Colonel V. Balck to suit the Swedish representatives.[58] In Greece the Swedes, on the other hand, accused Norwegians of intrigues, envy and 'unfriendly behaviour'.[59]

The appearance in Athens was the first performance by Norway as an independent nation in the Olympic arena. The experience was considered fairly successful both by political and sports officials. More of an accident, but a well-received part of the picture, was the fact that the first Norwegian

IOC member, captain Henrik Angell, was appointed after the IOC congress in Brussels in June 1905.[60]

In this connection developments concerning attitudes towards the Olympic movement are of some relevance. An influential perception of the Olympic Games in Norway was to view them as a controversial aspect of modern sport. Both before 1906 and after, there were strong tendencies, especially among Norwegian gymnasts, to regard the Olympics as far from a true and healthy element in the sports movement. Efforts to equate the Olympics with the unwanted face of sport were made as late as 1912,[61] and had an even longer effect.[62] Gymnast officials, as well as other national-minded sport conservatives, saw it as a natural prolongation of their former 'national stand' to oppose the phenomenon of Olympic Games as an example of all they had warned against in international sport. To them the Olympics were 'competition and sport' promoting specialization, circus and fanaticism, in contrast to healthy and versatile 'idræt':[63]

> ... Few ask whether the Olympic participant's physical development goes in a healthy and harmonious direction. If he succeeds in setting a new world record in a distinct sport, it seems irrelevant whether he has a deformed body, a neglected spirit and a dissolute character'.[64]

Still, such attitudes were waning after 1906. The experience of the extra-Olympics in Athens won support for Norwegian participation and ensured continued official support of Olympic involvement.

For the Olympic Games in London in 1908, the Ministry of Defence increased financial support for Norwegian participation from 3,000 to 5,000 kr.[65] At the same time the Swedish sports organizations sought governmental financial aid, arguing that it was important to show the world who was 'big brother' in Scandinavia. Reports that Norway and Denmark had made a bid for the London Olympics seems to have ensured state support in Sweden.[66] Through the three Olympic Games between 1906 and 1912 Norway became visible on the international sports scene. Seventy-three athletes were sent to London, and no less than 207 participants constituted the Norwegian team in 1912, which made it the third largest.

The Stockholm Olympics witnessed the first major Norwegian sports appearance in Sweden since the breakup of the union seven years before, and as such embraced as significant by both nations. The Norwegian government actively promoted extensive participation by granting three times as much as for the London Games, namely 15,000 kr, despite the fact that travel expenses could be kept at a much lower level. The increased amount created opposition in parliament. Forty-three members voted for a lower grant or none at all. Still, the government, composed of conservatives and moderates, could rally 68 members behind their contribution. The conservatives clearly used national sentiment as an argument for extended official support: 'Precisely in this, our neighbouring country, it is of vital interest that we meet with representatives in most or all sports ... on this occasion Norway must not lag behind.'[67]

The sporting rivalry between Norway and Sweden was not confined to participation, but also involved performance. Inherent in the amount applied for by the Norwegian Olympic Committee,[68] was a sum of 8,000 kr for 'coaches in athletics, rowing, fencing etc.' To perform well on what was really an away ground, skilled trainers were imported from abroad.[69]

Still, little could be done to match the neighbour. Sweden was the highest ranked nation in its own Olympic Games. Statements by Swedish sports officials implied that this achievement was a long awaited Swedish revenge for 1905 and recession. It had at least been established that Sweden was 'big brother' in Scandinavia.[70] This now confirmed, Norwegians could again be invited to take part in the Nordic Games in 1913 – an invitation that was accepted.

Functions of Nationalism: Identity or Identification?

The image of Norwegian sport after 1905 was built to a large extent upon the national identity that had been established in the decades before full independence was achieved.

Sport, and especially skiing, were part of this identity. One example illustrating the significant role played by this activity in creating 'Norwegianness' should be mentioned here. It was not accidental that the new royal family, imported from Denmark and England after independence in the late autumn 1905,[71] made a visit to the Holmenkollen ski-jumping hill in winter 1906, as one of their first public appearances. In this way the foreigners were attempting to assume a Norwegian identity by experiencing winter sport the Norwegian way, attending a ski-jumping competition in weather conditions which most non-Nordic visitors would consider unacceptable. The royal family's regular appearances in Holmenkollen, which became a tradition, and the later King Olav's actually jumping the hill, identified the royal family with a national athletic event, and was an important part of their acculturation as Norwegian royals.[72]

The beginning of the twentieth century had brought full political independence, gradually bringing Norway into the established fold of European nations. Simultaneously a positive national identity with a close relation to nature and outdoor activities had been generated. In this situation, was there anything more required to arouse nationalist feeling? One question, which deserves to be raised, concerns nationalism's function. Was it a 'vicarious purpose', disguising other purposes? Such a role has been suggested for nationalism in other fields by the historian J.A. Seip.[73] Here it would mean that nationalism in sport was encouraged in order to advance certain political ambitions that were more controversial and for which it was harder to gather public support. Should, for example, Norwegian nationalism in the sport of skiing, be seen as political conservatism or practical resistance to innovations in the sport?

Skiing was the one field in which a national identity seems to have been asserted strongly from time to time. In matters concerning the national 'idræt' of skiing, the Norwegians, as inventors of the sport, felt they had little to learn from abroad. And from their own point of view Norway was the natural governing nation of skiing as an organized sport. This led to conflicts when the sport developed in other parts of the world. Ski officials worked hard to translate the Norwegian standards for ski competitions into international standards stressing versatility as opposed to specialization as the norm.

Norway, therefore, together with other Scandinavian countries in the 1920s, opposed the idea of introducing a Winter Olympics. The Norwegian Ski Federation did send a team of skiers to compete in Chamonix in 1924, later claiming ignorance of the intention that the International Winter Sports Week was to be announced (in retrospect) as the first Winter Olympic Games.[74] Before the next Games an ill-tempered discussion about taking part arose. In the final decisive debate in the Federation, Norway's participation at St. Moritz in 1928 was approved with the smallest possible majority (29 to 27), and led to the board's resignation.

The background to the strong national opposition to a Winter Olympic Games seems to have been a general conservatism. Fear of losing prestige due to the reduced stature of the Holmenkollen events in international skiing played its part. However, the matter was presented to the public as a failure of the world at large to understand Norwegian standards of skiing, which, of course, were the 'true and natural' norms of the sport.[75] A parallel example of sports nationalism as isolationism was English attitudes towards organized international football co-operation, when the Fédération Internationale de Football Association (FIFA) established itself as the governing body of the sport. Like the (English) Football Association, influential parts of the Norwegian Ski Federation preferred to live in 'splendid isolation'.[76]

Quite another example illuminating the function of sports nationalism was the emergence and cultivation of 'national sports stars' in the period between the two World Wars. This was a time when the radical workers' sports movement was strong, driving their political counterparts to stress the need for a national assembly. Such a reaction was mostly a right-wing phenomenon. However, the development of a national stand in the workers' political parties was also evident in the 1930s.[77] At the same time, sports star enthusiasm was strongly nurtured in the press during the controversial participation in the 1936 Olympics. The success of Norwegian athletes in the Winter Games, and especially the victory over Germany in the football competition, rapidly overcame national doubts about participating in the events in the Third Reich. With Hitler present on the terraces the match became a pre-war struggle between Norway and Germany on the football ground. The Norwegian triumph was seen as symbolic in other small nations in Europe.[78] At home one outcome of taking part in the 1936 Olympics was clearly diminished national political tension in the sports movement.

In the decades after 1905, then, sports nationalism entered a new phase. In the long run some of the indigenous traditional sports creating internal identity lost their partisan-function, although they were not totally abandoned. This development implied that the question of a sport's origin was no longer an urgent problem. From around the First World War English sport gradually had been accepted as a natural part of the Norwegian sports movement, and as such established another phase of sports nationalism. With a growing number of international contests, football, regardless of its foreign origin, functioned as a factor of national identification.

That sport after the First World War has been a 'uniquely effective medium for inculcating national feelings' is an unremarkable claim.[79] However, it should be added that there are earlier examples of this function of sport. More precisely, it could be argued that the function of sports nationalism entered a new phase in the period between the two wars. With the growing internationalization of sport, the inherent identity in sport itself could no longer be the chief function.[80] As development became uniform among national sports cultures, the expression of national identification through rival flags, colours, uniforms and a national team became the common phenomenon.

Benedict Andersson's concept of 'imagined communities'[81] can be discussed.[82] Interpreted as a 'wanted community' it certainly has relevance, with reference to the earlier phases of sports nationalism. However, Hobsbawm's observation that 'the imagined community of millions seems more real as a team of eleven named people'[83] appears to be of uniform significance, underpinning both post-Second World War Eastern European sports efforts[84] and more spontaneous sports enthusiasm in other parts of the world.[85]

A Nordic Self-Assertion Perspective

After the First World War Norwegian sports nationalism, meaning self-assertion, mostly surfaced in the international matches between Sweden and Norway. The first football victory over Sweden in 1918 was taken as a decisive step towards 'equality of worth'.[86] In the whole of the twentieth century, Sweden has been the country to beat in international Scandinavian matches. There were striking similarities in this respect between the Norwegian position and Finnish attitudes to beating Sweden in athletics and icehockey.

Norway, Sweden and Finland, therefore, each used sport to national assertive ends.[78] Finland, which has had the most demanding route to national independence of the three, has been the nation which has pursued national assertion through sport most vigorously. Its success in putting Finland 'on the map' is well known. Finnish historians and writers' acknowledgement of this function of sport is evident. 'Sport as an Exponent of National Strength', an essay by Arthur Eklund in 1913,[88] was typical.[89] Sweden, on the other hand, after 1905 has had more of an inhibited attitude to outspoken national assertion through sport. It was considered important, but not vital, to do well. The country's position as the rich big brother among the Nordic countries was unrivalled in sport as in other fields. With such a status undisguised assertion would be undignified.[89] Norway seems to have found itself in a position between Finland and Sweden. Norwegian winter sportsmen have been expected to be the guardians of a national identity of a forceful people with winter capacities, although as the twentieth century has progressed, this image has become less vital for the nation's well-being.

Conclusion: Sport – An Arena for National Expression?

Nationalism as a historical phenomenon has proved many-sided. It can be seen to have different functions in different countries. One is the contrast between new and established nations. W. Baker has suggested that in the nation-building phases of new African states, success in sports has played an important role by, amongst other things, creating unifying national heroes.[90] This phenomenon can be seen in the history of established nations. From other parts of the world there have come reports of seemingly successful strategies for creating some sort of unification. We have briefly touched upon the Finnish athletes' success in making Finland known to the world from 1912 as the most outstanding example of 'peaceful assertion' in the Nordic countries. Far less triumphant in the long run was the history of nation building through success in sport in the former GDR.

However, attention should also be drawn to another antagonism inherent in the nationalism concept. If we return to Norway and the nation-building phase in the late nineteenth and early twentieth centuries, nationalism, expressed as 'national sentiment', meant and was associated with struggles for independence and democratization. Some time after independence had been secured, however, nationalism, now of a new type, was embraced by small right-wing chauvinist and expansionist groups. The Second World War illustrated a drastic dichotomy; between a national stand, in firm defence of the fatherland, and a nationalistic posture, involving aggressive expansion. The war made the right-wing nationalistic position synonymous with treason, and has ever since marginalized everything that resembles it.[91]

In these historical connections it is of interest that sport, to such a marked degree, stands out as a representative symbol of nationalism. There are few, if any, cultural or social arenas where encouragement for nationalist expressions is so intense. Likewise, tolerance for the same manifestations seems to be equally high, if we limit our views to the modern Western world. Even in these days of attempted unity in Western Europe, sport is a suitable stage for displaying, provoking and asserting national sentiment.[92] Although this may be no more than '90 minute nationalism',[93] it is an expression of an underlying reality which still exists.

Through the twentieth century the earlier self-assertive aspect of sports nationalism has gradually declined as a vital element of Norwegian sport, even in traditional national sports closely associated with national identity.[94] Is one feature of twentieth-century sports history that an autonomous state with a high degree of legitimacy and strong public support regards its success in sport as little more than a transitory glimpse of glory? If this is the case, national symbols nevertheless are still energetically and enthusiastically displayed through the medium of sport, although their significance and meaning have changed. Nevertheless short-lived moments can live a long time in a nation's collective memory.

NOTES

1. Laurentius Urdahl: *Idrætsbladet,* 4 (1892).
2. Captain Johan Sverre at the outset of the 'Athenian expedition' 1906, quoted in Karl Johan Haagensen, *Athenerfrætrden 1906* (Kristiania, 1907).
3. Eric Hobsbawm, 'Mass-Producing Traditions: Europe, 1870–1914', in E. Hobsbawm and T. Ranger (eds.), *The Invention of Tradition* (Cambridge, 1983).
4. E. Renan, 'Qu'est-ce qu'une nation?' (Paris 1882) (English version: What is a nation?) in Alfred Zimmern (ed.), *Modern Political Doctrines* (Oxford 1939), p.203. For M. Weber, see David Beetham, *Max Weber and the Theory of Modern Politics* (London, 1974). 'Mobilization of the masses' was a central element in Stein Rokkan's interpretation of 'nation building', see S. Rokkan, *Citizens, Elections, Parties.* (Oslo, 1970) and S. M. Lipset and S. Rokkan, *Party Systems and Voter Alignments* (New York, 1967). As a general reference on nationalism, see Øyvind Østerud, *Nasjonenes selvbestemmelsesrett. Søkelys på en politisk doktrine.* (Universitetsforlaget Oslo – Bergen – Stavanger – Tromsø, 1984).

5. Both Ernest Gellner, Anthony D. Smith and Eric Hobsbawm seem to regard this as a common starting point, despite their other disagreements. Ernest Gellner, *Nations and Nationalism* (Oxford,1988), Anthony D. Smith, *Theories of Nationalism* (London, 1983), Eric J. Hobsbawm, *Nations and Nationalism since 1780* (Cambridge, 1990).
6. To apply another of Eric Hobsbawm's statements of invented traditions in 'Mass-producing Traditions: Europe, 1870–1914' in Hobsbawm and Ranger (eds.), *The Invention of Tradition*, p.264.
7. An example of the latter is Ragnar Stara 'Nationsbegreppet – en social helhetslogik' (Ph.D. Uppsala, 1980. Ekenäs, 1980).
8. E. H. Carr, *Nationalism and After* (London 1945) Cf. Østerud, p.12–13.
9. K. Lunden, *Norsk grålysning. Norsk nasjonalisme 1770–1814 på allmenn backgrunn* (Oslo, 1992).
10. Gellner, op. cit., 1983.
11. Hobsbawm, Introduction, in Hobsbawm and Ranger, p.13.
12. Gellner, uses the term 'congruent', p.1.
13. Østerud, p.69.
14. Østerud, p.60.
15. Applying Weber's theories in a Nordic context. Eugen Weber, *Peasants into Frenchman. The Modernization of Rural France, 1870–1914* (London, 1977).
16. Foremost among the 'national' historians of the nineteenth century was Ernst Sars, *Historisk Indledning til Grundloven* (Christiania, 1882), *Udsigt over Den norske Historie* (Christiania, 1873–91). For the current discussion cf. Lunden (1992), and Trond Nordby, *Norsk nasjonalisme som historisk problem* (Nytt Norsk Tidsskrift, 1986).
17. Lunden, p.34. Miroslav Hroch, *Social Preconditions of National Revival in Europe* (Cambridge, 1985).
18. S. Aarnes, 'Nasjonen finner seg selv', in Semmingsen *et al.* (eds.), *Norges kulturhistorie 4* (Oslo, 1979), 136.
19. The third largest in the world already in 1879, after Great Britain and the USA. Hans Try, 'To kulturer – en stat 1850–1884', in K. Mykland (ed.), *Norges historie* (Oslo, 1979).
20. For most of the nineteenth century the right to vote was restricted to men with property, excluding women, rural workers, cotters and town workers. Universal suffrage for men over 25 was introduced in 1898, after gradual reforms since 1884, and for women in 1913.
21. See Henning Eichberg and Ejgil Jespersen, *De grønne bølger* (Slagelse, 1986).
22. Sigurd A. Aarnes, 'Hu hei! Kor er det vel friskt og lett uppå fjellet!', *Nytt Norsk Tidsskrift*, 1 (1991). Nina Witoscek, 'Der kultur møter natur. Tilfellet Norge', *Samtiden*, 4 (1991).
23. Finn Olstad og Stein Tønnesson, *Norsk idretthistoire, 1861–1939, 1939–1986*. 1–2 (Oslo, 1986–87). Matti Goksøyr, *Idrettsliv i borgerskapets by. Idrettens utvikling i Bergan på 1800-tallet* (Oslo, 1991).
24. H. Eichberg, *Die Veränderung des Sports ist gesellschaftlich* (Münster, 1986). A recent article by Eichberg, 'Towards a Historical Materialism of the Folk Question', 1. International ISHPES Seminar, Turku, Finland 1992, *Sport and Cultural Minorities*, is of relevance to the broader theme of this article.
25. M. Goksøyr, 'Popular Pastimes or Patriotic Virtues? The Role of Sport in the National Celebrations of Nineteenth-Century Norway', *International Journal of the History of Sport*, 5, 2 (1988).
26. M. Goksøyr (1991), p.131ff.
27. S. Rokkan, op. cit.
28. Giving the word union a definite negative connotation, still alive in current discussions about the EU.
29. Centralforeningen for Udbredelse af Legemsøvelser og Vaabenbrug.
30. Nansen in, *Centralforeningens årbok 1902/03*, p.1. Urdahl in, *Idrætsbladet*, 4 (1892). The view that sport was 'entartete' idræt was widespread. See *Norsk Skyttertidende*, 5/1903.
31. In Norwegian 'nationale idræter', one example being rowing: 'national Roning'.
32. Four-oared traditional rowing boat used for domestic fishing and transport.
33. Njørd: Files, 'Journal 1880–1901', p.189 (emphasis added).

34. Eichberg and Jespersen (1986), pp.155–6. Leif Yttergren, *Från skidsport til skogsmulle. Friluftsfrämjandet 1892–1992* (Stockholm, 1992), mentions this influence.
35. Fridtjof Nansen (trans. Hubert Majendie Gepp), *The First Crossing of Greenland* (London, 1890); in Norwegian, *Paa Ski over Grønland* (Kristiania, 1890).
36. Nansen naturally used the term 'idræt'.
37. Nansen, p.83f. The translation of this passage is my own, since the original translation was a loose rendering of the Norwegian.
38. A general reference to this field is L. P. Kirwan, *A History of Polar Explorations* (Harmondsworth 1962). A specific study is Einar-Arne Drivenes: 'La Recherche' Forskningsekspedisjonen Frankrike glemte'. (Norwegian, *Historisk Tidsskrift* 1 [1992]).
39. The Norwegian and Nordic special 'method' in polar explorations was different to the English method, and applied techniques developed by people living in the Arctic region. Apart from literature on and by Nansen and Amundsen, *see also* Kirwan, p.210ff., Drivenes, pp.17–18.
40. When in 1891 the club Norrøna unfurled its new standard, a Norwegian flag without union symbols, it was 'to be the banner, under which sport was now to be staged', *Bergensposten*, 15 May 1891.
41. 'Invented traditions' like this were important parts of the Norwegian sports movement around the turn of the century. Cf. E. Hobsbawm and T. Ranger (eds.), 1983.
42. From the 10th to 13th centuries Norwegian kings ruled for long periods over large parts of the northern Atlantic ('Noregsveldet'): Iceland, Greenland, the Faroe Islands, Shetland, The Hebrides, and the Isle of Man as well as temporary settlements in Britain, Ireland and Brittany. The Black Death (1349) and union with Denmark and Sweden (1372) ended the Norwegian sovereignty and started what Henrik Ibsen in *Peer Gynt* named the '400 years' night'.
43. Some exceptions could be made. The Norwegian skaters Axel Paulsen and Harald Hagen drew large crowds when competing against foreign rivals. On quite another scale was the cultural rivalry between town and rural people, notably in ski and rowing competitions.
44. 'Brödrafolkens Väl'. See Jan Lindroth, 'Unionsupplösningen 1905 och idrotten', *Sveriges Centralförenings för Idrottens Främjande årsbok 1977*.
45. Quoted in Lindroth (1977), p.4 (emphasis added).
46. Lindroth (1977), p.6.
47. *Morgenbladet*, 12/1 (1905). See Lindroth (1977), pp.6–7.
48. *Norsk Sportsblad*, 1 (1905).
49. The preparations had already 'taken place' when the grant was given *Stortingsforhandlinger*, 1904/1905, 18 March.
50. Constituting less than 0.0005% of the voters.
51. 'Norskfjäsk', as he called it. Lindroth (1977), p.8.
52. Leif Yttergren (1992), pp.26, 54.
53. The sports leader Ivar Berger in 1907, quoted in Lindroth (1977), p.11.
54. Most often these meetings were staged in the country, a long way from the two capital cities.
55. In addition some Norwegian emigrants competed in the Olympics of St. Louis in 1904, unknown to the homeland until some time later.
56. The term 'Athener-Færden' or 'Athener-ekspeditionen' was used both in official, departmental publications as well as in records of the sports organizations. A participant's diary is Karl Johan Haagensen *Athenerfærden 1906* (Kristiania, 1907).
57. *Stortingsforhandlinger* 1905/1906, 21 April. The grant of 3,000 kr. was approved by 92 votes to 18. Objections varied from general sports reluctance to opposition to sport's military dominance and exclusive social character. See M. Goksøyr, *Staten og idretten 1861–1991* (Oslo, 1992), pp.27–9.
58. *Norsk Idrætsblad*, 4 (1906). 'Who are really the organizers of the Olympic Games, the Greeks or the Swedes?', *Norsk Idrætsblad. 10 (1906)*.
59. *Stockholms* Dagblad 13/9, 14/9 (1906) and *Balck* 13/9 (1906), quoted in Lindroth (1977), pp.8–9.
60. Angell was sent by the Norwegian government to the IOC conference in Brussels in June

1905 at the request of the Belgian authorities, and was the same year appointed as IOC member. He was replaced in 1907 by Thomas Heftye, a merchant. The Brussels congress had other ingredients which the Norwegian observer perceived as tokens of far-reaching foreign recognition of the Norwegian nation. For the first time honorary diplomas of sport were awarded by the IOC. Fridtjof Nansen was one of the four honoured, together with President Roosevelt, Santos Dumont and Herbert Greenfeld. Afterwards the Norwegian flag and national anthem were seen and heard. A memorable event for the Norwegian observer in the June days of 1905 (*Norsk Idrætsblad* 1905, no.7 and no.26).

61. The plans to participate in the scheduled Olympic Games in Berlin 1916 were the first to pass unopposed through the Norwegian sports federations (*Norges Riksforbund for Idræt. Rundskriv*, 33, 15/16–1913).

62. Johan Martens, president of the sports federation Norges Riksforbund for Idræt 1910–1914, was not re-elected partly due to his opposition to 'too frequent' Olympic Games.

63. See *Turnbladet* 1906 (Official magazine for the Norwegian Turners and Gymnasts Association), Centralforeningen for Ubredelse af Idrætm, Årbøker 1905–1912. The reluctance shown by the 'nationals' and their stronghold, the Central Association, to organize Norwegian participation in 1906 and 1908 was one of the reasons why the Central Association was replaced by a new federation, Norges Riksforbund for Idræt, in 1910 as the leading and official sports organisation.

64. Captain (of horse) Jacob Grøttum in *Dagbladet*, 6 April 1913. See also Finn Olstad, *Norsk idrettshistorie*, Vol.1 (Oslo, 1987), pp.159–6.

65. Stortingsforhandlinger 6 D, 1908, 27/5. In 1908 there was much less debate, and the opposition had gone down from 18 to 11.

66. Lindroth (1977), p.17.

67. Prime minister J. H. Bratlie in the parliament, Stortingsforhandlinger 1912, 31/5.

68. Still in an *ad hoc* phase of its development.

69. Norges Riksforbund for Idræt, *Rundskriv*, 12, 28/7 (1911). Already in 1908 the Norwegian rowers hired a foreign coach. Olstad, p.159.

70. V. Balck 1913, quoted in Lindroth (1977), p.16.

71. The 12–13 November plebiscite produced a majority of more than 75 per cent in favour of a monarchy. Berge Furre, *Vårt hundreår. Norsk historie 1905–1990* (Oslo, 1991), p.21.

72. A much later, but relevant incident, was the same king Olav's famous tram trip on regular public transport to do his Sunday skiing tour in Holmenkollen during the oil crisis in winter 1973–74 (private car driving was prohibited on Sundays) – illustrating both popularity and skiing interest, two essential and legitimizing elements in Norwegian royal identity.

73. Jens Arup Seip, 'Nasjonalisme som vikarierende motiv'; in *Fra embedsmannsstat til ettpartistat og andre essays* (Oslo Bergen - Tromsø, 1974).

74. It was the IOC meetings in Prague 1925 and Lisbon the year after that gave the Winter Sports Week status as the first Winter Olympics.

75. Kristen Mo, 'Norsk motstand mot vinter-OL', in Goksøyr og Mo (red.), *Norsk Idrettshistorisk Årbok*, 1989.

76. R. Holt, *Sport and the British: A Modern History* (Oxford, 1989), p.273.

77. Tore Pryser *Klassen og nasjonen, 1935–1946*. Vol.4 *Arbeiderbevgelsens historie i Norge*, Vols.1–6 (Oslo, 1988), p.13ff, gives the time when the workers' organization started to take part in national celebrations like 17 May, as 1935–36. These were celebrations which previously had been considered 'bourgeois'.

78. For example, Jean-Claude Bussard, 'Les Jeux de 1936 dans le presse Suisse de langue Francaise', R. Renson, M. Lämmer, J. Riordan, D. Chassiotis (eds.), *The Olympic Games through the Ages: Greek Antiquity and its Impact on Modern Sport. Proceedings of the 13th International HISPA Conference*, Olympia 22–28 May 1989, pp.363–4.

79. Hobsbawm (1990), p.143.

80. For a general introduction on globalization of culture, see Mike Featherstone (ed.), *Global Culture. Nationalism, Globalization and Modernity. Theory, Culture and Society* (London, 1990).

81. Benedict Andersson, *Imagined Communities* (London 1983, extended version London/New

York 1991). Andersson stresses a broad interpretation of the term 'imagined'.

82. See Lunden, pp.30–4, for a critical view on B. Andersson (and others).

83. Hobsbawm (1990), ibid.

84. Recent developments in Eastern Europe suggest that success in sports is indeed a flimsy foundation on which to build a nation when most of the other fundamentals are lacking. Recent European history requires more empirical and theoretical research about the outcomes of national assertion strategies through sport.

85. Cultural uniformity has not left the sports identity question totally behind. Some sports are still considered more important than others in certain parts of the world. Consider for example Cuban journalists in the Barcelona Olympics 1992, stating that the baseball gold medal was 'more important than ten boxing medals' (Swedish TV2, 5 Aug. 1992). Norwegian sports officials attempted a 'modern' perspective after the successful Winter Olympics of Albertville the same year, downplaying the importance of winning in cross-country skiing and speed skating. 'It is winning the alpine events that counts', they remarked, dangerously abandoning a national heritage that had thus far legitimized their own professions.

86. 'Also in sport', Norges Fotballforbund XXV aar, 1902–1927. Oslo 1927. Although the seriousness of the national honour involved in these meetings gradually declined, the special meaning lingered by the revitalized Swedish attitude to international sports during the Second World War. The fact that the Swedes had kept the world championships in skiing going, in collaboration with Germany and Italy, gave the first post-war matches an extra sense of national pride. It also made Swedish participation at the first Holmenkollen Ski Festivals after the war controversial.

87. A useful reference to Nordic 'nationalisms' is Stein Tønnesson, 'History and National Identity in Scandinavia: The Contemporary Debate', D.phil. lecture presented at the University of Oslo, 25 Oct. 1991.

88. Arthur Eklund, 'Idrotten som nationell kraftexponent (1913)' in Edklund: Idrottens filosofi (Helsingfors, 1917). See also Juhani Paasivirta, Finland och de olympiska spelen i Stockholm: Diplomatin bakom kulisserna (Ekenäs, 1963), Leena Laine, 'Idrott för alla – men på olika villkor? Idrott, samhälle och social kontroll i Filand 1856–1917', in Idrott, historia, samhälle. Svenska idrottshistoriska föreningens årsskrift 1988.

89. After Victor Balck had withdrawn in 1913, the Swedish sports organisations were most reluctant to express any national (ideological or political) opinions at all. Per Olof Holmäng, Idrott och utrikespolitik. Den svenska idrottsrörelsens internationelle förbindelser 1919–1945. Göteborg 1988. Jan Lindroth, Idrott mellan krigen (Stockholm 1987).

90. W. Baker, 'Political Games, The Meaning of International sport for Independent Africa', in W. Baker and J.A. Mangan (eds.), Sport in Africa (New York, 1987). However, questions should be raised. One might, for example, ask whether the African export of national prestige on the sports field has had any local social effects. In other words, does sport work here as an old type of enclave economy, where national glory is exported without any local social outcome?

91. Ø. Østerud, '9 April – Wergeland eller Quisling?', Dagbladet (1989). Also Østerud, Nasjonenes selvbestemmelsesrett: Søkelys på en politisk doktrine (Oslo, 1984).

92. Nordic sports nationalism has been good-tempered, illustrated by the Danish Foreign Secretary's statement after the soccer final against Germany in the European Nations Cup in June 1992: 'If you can't join them, beat them!' (Uffe Ellemann Jensen, having previously lost the referendum over signing the Maastricht Treaty in June 1992, Fædrelandsvennen 4 July 1992). Even more illustrative is the Norwegian outburst after beating England in a World Cup qualifier in 1981: 'We are the best in the world! Lord Nelson, Lord Beaverbrook, Sir Winston Churchill ... etc. Maggie Thatcher, can you hear me ...!' (Bjøge Lillelien of the Norwegian Broadcasting Corporation, 9 Sept. 1981).

93. Grant Jarvie, 'Sport, Nationalism and Cultural Identity', in Lincoln Allison (ed.), The Changing Politics of Sport (Manchester University Press).

94. The 1988 forthcoming Winter Olympics in Calgary, when for the first time Norway did not win any gold medals, brought no revolution in the Norwegian sports organizations.

Nature, Skiing and Swedish Nationalism

SVERKER SÖRLIN

Skiing is a part of life in the Nordic countries, and it has been for a long time. A ski from Kalvträsk circa 3200 BC is one of the oldest preserved artifacts from this part of the world. In his sixth century description of Thule, Procopius speaks of the *Skrithifinoi* – the gliding Finns, namely the Saami gliding on snow! Paulus Diaconus, circa 780, Adamus Bremensis (eleventh century) and Saxo Grammaticus (thirteenth century) all have similar descriptions. In the tenth century the daughter of the Norwegian king Gunhild is said to have claimed that the Saami were such good skiers that they could be outrun by neither beasts nor humans.[1] The langobardic monk Paulus Diaconus claimed that the name of the people in the far north was derived from the word 'to jump, because as they are jumping they overtake wild animals'. It is not certain that he had seen people skiing, but it is a clear possibility.[2]

These sources all date back to the period well before the Nordic nation-states. Skiing is something that the Nordic countries have in common. The basic explanations are, quite certainly, functional and ecological. Hunting and transportation required ski equipment in the long winter months. In all the Nordic countries there have been studies of the history and prehistory of skis and skiing. In Norwegian, for example, there is M. Breili and T. Schjelderup's *100 år med ski på bena* (1982), Olav Bö's *På ski gjennom historia* (1992) and F. Olstad's *Norsk idrettshistorie: forsvar, sport & klassekamp* (1987).

This study willl concentrate mainly on Sweden. Skiing, even wilderness skiing, cannot be detached from the ideological and social contexts of the time, especially that of nationalism. Therefore, rather than skim superficially over the entire North, we have chosen to discuss Sweden in detail.

Skiing as an Element of Identity

If skiing has always been part of the Nordic experience, when and why did it enter the consciousness of the Swedes? It happened at a late stage. We should note, of course, that Linnaeus, commenting on skiing in his Lapland diary of 1732, praises the Nordic winter, when he observes that people can move swiftly on the 'crystal ice'. He notes that there is snow, but he does not make much of that fact. In the eighteenth century, when the Academy of Sciences in Stockholm with patriotic zeal stimulated the development of practical technology and skills of all kinds, they did not mention skis or skiing; likewise, there is no entry in the Academy archives nor in the voluminous index to Sten Lindroth's 2,000 page work on the history of the Academy between 1739 and 1818. One might expect the early nineteenth-century Romantics to have shown an interest in this noble art of Swedishness, but apparently they did not.

A clue to the Swedish silence on the topic can be found in Olaus Magnus's multi-volume work *Historia om de nordiska folken* (History of the Nordic Peoples) [1555]. He has several entries about skiing, but they all concern skiing among the Saami, not among the Swedes. He quotes Procopius and other classical authors and notes especially that the Saami are skilled skiers (Vol.1, books 4, 5). He furthermore states explicitly that those who ski with 'bent wooden ribs' are 'people from the woods or Laps' (Vol.1, book 25). This is to distinguish them from the people who ran with skates on ice, a practice which was common in other parts of Sweden. In other words, Swedes did not ski, according to Olaus Magnus, and to a large extent he was right. In 'real' Sweden, south of Norrland, the North, skiing was not as common as one might expect.[3]

The Norwegians were different. The Norse sagas – Eigil Skallagrimsson's and Håkon Håkonsson's for example – contained episodes in which people skied. Heming, the popular saga hero, fought with Harald Hårdråde and was a superb skier. Norwegian lore in the eighteenth and nineteenth centuries is full of evidence of skiing (Bö, 16, 20). The Norwegian military, at least up to the Napoleonic wars, were more ski-bound than their Swedish counterparts.[4] From the sources one gets the impression that skiing was not part of Swedish consciousness but rather of the consciousness of the Norwegians and of the Finns.

In the nineteenth century Sweden's consciousness of skiing changed gradually. References to wilderness, to snow, and to skiing as elements of Swedishness become more common in the closing decades of the century. They coincided with the growing importance of the North, especially Lapland. The region became important not only for its natural but also for its spiritual resources: the wilderness, the forests, waterfalls and high mountains.

Skiing as a *sport* was launched after the return of the Nordenskiöld expedition to Grönland in 1883. Two Saami men, Pava Lars Tuorda and Anders Rossa, were reported to have crossed a large part of the ice cap on skis, covering 460 kilometres in 57 hours.[5] This was considered so incredible that a race was arranged the following year in Lapland, between Jokkmokk and Kvikkjokk, a distance of about 220 kilometres. Sufficient competitors succeeded in going the full distance to silence the sceptics. Tuorda won.[6] The race is sometimes referred to as the first Swedish ski competition, but this is contentious. The first competition in Stockholm was certainly held in 1879, and races for school children in the Norrland city of Sundsvall date back to 1877.[7] But it is certain that Sweden had no traditions to match Norway, where there were competitions from at least 1834, a year which featured three races in Tromsö alone. Later, in the 1880s, Swedish sports promoter Viktor Balck's multi-volume work on sports included a note on skiing. The avalanche had started rolling. In novels, art, hunting literature, historical narrative and in children's books skiing quickly became a topic.

Noteworthy, not least for its moral and didactic dimensions, is the book *Olles skidfärd* (1907; 'Olle's Ski Trip') by Elsa Beskow, the enormously popular author of children's books. Olle, a young Swedish boy, not a Saami, has longed for a pair of skis and he is given a pair by his father on his sixth birthday. Olle then embarks on a mythical journey with Old Man Frost. He is given the opportunity to meet King Winter and he peeps into the busy workshop where Saami boys are making skis. Winter and snow are associated with purity and innocence, beauty and order. When Olle comes across rain and warm weather, in the incarnation of a woman, the witch-like Old Woman Thaw, he becomes sad and starts sneezing and the world around him loses all its splendour.

In the same decade the historian Carl Grimberg published the first volumes of his work *Svenska folkets underbara öden*. In it he included a fleshed-out version of Gustav Vasa's attempt to escape, skiing, from Danish soldiers in Dalarna. It endowed the seemingly plebeian practice with a royal dignity.

By the early years of the twentieth century it was obvious that snow, skiing and the chill of the North had become components of some elevated northern quality. This quality most certainly had its forebears in the old Nordic Gothicism of previous centuries, but what was now added was frost and snow, indeed the world of skiing, that was no longer the privilege of the Saami but was more and more associated with Sweden and the North as a whole.

The Origins of Skiing as National Sport

We have identified the answer to 'when'. The question remains 'why' this growth of interest in skiing occurred. It is hard to escape the impression that skiing became, in a general sense, part of a national mobilization, triggered by competition among the leading countries in the era of industrialization. Competition took place in the economic arena, but in a symbolic sense progress and power were manifested in other achievements as well. Polar exploration was one of them, and the ski was identified at an early date as the special means (together with the use of dogs) by which people from the Nordic countries outdid their more numerous and more powerful American and European competitors.[8] The theme of mobilization was also the cornerstone of the leading skiing organization formed at this time: the Swedish Association for the Promotion of Ski Sports, founded in March 1892.

Why skiing? Why not other sports? What was it about this particular kind of activity that made it useful as a cultural and symbolic tool to promote national mobilization? There are four reasons:
1. Skiing was virtuous: it was connected with snow, winter, purity and wilderness.
2. Skiing was manly: it was constantly described as a masculine activity, like hunting, sport and war.
3. Skiing was heroic: it was connected with polar exploration and great journeys.
4. Skiing was Swedish: the king who founded Sweden did so on skis. The fact that skis were in those days no ordinary royal mode of transport in no way contradicted this. On the contrary: when skiing the people were as noble as the king.

Perhaps a fifth factor should be added that has little to do with mobilization or with northern identity: skiing was silent and peaceful, on skis you entered the wilderness on its own terms. The hunter is, in Nordic iconography generally, at the same time both exploiter and part of nature.

The 'Feeling for Nature'

The 1890s in Sweden were a time of both strong national sentiment and a growing awareness of the values of nature and natural resources. The economic importance of forests, iron ore, hydro-electric power and peat bogs became increasingly apparent as industrialization progressed, and natural resources became a recurrent theme in national propaganda, school books, education pamphlets and the mass media. This theme is also clear in the various scientific disciplines in which researchers mapped and described natural resources and their possible use for the benefit of the country. The economic value of these resources and their role in the economic history of Sweden have been closely analysed in previous research. The national rhetoric of economic nature has also been described and examined.[9]

Whilst the economic value of Sweden's natural resources has been the subject of extensive research, the same is not true of outdoor leisure activities and the recreational use of nature. To date we have had to make do with clichés and simplifications. For example, conventional wisdom has it that the Swedes generally enjoy an intense and intimate relationship with nature and frequently use natural locations for leisure, worship, sports and other types of recreational activity. This has been the refrain in countless texts and contexts throughout this century. However, there is actually very little empirical evidence of the Swedes' outdoor activities. Official statistics of outdoor leisure activity go back less than a decade. Other indicators – ownership of cabins and summer houses, the number of visitors to lodges run by the Swedish Tourist Association, membership of organizations promoting outdoor activities – offer supplementary, if partial, information.

That Swedes do indeed enjoy the outdoors, and have done so for the better part of this century, is indisputable. However, should this behavioural feature of the Swedes be studied in terms of recreational sociology, or would it be advantageous to view the strong tradition of 'feeling for nature' and its companion 'the outdoors' as ideological constructs that have helped shape a new Swedish identity in the transition from an agrarian to an industrial economy?

The question is pertinent.[10] But even without further empirical investigation one may note the contrast between complaints about the peasantry's ('allmogen') lack of interest in nature during the latter half of the nineteenth century and the Swedish gospel of 'feeling for nature' ('naturkänsla') in the early decades of this century. Often quoted, and rightly so, is the widely circulated pamphlet *Det svenska folklynnet* (Swedish Mentality) written in 1911. 'The love of nature is deeply rooted in our people,' claims its author, Gustav Sundbärg. He goes on to say that this passion may have been sparked by Linnaeus but that it is probably older: it 'lies in the character of our people from the beginning'. He quotes popular songs and psalms, mentions that family names are derived from features of the landscape, and that in Sweden – more than anywhere else, he presumes – there is a general need to escape the cities and spend the summer in 'nature' ('i naturens sköte').[11]

Sundbärg's book was originally published as a part of a public inquiry into the problem of emigration. If there was an official point of view on folk character, Sundbärg's came very close to it. And his ideas did not pass unnoticed, in its first year of publication the book was reprinted eleven times. Mythology sold well.

Sundbärg's uncompromising version should be interpreted as the canonization of an ideology of the Swedish *Volkscharakter* that had been in the making for about half a century. The previous decades had already seen the publication of several works expressing a similar viewpoint, albeit not so distinctly stated.[12] In 1912 Carl G. Laurin published his *Svensk själf-pröfning*, in which he applauded Sundbärg's work and drew attention to ideological precursors of the Swedish *Naturgefühl* like historian Erik Gustaf Geijer and writer C.J.L. Almqvist; the latter who claimed that Sweden could never be part of Europe: 'It is our fate to go by sledge.'

Organizations for Nature

A number of organizations with activities related to nature and the outdoors were formed during this period: the Swedish Tourist Association (STF, 1885); the Swedish Ski Association (1892); the Swedish branch of the Scout movement (1908), the Swedish Nature Conservation Society (SNF, 1909). The more exclusive Svenska Fjallklubben – The Swedish Alpine Club – was founded somewhat later, in 1927. Organizations for various kinds of outdoor sports – climbing, sailing, skating, orienteering and the like – were established in the first quarter of the century. Membership was fairly limited compared with the total Swedish population and in relation to membership figures in the post-Second World War period. SNF remained an expert organization until well after 1945; not until 1942 did membership reach 4,000.[13] The Ski Association had about 5,000 members in 1912. STF was the most successful in terms of membership and counted 50,000 members in 1910 and 100,000 in 1924, when its concept of tourism had widened to include not only hiking tours and skiing in the high wilderness areas of northern Sweden (a main preoccupation of its yearbook before 1900) but also bicycle outings and walking tours in the nearby countryside ('hembygden'), a shift of focus that apparently increased its folk appeal.[14]

Skiing and Outdoor Life

The Swedish Ski Association was representative of a particular strand of this growing interest in nature and leisure: skiing, in a wider sense, included everything that had to do with snow. From its outset it had strong patriotic associations and throughout its first half century or more of existence this remained especially true, not least during the Second World War. The post-war period has seen an interesting shift away from the patriotic and heroic to a concern with nature's holistic, aesthetic and ecological dimensions. One very obvious symptom of this shift of emphasis is the very name of the organization. After 1939 it was called the Swedish Ski and Outdoor Life Association and incorporated a wider range of nature-related activities. In the 1980s the word 'ski' was removed from the name, thus emphasizing a non-exclusive, non-specialist approach to nature.

The Association can be viewed as a prism through which leisure ideology and attitudes to nature in Sweden can be identified and analysed. If it is true, as stated above, that the Swedish 'feeling for nature' is an ideological construct, it should be possible to detect this in texts and documents from the Association. The ideology of the recreational use of nature changes significantly in the course of the one hundred years of the Association's existence. A further problem, one that is important but lies outside the scope of this essay, is the extent of the connection between ideology and practice within the Association and the shaping and growth of environmental consciousness and its popular appeal. That problem is in itself part of a wider complex of relationships making up the pre-history of Swedish environmentalism, a topic hitherto only partly analysed.[15]

Founding Fathers

The founding fathers of the Association were solid pillars of society. Among the fourteen members of the first board were six military officers, three men from financial circles (among them one of Sweden's leading industrialists, Frans Kempe) and two scientists. When the network spread over the country it relied mainly on the higher ranks of society – officers, doctors, engineers, and so on. There was a particular interest in promoting defence. The Association's first president, Captain Adolf Heijkenskjöld, published several articles in the early volumes of the Yearbook[16] where he stressed the importance of trained ski runners in the military and generally advocated the old and traditional art of skiing as a means of fostering a patriotic spirit and physical strength in young men. The full force of the militaristic and patriotic sentiments of the early years can be amply exemplified by the expulsion in 1905, following the dissolution of the Swedish–Norwegian union, of Fridtjof Nansen who had been an honorary member.

The association sponsored and stimulated winter tourism, notably in the mountainous parts of Sweden. It arranged exhibitions abroad, sometimes in co-operation with STF in order to market a Swedish ski industry in foreign countries and to publicize Sweden as a country for winter tourism. Youth activities were considered of great importance. Board member Carl Svedelius organized ski outings and competitions and initiated tours to the 'alpine regions' for Stockholm school children. These eventually became an annual institution.

The grip of the military on the ideology and style of the Association did not relax in the first fifty years of the Association's existence. During the Second World War, for example, Swedish ski teams travelled to Italy and Germany for competitions. In the eyes of the Association there was nothing to be ashamed of in this; pro-German tendencies had been strong from the outset. However, a lot of the Association's activities were more popular and, like those of STF, geared to recreation. This made the Association attractive to wider groups of people and in the late 1930s membership figures rose to more than 20,000.

Leisure Time and Welfare

It came as no surprise, therefore, when in 1939 the Association changed its name to include the expression 'Outdoor Life' ('Friluftsliv'). This change facilitated the Association's diffusion to the warmer southern parts of Sweden where skiing was rarely possible. The immediate stimulus, however, seems to have been the official public inquiry into 'leisure' ('Fritidsutredningen') ordered by social minister Gustav Möller in 1937. Carl Nordenson of the Association was among the seven members of the committee which proposed, among other things, an official foundation to promote outdoor life financed with income from the state-run betting system ('tipsmedlen'). Outdoor organizations could apply, it was suggested, for grants from the foundation for an outdoor life infrastructure: trails, cabins, playgrounds, and so on. This particular proposal came in 1939 (the main report was published in 1940), the year the Association changed its name.[17] It failed, however, to win sufficient support in Parliament, and state support only came gradually in the post-war period.

Mobilization

A remarkable example of how skiing could be considered part of a wider mobilization of the outdoors is a contribution by minister Artur Engberg to the fiftieth anniversary volume of Education and Culture published in 1942. Engberg referred to the Finnish-Soviet War of 1939–40 when the Finnish soldiers, 'sons of the snow', moved swiftly over their natural element. 'During that winter the ski wrote a chapter of world history.' The Finns had enjoyed great support in the Association which had organized campaigns to collect skis and rucksacks for the troops and had even lobbied to have Sweden enter the war on the Finnish side.

Engberg utilized this example to declare his conviction that a nation's efforts in peacetime paid off in times of war: 'The personal skills, endurance, moral strength, civil courage and ability to sacrifice, insight, wisdom and sense of responsibility – everything will be utilized, everything will prove its value, when the day of evil is here.' He went on to compare skiing to shooting; both sports released, as it were, the 'natural' powers of self-defence that lay hidden in the people and in the country herself. The ski was, he argued, in this context, 'a bulwark of freedom', and in consequence he expressed the hope that skiing would become a 'giant popular movement in our country'.[18]

Engberg's rhetoric was naturally affected by the ongoing war. But it could not simply be reduced to a product of the war. Similar words had been heard in the Association right from its inception. In its first year of operation it organized competitions in cross-country skiing as well as in ski jumping.

På skidor, the Association's yearbook, contained numerous articles stressing the need for a specially trained ski force in northern Sweden (where the eternal Russian enemy was expected to strike), for learning how to survive in snow bivouacs and so on. As late as 1942 one writer, Sven Nissing, could claim that the Association 'promotes defensive abilities by working for an outdoor life on skis in the wintertime, and thereby contributes to the strengthening of the country's winter defence'.[19] The wilderness experience was becoming part of the country's self-defence.

Health

A recurrent theme in the annals of the Association is the value of the outdoors for the physical well-being of the Swedish population. The Swedish term 'konditionsuppbyggnad' (literally, 'improving physical fitness') is close to what in German was called *Leistung*, the effort to prepare the population physically for battle with other nations. As John Hoberman has shown, this is a constant preoccupation throughout twentieth-century German history.[20] Sound physical health in both Sweden and Germany had military connotations.

It would seem illogical not to prepare the body at other times of the year as well as winter. So, in 1930, the Association decided to expand its activities – both in space with the foundations of local committees (110 of those were in existence in 1942), and time (year-round activities were introduced, attention was given to military or paramilitary events, like orienteering and 'field sports' – the Swedish connotation of the concept of 'fältsport' is a military one). The latter was normally organized by shooting clubs or military organizations. To promote year-round activities, especially designed cottages (combined ski cottages and cabins for use throughout the year) were established all over the country, often with municipal or community support.[21]

Youth

A special interest was taken in the outdoor life of the young. In the 1930s there was a heated debate about the leisure pursuits of the Swedish teenage population. Worthy citizens, such as teachers and priests, those conservative pillars of society, claimed that a serious behavioural decline could be discerned, typically symbolized by the prevalence of dance halls and the growing popularity of jazz.[22] Outdoor life was considered an important antidote. The State Bureau for Medical Affairs declared in 1936 that outdoor activity was a valuable counterbalance to the closed and unhealthy indoor lifestyle of the cities. Its reports advocated relaxing the regulation of working hours in the hope that this would trigger an increased involvement in outdoor pursuits and establish a mass movement.[23]

It was also considered that outdoor activity would help to rehabilitate people with social, psychological and drug problems. As early as 1924 it was proposed that outdoor pursuits would eliminate juvenile crime.[24] The Association directed its efforts towards raising standards of health at all levels of society and was thus parts of an effort towards class integration. This gospel was not political in the sense that it was associated with any particular party, but it was nevertheless conservative in its view of society as basically an organism. It stressed co-operation between social groups and classes, rather than confrontation. At the same time it was hostile to anything that had to do with pacifism and neutrality.

Hygiene, Resorts

The estate of Storlien in the province of Jämtland, close to the Norwegian border, was donated to the Association by Countess ('friherrinnan') Louise Falkenberg in 1928. It had already been offered to the Military Sports Organization (Sveriges Militära Idrottsförbund) which had declined it, claiming that for reasons of expense it was not able to maintain the land and its buildings. Storlien had been a resort well before the turn of the century. Other places with health and medical facilities in the area were Åre, Mörsil and Bydalen, where special hospitals for the treatment of tuberculosis were established. Thus tourism and health developed hand in hand in this mountainous part of Sweden. It formed an important part of the image of western Jämtland, Åre being called 'the Davos of Sweden'.[25] As late as in the 1960s the tradition was enlarged when the Association started 'Hålliform', a combination of walking, jogging, workout, testing of physical condition and sauna, sometimes with medical observation.

Women

One important feature of Swedish outdoor life is that from the outset it was open to both sexes. It attracted a fair number of women. They had their problems, however. Skiing, as well as other sports, had to be practised with an adherence to particular rules of behaviour and dress that befitted 'the weaker sex'. For almost half a century there was a heated debate on women's ski-dress. Only in the late 1920s and 1930s were women finally freed from the skirt and the large hat.[26] Inevitably, traditionalists, ever appalled by women athletes ('monstrosities'), warned against physical training likely to give women the square and bulky physique of men.[27]

However, there were compelling arguments in favour of women's skiing, sport and outdoor life – not least enhanced personal and public health. In 1885 the public inquiry into high school education presented a report[28] which contained the upsetting fact that 80 per cent of high school girls were suffering from psychological defects and problems which could have been avoided by physical exercise.[29] Women did not, however, play any important role in the Association until after the Second World War. After 1945 the paramilitary character of the organization gave way to an emphasis on a more general outdoor life, focused in part on pre-school children which encouraged mothers to join.

After 1945

The development of the Association in the post-Second World War period is typical of a more general tendency in outdoor life in Sweden: a shift from the military and athletic to the popular and recreational. One aspect of this was diversification in outdoor activities.

In 1935 the Association helped form the Association for the Promotion of Cycling (Cykelfrämjandet), and in 1937 the Association became a member of the National Organisation for Protection of Nature (Riksförbundet for naturvärn). At once, the Association started to work more actively to popularize nature conservation. This new interest should be seen against the background of the new 'social outdoors' approach, that, as mentioned above, was introduced as part of social policy in the 1930s. This development coincided with the trends that have already been identified above: better hygiene, broadening of the membership in terms of age, sex, and social class, year-round activities and so on. But it also ties in with another, quite fundamental, transformation of the concept of nature that occurred in Sweden in the mid-twentieth century. At this time the age-old concept of 'everyman's access to nature' ('allemansrätten') came to the fore. It was preached in the yearbook and at meetings and practised on excursions within the Association by leading members like Folke Thörn. This new ideological emphasis was termed 'Nature and us' ('Naturen och vi'). Karl-Erik Forsslund, poet and radical advocate of preservation and holism, was hailed as a persuasive ideologist. In ski lodges across the country one could read his plaintive preservationist aphorisms and poems, sometimes carved in wood or burned into birchbark wallpaper. In 1944 *Friluftsboken* (The Book of the Outdoors) was published and became an instant success. A special emblem, 'Friluftsmårket', was also introduced. Whoever acquired the gold variant of it was not simply a skier but an 'open air all-rounder'.[30]

This trend developed during the years that followed. In 1952 another new book was launched, *Bortom vardagen* (Beyond Everyday). It was yet another publishing success. In 1958 the Association joined with the Swedish Tourist Association to publish *Hygienisk revy* (Hygienic Review). And in the same year Bengt Sjögren's *Friskt vatten – ett livsvillkor* (literally, Fresh Water: Necessary for Life) appeared, marking a new role for the nature conservationist: the ecological.

Decline

The war had preserved the older values and concepts but immediately afterwards there was a rapid shift towards a new, broader, social orientation. The social policies of the 1930s now burst into full blossom. *I alla väder* ('In Any Weather'), the Association's popular journal, appeared in 1952, and in 1958 the membership rose to an all time high of 44,000. Thereafter the importance of the Association declined, despite efforts to woo the very young with educational walkabouts, the 'Mulle'-school, and ever more impressive ski lodges and mountain hotels. The patriotic and puritan ideology of recreation that the Association represented was no longer attractive. Other interests in nature had grown stronger. On the one hand there was a whole new repertoire of sports activities, both winter and summer, that Swedes had learned and could afford. On the other hand the environmental movement presented a new and different ideological gospel that indeed contained elements of the ideology long held by the Association, but also added the alien, or at least novel, ideas of social consciousness, global solidarity and political radicalism.[31] The momentum lay no longer with the Association, and certainly not with an organization promoting the noble art of skiing, which was why the word 'ski' was finally deleted from the name of the Association in the 1980s.

The full story of decline is, of course, far more complicated, but lack of space precludes full consideration here. It is evident, for example, that important values were inherited by the environmental movement from the older conservation and outdoors organizations, and in the 1980s and 1990s with political radicalism losing ground, it seems an era of convergence has been dawning upon most camps of environmentally concerned citizens.[32]

Periods and Perspectives

This exploratory inquiry into the history of the Swedish Association for the Promotion of Outdoor Life and Ski Sports reveals three distinct phases during the organization's one hundred years of existence. The first period, 1892 to the 1930s, focused on the patriotic, militaristic, and heroic dimensions of ski sports and outdoor life. The Association was narrowly defined and neither sought nor found a wide following during these years. The second period started slowly in the 1930s and gained momentum only after 1945. It was characterized by the social welfare dimension of the outdoor life: personal health and family-orientated leisure activities. The competitive and military elements were progressively reduced. The third period was anticipated in the 1950s but only developed fully in the 1970s and 1980s. It still retained much of the social policy ingredients of the previous period, but it was also characterized by environmental concern and a global outlook.

The most significant period was that which preceded the Association's decline in the late 1960s and the 1970s. Until then the three essential interconnected ambitions of the Association were: nation building, mobilization, and social well-being.

Nation Building

Forming communal identity, namely 'constructing' nations and regions, is a concern that has increasingly become the object of historical analysis over the past decade.[33] During its first decade of existence the Association fits nicely into such an analysis. It was one among a whole array of organizations and societies which through rhetoric and action gave the Swedish environment, especially in terms of its extreme and wild nature, national significance. Furthermore, making much of the Nordic climate of snow and harsh winters, the Association saw the Swedes as a people who from the outset had adapted successfully to the Nordic climate and who had been among the first to use skis. The identity of the Swedish nation that emerged from this interlocking view of nature, history and anthropology was one of a distinct northernness where the relationship with nature and climate typified the people and set them apart from all other nations and peoples of the world. At the same time nature and climate were linked to the idea of internal social integration. It was generally considered that both the social classes and geographical regions of Sweden were too loosely integrated. Nature, climate and the outdoor life could serve as cohesive agents in cementing society to create a united and strong Sweden.

Mobilization

The concept of mobilization relied on the basic assumption that it, like the Tourist Association and (to some extent) the Nature Conservation Society, hailed nature and the outdoors as being for the spiritual and physical good of the Swedish people and the Swedish nation. The people were considered a resource for defence, production and reproduction. Nature and the outdoor activities associated with it, especially skiing, were means of keeping this valuable resource in good condition. This explains the Associations early obsession with health, endurance and physical condition. It also explains the great attention given to the national team's performance in ski competitions both in Sweden and internationally. The national ski team was, in a sense, a barometer of the physical condition of the nation. The ultimate goal of mobilization was, according to this implicit ideology, victory in war.

Social Welfare

This concern emerged in the 1920s and 1930s with social liberalism and social democracy gaining ground in the political arena. These ideas arose out of a genuine ambition to utilize the newly acquired spare time – from 1920 the eight hour working day was the rule and the first general vacation law came in 1938 – for the benefit of the people. The Association responded to this new policy rather than initiated it. In fact the idea of social well-being was not difficult to combine with the older value of outdoor recreation. It had the same objectives of making people function better in society, of improving interaction between social classes, preventing social unrest and maintaining the health and sobriety of the nation.

A Swedish Ideology of Nature?

Did skiing represent a specific 'Swedish ideology' of nature and the outdoor life? In the absence of adequate comparative studies this is difficult to say. What can be said, without fear of correction, is that nature was an unusually strong element in the case of Sweden. Nature became a primary national symbol in Sweden, to an extent probably matched only in Finland and Norway.

Further comparative studies on the ideology of the outdoor life should be rewarding. An important focus would be the role of nature and the outdoors in nation building and military mobilization in a global setting. In this context the United States is of interest. In his classic work *Back to Nature*, first published in 1969, Peter J. Schmitt noted that in the United States 'back-to-nature' was indeed a movement, albeit diverse and varied. It consisted mainly of city dwellers who wanted to improve on urban life by bringing nature closer, through suburban living, country houses, outings, bird-watching, fishing, sports and so forth. However the wilderness, in itself, received little attention.

'Back-to-nature' in America had certain features, like those mentioned above, in common with the Swedish ideology of nature and recreation. But there are differences too. The nation-building element does not seem to have been so strong in America, where nature's role as a key symbol of American identity dates well back to the nineteenth century and beyond. The paramilitary character of the early Swedish outdoor movement does not seem to have played a major role in America.[34] In America 'back-to-nature' was also closely tied to social planning, suburban commuting, and garden cities, which was not the case in Sweden. A reasonable conclusion would seem to be that the Swedish Association for the Promotion of the Outdoors was something of a mix between the German *Leistung* tradition, which focused on the body and on physical performance, and the American 'Back-to-nature' tradition.

Nature and outdoor life – rooted, as was often stressed, in 'allemansrätten' and old rustic traditions – became part a myth of Sweden. As such it was channelled through school books, media, the semi-official

Radiotjänst (Radio Broadcasting), and protected by royal and other leading members of society.

If a full understanding of the importance of outdoor life for post-1960 environmental concerns and activities in Sweden is required, then it will be achieved by scrutinizing not only the environmental practices of the Swedish people, but also the Swedish ideology of nature.

NOTES

1. Erik von Wolcker, 'Anteckningar om skidkidrott i Sverige före Skidföreningens tillkomsf', *På skidor* (On Skis), 1925.
2. Phebe Fjellström, *Samerna* (The Saami) (Stockholm: Norstedts, 1985), p.52.
3. See, however, Marie-Anne Condé, 'Folkets skidor och herrskapets' (Skis among the people and among the upper classes), *Folkets Historia* (History of the People), 1994:1. Condé refers to several types of popular skis, mentioned by local informants, yet with scarce examples from before c.1850.
4. Marie-Anne-Condé, *Skidåkning i Sverige: Från Hedenhòs till Heijkensiöld* (Skiing in Sweden: From Ancient Times to c.1900) (Stockholm: Institute of Ethnology, Stockholm University, 1991), pp.45–8, confirms that the Swedish military rarely used skis and that the units that did were recruited from the northern provinces of the country.
5. Axel Hamberg, 'Till skidans 50-årsjubileum såsom redskap vid arktisk forskning' (On the fiftieth anniversary of the ski as a tool in Arctic research) (*På skidor*, 1933).
6. H. Grundström, 'Den stora skidtävlingen Purkijaur-Kvikkjokk och åter' (The big ski competition from Purkijaur to Kvikkjokk and back), *På Skidor*, 1934.
7. Von Wolcker, 'Anteckningar om skididrott', pp.71–9.
8. This theme interested Fridtjof Nansen, the Norwegian explorer. The theme also looms large in Roland Huntford, *Scott and Amundsen* (London, 1979).
9. Sverker Sörlin, *Framtidslandet: Debatten om Norrland och naturresurserna under det industriella genombrottet* (With a summary in English: The Land of the Future: The Debate on Norrland and Its Natural Resources at the Time of the Industrial Breakthrough) (Stockholm: Carlsson Bokförlag, 1988); the bibliography includes a quite exhaustive list of previous research.
10. An attempt to answer it is Klas Sandell and Sverker Sörlin, 'Naturen som fostrare: Friluftsliv och ideologi i svenskt 1900-tal' (Nature as Fosterer: Outdoor Life and Ideology in Twentieth Century Sweden), *Historisk tidskrift* (Journal of History), 1 (1994), 4–43.
11. Gustav Sundbärg, *Det svenska folklynnet: Aforismer* (Swedish Mentality: Aphorisms), 4 ed. (Stockholm, 1911), p.8f.
12. Among them Verner von Heidenstam, 'Om svenskarnas lynne' (On Swedish Mentality), *Ord & Bild* (1897).
13. Désirée Haraldsson, *Skydda vår natur!: Svenska Naturskyddsföreningens framväxt och tidiga utveckling* (With a summary in English: Protect Our Nature!: The Swedish Nature Conservation Society, Its Background and Early Development.), (Lund: Lund University Press, 1987).
14. Sverker Sörlin, *Naturkontraktet: Om naturumgängets idéhistoria* (The Natural Contract: A History of Environmental Ideas) (Stockholm: Carlsson Bokforlag, 1991), Ch.10 and literature quoted therein.
15. On this particular aspect on Swedish environmental history see: Thomas Söderqvist, *The Ecologists: From Merry Naturalists to Saviours of the Nation* (Stockholm: Almqvist & Wiksell, 1986); Bo Rosén, *Den glömda miljödebatten* (The Forgotten Environmental Debate) (Solna: Naturvårdsverket & Bra Böcker, 1987); Bosse Sundin, 'Från rikspark till bygdemuseum: Om djurskydds-, naturskydds- och hembygdsrörelserna i sekelskiftets Sverige' (From national park to local museum: On the movements for animal protection, nature conservation and preservation of the local heritage), in *Naturligtvis* (Umeå

University: Department of History of Science and Ideas, 1981), pp.152–93. My own interest
in the field can be studied in Sörlin, *Framtidslandet*, esp. Chs.3 and 4, and in
Naturkontraktet, Ch.10.

16. *Föreningen för skidlöpningens främjande i Sverige: Program och årsskrift* (The Swedish
Ski Association: Program and Yearbook); the first issue (1893–94) contained only 64 pages
but the *Yearbook* grew within a decade to substantial volumes of about 300–400 pages.

17. Hans-Erik Olson, *Staten, turismen och rekreationen: Producenter och konsumenter i kamp
om makten!* (State, Tourism, and Recreation: Producers and Consumers Fighting for
Power), Fritidspolitiska studier 2, (Stockholm: Forvaltningshögskolan, 1988).

18. Artur Engberg, 'Skidlöpning, den väldiga folkrörelsen' (Skiing, the giant people's
movement), in *I svenska skidspår* (In Swedish Ski-tracks) (Stockholm: A-B Svensk
litteratur, 1942), p.111.

19. Sven Nissing, 'Friluftsliv åt alla året om' (Out of doors for everybody all year round), in *I
svenska skidspår* , 119.

20. J.M. Hoberman, *Sports and Political Ideology* (University of Texas Press: Austin, 1984).

21. Nissing, 'Friluftsliv', 120f.

22. Jonas Frykman, *Dansbaneeländet: Ungdomen, populärkulturen och opinionen* (The Misery
of the Open-air Dance-floor: Youth, Popular Culture, and the Opinion), (Stockholm: Natur
& Kultur, 1988). Alf Arvidsson, *Sågarnas sång: Folkligt musicerande i sågverkssamhället
Holmsund 1850-1980* (The Song of the Saw-mills: Popular Music-making in the Saw-mill
Community of Holmsund 1859–1980), Umeå Studies in the Humanities (Umeå, 1991). Jan
Ling, Märta Ramsten and Gunnar Ternhag (eds.), *Folkmusikboken* (The Folk Music Book)
(Stockholm, 1980).

23. Nissing, 'Friluftsliv', 121f. Ruben Wagnsson, 'Skidfrämjandets ungdomsverksamhet' (The
Ski Association's youth activities), in *I svenska skidspår*, 135–40. For a more detailed
analysis, see Sandell and Sörlin, 'Naturen som fostrare'.

24. Bo Rosén, 'De moderna skidorna kommer' (The Modern Skis are Here), *På skidor* (1968),
89, citing Association minutes of 19 Dec. 1924.

25. Martha Järnfeldt-Carlsson, *Landskap, jaktvillor och kurhotell: Arkitektur och turism i
Västjämtland 1880-1915* (With a Summary in English: Landscape, Hunting Villas, Resort
Hotels: Architecture and Tourism in Western Jämtland 1880–1915) (Umeå, 1988). Göran
Rosander, 'Medicinsk turism' (Medical Tourism), *Folkets historia* (1988).

26. Kid Bruncrona, 'Från den "rationella skidlöparedrägten för fruntimmer" till
"fortåkarbyxan" (From the 'rational ski-dress for women' to 'the speed pants'), in *i svenska
skidspår*, 267–74.

27. Hanna Rydh, 'Kvinnan och friluftslivet' (Women and Out of Doors), in *I svenska skidspår*,
188.

28. 'Bilaga E till läroverkskommitténs betänkande' (Appendix E to the Report of the
Committee on High School Education).

29. Rydh, 'Kvinnan och friluftslivet', 188.

30. *På skidor* (1968), 112.

31. Andrew Jamison *et al.*, *The Making of the New Environmental Consciousness: A
Comparative Study of the Environmental Movements in Sweden, Denmark and the Netherlands* (Edinburgh: Edinburgh University Press, 1990), Ch.2.

32. Sverker Sörlin, 'Sveriges moderna miljohistoria' (An Environmental History of Modern
Sweden), Ch.14 *in Humanekologi: Naturens resurser och människans försörjning* (Human
Ecology: Nature's Resources and the Wealth of Man), ed. S. Sörlin (Stockholm: Carlsson
Bokförlag, 1992). For useful American comparisons see P. Shabecoff, *A Fierce Green Fire:
The American Environmental Movement* (New York: Hill and Wang, 1993).

33. I am referring in particular to the debate and research inspired by works such as Benedict
Andersson's *Imagined Communities* (London: Verso, 1983), to Ernest Gellner, *Nations and
Nationalism* (Oxford: Blackwell, 1983); and Eric J. Hobsbawm and Terence Ranger (eds.),
The Invention of Tradition (Cambridge: Cambridge University Press, 1983). See also the
subtle theoretical contribution by Anssi Paasi, 'The Institutionalization of Regions: A
Theoretical Framework for the Understanding of Regions and the Constitution of Regional
Identity', *Fennia* 164 (1986).

34. Peter J. Schmitt, *Back to Nature: The Arcadian Myth in Urban America* (1969), new ed. (Baltimore, MD: Johns Hopkins University Press, 1990). See also Roderick Nash, *Wilderness and the American Mind* (New Haven, CT: Yale University Press, 1963).

National Identity and the Emergence of the Sports Movement in Late Imperial Russia

JOHN D. WINDHAUSEN and IRINA V. TSYPKINA

Historians often examine the features of late tsarist Russia with respect to its national pride. Russian national feelings were virtually indistinguishable from the much discussed inferiority complex that plagued the educated Russian public for over a century. Despite the cultural achievements of the previous two generations, Russians in 1900 were painfully aware of their backwardness in sundry ways to the modern West. Not far from the speculations of historians, of course, was the future of Tsar Nicholas' empire without the alleged 'accident' of the world war. And so pan-Slavism, a national school of art, Russification of ethnic and religious minorities, concern over dependency on foreign capital, the humiliation suffered by the war with Japan in 1904–5, the tawdry chauvinism of the imperial council, including its links to the reactionary nationalist group called the 'Black Hundreds', have all been subject to the historians' microscopes. One neglected topic has been the early development and evolution of the European sports movement in Russia under the last Romanov.

Russian Westerners urged Russia's participation in the new Olympic Games and in other international sporting competitions. Slavophiles distrusted the commercial and aggressive character of European sports and promoted the revival of national games like gorodki, svaika, and lapta. This same phenomenon was found in Ireland in this generation where nationalists even more aggressively discouraged international (English!) games in favour of national ones.

Nearly twenty years ago Eugen Weber wrote a seminal article in the *American Historical Review* tracing the nature and impact of the modern sports movement as a reflection of national identity and another measuring rod of national consciousness.[1] This study describes some of the initial spade work for the Russian scene and suggests the applicability of the Weber approach for a study of that country before the First World War.

First some clarification of terms is in order: sports, modern sports, the sports movement. As for the first, this writer accepts the limitations of the word explored by Bernard Jeu, a philosopher of sports at the Université de Lille.[2] Jeu writes that sport is used in three senses: as a free, physical activity; as the systematic discipline of one's own body; and thirdly, as a combination of the first two notions culminating in competition. This competition, he notes, has been symbolic of human tragedy and marked by free compliance to rules. Less philosophical but similar to the Jeu description in its implications is the definition of sport by Allen Guttmann of Amherst College in North America.[3] He calls sport a non-utilitarian physical contest. By accepting the competitive nature of sport this essay necessarily ignores the rich contributions to the theory and practice of physical education advanced by such Russians as Pyotr F. Lesgaft and Varnav Efimovich Ignatiev.

Modern sport is characterized by secularism, specialization of roles, systematic regulations, a zeal for quantification and record setting, the rise of sporting heroes and, above all, by bureaucratic structures.[4] Finally, the term sports movement herein means the development of fan interest and the inter-nationalization of modern sports that matured in the last decade of the nineteenth century and which mirrored the values of English and French societies, in particular.

What was the relative state of sports and athletics in Russia under the last Romanov? The dismal showing of Russian sportsmen at the Olympic Games at Stockholm in 1912, the last before the Soviet era, was often cited by Soviet sportswriters as evidence of the failure of the old regime to adapt to modern values. Was the state of imperial Russian sports in the early twentieth century another example of a cultural lag, another cause to sustain the image of national inferiority? Whether lag or no lag, the evolutionary development of Russia's sports heritage does not appear unique.

As in other western nations the phenomenon of organized recreation and sports was limited for centuries by the lack of available time for all but the leisured class. Horseback riding competitions, for example, had been organized by a Kievan grand prince in 1150, while universal sports like bonfire jumping, wrestling, fist-fighting, spear hurling, and swimming were frequently encountered in literature describing the lifestyles of the early nobles, the druzhiny and boyars.[5] Native Russian games like gorodki and svaika, which were less identified with the upper classes, were similar to their western counterparts, bowling and throwing the disc or hoop. Lapta, too, may be imagined as a distant relative of American baseball. By the fifteenth and sixteenth centuries skiing was avidly promoted among the new service nobility called dvoriane since this activity was linked with the military exigencies of the time. Sources also reveal the popularity at that time of racing on ice without benefit of skates.[6]

As in England and New England, churchmen often feared the indulgent spirit of sport, and so certain athletic activities in Muscovy were prohibited by the Stoglav Sobor of 1551, and later by the Domostroi of 1580.[7] Patriarch Iob banned fist-fighting in 1604 and that prohibition was reaffirmed by Tsar Alexei Mikhailovich in 1648.[8] By the time of Peter I there was a marked change in attitudes, partly due to the tsar's somewhat secular outlook, and partly due to the publication of the first pedagogical analysis of sports and games by the Ukrainian scholar Epiphanii Slavinetskii of Moscow's Chudov Monastery.[9] When Tsar Peter visited England in 1689, as a result of a challenge at a dinner party he arranged on the evening of 20 April in the garden of the Marquis de Camarthen a contest that has been called the first international boxing match. One of Peter's grenadier guards defeated a Scotsman regarded as the unofficial champion of England and Scotland.[10] Unfortunately the names of both participants are unknown.

Encouraged by this British experience the Tsar Reformer now introduced physical education and athletics as regular training for his soldiers and, at the School for Mathematical Sciences and Navigation which he had established in Moscow the curriculum included swimming, fencing, sailing and rowing.[11] Throughout the eighteenth century fencing and horseback riding were normal skills taught for the education of the nobility. By the nineteenth century two Russian fencers, Tarasov and Sokolov, even enjoyed international reputations.

Thus far, the state of sports was either non-organized recreation or else organized for utilitarian ends. Only in the nineteenth century does sport, organized for non-utilitarian competition, gain popularity in Europe and in America. Allowing for the familiar cultural lag the same pattern emerged in Russia. There, aristocratic circles formed societies to promote various athletic events and the list of those clubs founded in the nineteenth century is as follows:

Amateur Shooting Club	c.1800
St. Petersburg Horse Racing Society	1826
Neva School of Swimmers	1834
Imperial Yacht Club	1846
Officers' Fencing Gymnasium	1857
Neva Lawn and Tennis Circle	1860
Amateur Skating Club of St. Petersburg	1864
St. Petersburg Tennis and Cricket Club	1868
Russian Gymnastics Society (Moscow)	1883
Kraievsky Heavy Athletics Circle (St. P.)	1885
Petrov Running Society (Cross Country)	1886
Petersburg Circle of Amateur Sportsmen	1887
Moscow Club of Amateur Cyclists	1888
Petersburg Gymnastics Society	c.1894
Moscow Skiers Club	1895
Kiev Athletic Society	1895
Baron Kister's English Boxing Arena	1895
Hercules Weightlifting Club	1896
Sanitas Wrestling Club	1897
Victoria Football Club	1897
Petersburg Circle (Bandy Ice Hockey)	1898[12]

This information indicates increased organizational activity as the century drew to a close, as was the case elsewhere in Europe. Russian sport societies were heavily concentrated in the two capital cities, St. Petersburg and Moscow, and were closely identified with western sports. One sport, however, cycling, developed a national network of urban clubs before the end of the century. Clubs had appeared even in such towns as Odessa, Kharkov, Tula, Voronezh, Yaroslavl, Riga, and in far-off Tashkent.[13]

The national character of European sports is revealed by the emergence of national sport organizations. Note this comparative pattern for national associations founded in the nineteenth and early twentieth centuries:

	Britain	USA	Germany	Russia	Italy
Association Football	1863		1900	1912	
Swimming	1869	1878	1887		
Cycling	1878	1880	1884	1884	1894
Rowing	1879	1872	1883	1898	
Ice Skating	1879	1888	1888	1908*	
Athletics (Track)	1880	1888	1898	1911	
Lawn Tennis	1886	1881	1902	1907	
Skiing	1903	1904	1904	1910	
Olympic Committees	1905	c.1906	c.1906	1911	1907[14]

* The Russian organization certainly existed before that year; the originating date is unknown to this writer but national speed skating championships were held annually from 1889.

The data point to a modest cultural lag on the part of the Russians, due perhaps to the later spread of industry, but nonetheless shows considerable attention to the Russian organization of sports during the years when Tsar Nicholas II was reigning. Indeed, official society promoted the organization of sports from the mid-1880s until 1914.

After the turn of the century the growth of sport organizations accelerated. Within five years the number of sport societies had risen from fifty to one hundred.[15] Although Soviet sports historians insisted that tsarist authorities severely restricted athletic opportunities for the working classes, not a few popular sports heroes were, as Soviet writers admitted, 'emigres from the people'.[16] Frequently cited were wrestlers Ivan Poddubnii and Ivan Zaikin, skaters Alexander Panshin and Nikolai A. Panin-Kolomenkin (whose proletarian status is doubtful) and the cyclist, Mikhail Diakov.[17] Class discrimination in athletics was hardly unique to Russia in this age but a review of sporting activities among the railway workers in 1912 reveals widespread involvement in the following sports, ranked by priority: gymnastics, light athletics, walking, cycling, lawn tennis, football, rowing, skiing, ice skating, tobogganing, gorodki, Russian and Italian lapta, basketball, jumping, swinging, and swimming.[18] Many Soviet sports historians suggested that tsarist officials as well as western bourgeois factory owners in Russia provided funds to develop fledgling sport organizations in efforts to draw workers from revolutionary activities.[19] One would imagine that the leisure time and resources requisite for broad based sports participation were not available in a society still in its industrial infancy. Yet in a recent work, Stolbov notes that 46 per cent of the members of sport clubs in 1914 were composed of students and workers.[20]

What seems remarkable is the extent to which Russian athletics did develop at this time. The most popular sport in Europe by the turn of the century was cycling, and Russians held their first official race on Mars Field in St. Petersburg in 1882. Soon every large town from Odessa to Tashkent had amateur cycling clubs so that by 1896 Russian cyclists had won several European prizes, both in France and in England.[21] The first soccer football contests among Russian teams had taken place only in 1898,[22] the same year as the first Russian hockey (bandy) match,[23] the first organized Russian modern boxing bout,[24] and in several cities the first organized pistol shooting matches;[25] that was also the third consecutive year of national ski meets.[26] Finally, the Russian circus regularly employed weightlifters before the turn of the century.

By 1914 there were more than 1200 official sporting clubs, including hunting and fishing societies, in the Russian empire, not to mention the many *dikhie*, or unofficial, ones.[27] Aside from numerous societies in major cities like Moscow, St. Petersburg, Kiev and Riga, others were found in Yerevan, Armenia, and Tiflis (Tbilisi), Tashkent, and Minsk. Only two years after the All-Russian Football Union was formed in 1912 there were 155 soccer football clubs in thirty-three cities.[28] In 1907 Russian teams had begun to engage in international hockey matches and in 1914 the newly established All-Russian Hockey Union had incorporated 32 clubs, including one from the Pacific port of Vladivostok.[29] Other all-Russian unions were assembled for the 24 rowing societies,[30] for the 48 lawn tennis societies, and for numerous Sokol gymnastic societies which sent competitors to the international tournaments in Prague in 1907 and in 1912. At the first Czechoslovakian-sponsored championships a team from Kiev captured a first prize in one event and in the later tournament teams from Kharkov and Kiev finished fourth and eleventh in a field of 311 teams. By 1914 there were 42 Sokol clubs in the Russian empire featuring a variety of sports in addition to gymnastics.[31] There was even an All-Russian Society of Motorcyclists.[32] One should note, finally, that a touring basketball team from the United States was defeated in St. Petersburg by a team from the capital club called Maiak, associated with the international YMCAs and founded by a New York philanthropist named James Stokes.[33]

Early in the decade Olympic officials blamed the press for failing to generate enough interest in athletics to send many Russian athletes to the Games in Athens, Paris and St. Louis. When seven Russian athletes participated in the London Games of 1908 press coverage in Russia was minimal. Yet the growth of fan interest began to prompt more attention in the newspapers. During its short life in 1906–7, a twice-monthly journal in St. Petersburg, *Russkii Sport*, catered to the popular excitement over ice skating competitions. Daily newspapers like *Novoe Vremia* regularly reported the results of the horse races, often sponsored by members of the royal family, and there was a twice-weekly illustrated sports newspaper in Moscow called *Russkii Sport* that ran from 1907 to 1916; it was the official organ of the Society for Physical Enlightenment called Sanitas. Also published in Moscow from 1911 to 1916 was *K Sportu*, the official newspaper of the Moscow football league. The Olympic Games in Stockholm in 1912 received daily attention even in such imperial newspapers as the St. Petersburg *Rech, Zemschina, Zeitung, Kraft und Gesundheit,* and *Novoe Vremia*; the Riga *Rigasche Zeitung, Rigas Avise, Rigasche Rundschau, Rigaer Tageblatt,* and *Dsimtenes Wehtsnesis*; the Dorpat *Postimees*; the Lvov *Wedrowiec*; the Moscow *Metropolis Gossips*; the Reval *Tallina Teataja*; and the Tiflis *Horison*.

If such data do not indicate mass participation, they nonetheless reveal a rapidly growing sports industry and public not dissimilar to those in western countries. This trend persisted during the last years before the First World War and was further illustrated by the growth of state support and widespread Russian participation in the Fifth Olympic Games in Stockholm in 1912.

Russian involvement in the modern Olympic Games dates from the founding congress in 1894 but the tsarist Olympic story again demonstrates Russia's cultural lag in the sports field and the nation's somewhat frantic efforts to close that gap. In the very first year of the new reign of Tsar Nicholas II, two men were sent to attend the organizational meetings in Paris for the resumption of the Olympic Games: General Alexei Dmitrievich Butovsky and Alexei P. Lebedev of the St. Petersburg Gymnastics Society. Russia was one of only nine nations represented at this first congress.[34] Butovsky was chosen to be one of the founding members and he wrote to Pierre de Coubertin, the father of the movement, that he felt 'duty bound to accept such an honourable responsibility with gratitude on behalf of an institution devoted to a universal cause which has a great future.'[35] Six months later he would write to Coubertin expressing his regrets at his failure to generate much Russian interest in this project, blaming the situation, as noted above, upon the Russian press which was 'not at all seriously interested in bringing up the question of physical education'.[36]

Butovsky failed to send any Russian athletes to the first Olympic games in Athens in 1896 and four years later was succeeded in this international body by two men, Prince Sergei Beliossersky and Count de Ribeaupierre, who served for the next eight years. During their tenure three countrymen entered the second Games at Paris, two equestrians and one marksman;[37] none went to St. Louis in 1904; one competed in the unofficial games in Athens in 1906 (his name and event are unknown);[38] seven competed during the London Olympiad in 1908. This latter included one skater, one discus thrower, two athletes in track and field, and three wrestlers.[39] During this last Olympiad Beliossersky and Ribeaupierre were succeeded on the governing board of the International Olympic Committee (IOC) by Count Semen Trubetskoy and Prince Léon Oroussiev. These two would organize tsarist Russia's last participation in the Olympic games.

The organization effort for the Stockholm events in 1912 was clearly intended as another of those Petrine leaps into the future that so marked the Russian historical landscape. The energies of official society, frustrated by the blows to national prestige resulting from the revolution, the military defeat by Japan, both in 1905, and by continuing weaknesses in the economic structures, were directed to the recovery of international honour through international sports competition. Hence officials clearly were poised to overcome the embarrassment of scant Russian presence in the prior games and to demonstrate the new Russian commitment to the world sports movement. Oroussiev, the most successful of the Russian representatives to the IOC, helped to arrange the first Russian National Olympic Committee in 1911. That committee was placed under the direction of State Councillor Vasily I. Sreznevsky and National Secretary Georges Dupperron. These three men ensured the presence of a remarkably large Russian contingent during the Fifth Olympiad in Sweden. The Russian team of athletes, comprising 178 members, was the only squad outside Scandinavia participating in all 13 categories of athletic competition.[40] Russian participants included: 32 in athletics (track and field), 10 in cycling, 22 in fencing, 19 in soccer, 22 in gymnastics, 7 in horse riding (equestrian competition), 2 in lawn tennis, 5 pentathletes, 1 rower, 27 in shooting, 3 swimmers, 11 wrestlers, and 17 in yachting. What is more, Tsar Nicholas II was persuaded to make available to the Russians the royal four-tier ocean liner, the SS *Birma*, which served as a hotel in the harbour of Stockholm.[41] The latter gesture may have reflected two concerns in state circles, since sport societies were anxious to save money on lodging and, on the other hand, political leaders continued to harbour historic reservations about allowing large numbers of citizens easy access to the West; as noted in *Russkii Sport*, the ship made the issue of passports for foreign travel unnecessary.[42]

State support for the Olympic movement was a new development. Germans, and possibly Swedes, appropriated parliamentary funds for athletic preparations in 1912 and an English public fund was set up in 1913 to improve coaching in Olympic sports. State support for Norwegian athletes may have been given as early as 1906. Tsarist financial aid in 1912 then was neither an unusual nor a late development.[43]

To judge by the number of gummed labels for luggage which the Swedish hosts printed for visiting national groups, the Russians, with 600, appeared to outnumber all the other foreigners with the exception of the neighbouring Danes and the English.[44] Some forty of the Russians had official status at the games as judges or as representatives of the government or of sport societies, again, one of the largest such delegations.[45]

There were other signs in which Russia's role at Stockholm revealed an enhanced commitment to the world sports movement. In addition to providing the royal vessel the tsar's involvement was observed by his donation of one of the prized challenge cups to be presented to the winner of the decathlon.[46] Grand Duke Dmitry was a member of the equestrian team and Grand Duke Nikolai Nikolaevich took the Russian Olympic Committee under his personal protection.[47] Ninety members of the Russian delegation were military officers and the Russian army even held sporting competitions as part of the preparations for the Stockholm Games.[48]

Russian presence was yet noted in other ways. Among the foreign judges selected by the Swedes, only Great Britain and Germany had more than the Russians. That the Swedes recognized the growth of athletic interest among the Russian public could be illustrated by the fact that the host advertisers distributed a large number of large and small posters and advertising stamps in the Russian language.[49] Only four other nations received more (even though the Swedish consulate staff had to undertake itself to post them in restaurants and railway stations in and around St. Petersburg).[50] Finally, one notes that 28 nations dispatched journalists to the Stockholm contests and the Russians had the eighth largest number with 15. They came from a wide range of cities: five from the capital city, St. Petersburg, five from Riga, and one each from Moscow, Lvov, Dorpat, Reval and Tiflis.[51] Unfortunately the Russian athletes performed poorly but perhaps that was to be expected from their first major effort, and, for that matter, not very important in terms of the original spirit of the renewed games.

These would be the last Olympic Games in which the Russians would participate until their re-entry at Helsinki in 1952. Meanwhile, Sreznevsky and the Russian ambassador to France both attended the celebration in Paris in July 1914, the twentieth anniversary of the first modern IOC congress.[52] Present also was the Russian State Inspector General for Sports and Physical Development, General Vladimir Voiekov, whose post and appointment were announced by the tsar in 1912.[53] Under his supervision nation-wide sport festivals, similar to the modern Spartakiada, were held in

Kiev in 1913 and in Riga in 1914. Undismayed by the few medal-winning performances in Stockholm some 579 athletes, including women, were attracted to the Kiev competitions. At Riga over 1000 participants came from 24 cities to compete in national games that were interrupted by the beginning of the world war.[54] Local chauvinism in the Ukraine and in the Baltic region may have prompted Voiekov to stage the festivals in non-Russian cities. This not only satisfied particular regional contributions to the sport movement (a separate Baltic committee represented [35] Baltic athletes from the Russian delegation at Stockholm), but the festivals in Kiev and Riga were no doubt reminders that the various nationalities were part of an imperial community. Meanwhile, Dupperron served on the IOC from 1913 until 1915, as did Oroussiev who left Russia after the revolution for Sofia, and later for Paris, maintaining his ties with the international sports body until his death in 1933.[55]

It seems clear from the foregoing that Russians decidedly encouraged the rise of a bureaucratic sports structure and by 1912 regarded themselves as a part of the world athletic community. Although the ill-fated games of 1916 had been awarded to Berlin, *The Times* reported that the Russians had been earnestly working for St. Petersburg as the next site.[56] The host city has traditionally used the Olympiad to promote not just urban but national pride. The conjunction of the World's Fair with the Olympic Games in St. Louis in 1904 may have been the most famous example prior to the Berlin Games of 1936. If the organization of competitive sports provides another example of a Russian cultural lag in 1900, then solid evidence indicates that national pride was motivating official Russian society to close that gap in the last years of the old regime.

There remains, of course, the natural question: how well did the Russian athletes perform? Or, to put the question another way: did the Russian public discover its share of sport heroes to satisfy and fortify feelings of national pride?

Some Soviet sport historians argued that the tsarist government furthered the development of sport societies to draw the working classes away from politics. Realizing this, radicals sometimes penetrated the sport societies, as when S.V. Kesiur, a Bolshevik, captained the Kiev football team from 1910 to 1912.[57] Yet, ironically, Soviet historians also took a different point of view: namely, that by restricting athletic opportunities to the elite, denying the athletic aspirations of the broad masses, the tsarist administration foiled the efforts of Russians to compete successfully in international tournaments.[58] In fact, so they argue, the Stockholm Olympics fraudulently raised the hopes of the Russian sporting public. At the end of the games Russia had finished in a fifteenth place tie with Austria, having earned but two silver (team pistol shooting and wrestling) and three bronze medals (clay bird shooting, yachting and rowing) from 178 competing athletes. Soviet sport historians frequently took note of this effort as a failure, a kind of 'Sports Tsushima', a reference to the naval humiliation at the hands of the Japanese in 1905.[59] The lesson is clear. The Soviets, by contrast, opened sports to the masses and the results have been the authentic fulfilment of national pride.

That judgement may be faulty. How scarce were the Russian sports heroes in the last generation of tsarist Russia? And did Russian athletes garner few awards in international competitions? In 1896, when the sport of cycling was as popular as soccer is today, a Russian named Mikhail Diakov won the cycling prize of England and Muscovite P.M. Vashkevits won a major European cycling title in 1898.[60] V.A. Giliarovsky was acclaimed in Belgrade in 1897 as the greatest gymnast in the world. Weightlifter S. Eliseev, fencer P. Zakovorot, and oarsman M. Sveshnikov won international titles around the turn of the century. A Russian boxer named Ivan Grava had won international renown.[61] A Russian woman, Nina Vasilyevna Popova, set a world record for the 100-metre foot race at Kiev in 1913.[62] And another Russian, Leonid Romanchenko, had set a world record in marathon swimming.[63] In the world's newest sport, aeronautics, there were numerous Russian pilots who regularly captured popular attention, such as P.M. Nesterov, M.E. Zhukovsky, and K.K. Artseulov.[64] Nikolai Panin won the gold medal in special figure skating in the London Olympic Games of 1908 and two Russian Graeco-Roman wrestlers, Nikolai Orlov (lightweight) and Alexander Petrov (super heavyweight), won the first Russian silver medals at the Games in London. In 1912 Graeco-Roman wrestler Max Klein from Russian Estonia won the middleweight silver medal as did the Russian pistol shooting team at Stockholm (Amos de Kasch, Nikolai de Melnikov, Pavel de Voyloshnikov and Georgi de Panteleymonov). Harry Blau won a bronze medal for Russia in clay bird shooting as did the sailing squad (Ester Beloselsky, Ernest Brasche, Pushnitsky, Alexander Rodionov, Jossif Shomaker, Filipp Strauch and Karl Lindblom) of the yacht *Gallia II* in the 10-metre class. Mikhail Kusik, described as an oarsman with a 'beautiful style and great energy', lost a close semi-final race to a Belgian but still managed to tie for the bronze in the single sculls event.[65]

Russian prowess was especially noticeable in ice skating, both in speed and figures. One widely repeated story is that Tsar Peter I, who was skating by the age of nine, invented a metal ice skate when he was living in Holland in 1697–98.[66] There he could not be indifferent to the popular enthusiasm for racing on skates, then not practised in Russia. Russians skated only for enjoyment but not yet for competition. After Peter's subsequent return home he sponsored racing on skates and it became quite fashionable among the aristocracy. Nevertheless, after his death the phenomenon vanished for about a century in Russia. Racing was revived in the 1820s and 1830s and even found a prominent place in a manual on winter gymnastics designed for cadets in 1839.[67] The first unofficial races may date from the opening of an ice field on the basin of the yacht club in the Yusupov Garden in St. Petersburg in 1865.[68] The St. Petersburg Society of Amateur Ice Skaters was formed in 1877, and in 1890 it hosted an international competition for speed skaters from America, England, Austria, Holland, Germany, Sweden and Norway in honour of the twenty-fifth anniversary of the first races in the Yusupov Garden.[69]

As early as 1883 Alexei P. Lebedev, competing in Helsingfors, won the unofficial world figure skating title, a feat he accomplished a second time in 1890.[70] St. Petersburg resident Aiexander Nikitich Panshin won the unofficial speed skating title in 1889. In his first competition, on 9 February 1886, Panshin raced 1609 metres (one mile) in 3:53.8 (minutes/seconds). He bettered this mark by 22 seconds the next year. The Yacht Club society sent him to world competition in Austria in 1888 and he easily won first place, outdistancing his next rival by 17 seconds. Panshin's thirst for competition took him to many other tournaments, all of which he won, including the famous match in January 1889, where he defeated an American champion named Joe Donahue for the world title in Amsterdam. Donahue, ten years younger than Panshin, challenged Panshin to a rematch a few weeks later in Vienna. But Panshin won again and then returned home to win the Russian national title that same year. Over a distance of three versts he defeated the second place finisher, Sergei Puresev, a young physician from Moscow. Panshin was also the Russian national figure skating champion for four years, 1897–1900.

Nikolai Alexandrovich Panin-Kolomenkin was his successor as national title holder in 1901. Panin became Russia's only pre-revolutionary gold medalist in Olympic competition when he won the special figures event in ice skating at the London Games of 1908.

The Russian skater surprised the world skating enthusiasts when he defeated the perennial world champion figure skater from Sweden, Ulrich Salchow, who came to St. Petersburg in February 1908 to challenge for the cup named in honour of Panshin. Although the match included six skaters, in essence it was a contest between Panin and the Swede. Panin's unexpected victory in the special figures so upset Salchow that, despite winning the free figures, he performed poorly in the compulsory part of the contest and all five judges placed him second to Panin.

When controversy erupted in this sport public attention was heightened considerably. The much heralded rematch was held at the London Olympic Games in the autumn. A Viennese newspaper reported that 'Mr. Salchow has every reason to be worried about the outcome, having such a formidable competitor as Mr. Panin.' Londoners too were conscious of the rivalry as *The Times* reported that Panin's arrival 'is eagerly expected as he took upon himself to defeat no less a person than Mr. Salchow...last winter'.[71] The Olympic officials divided the figure contests into two separate events – compulsory and free figures in one event, and special figures in the other; Salchow and Panin registered for both events.

Russian accounts, including Panin's own recollections, relate the story on 10 October. According to Panin, throughout his compulsory performance Salchow tried to unnerve him by a barrage of verbal assaults that elicited a protest from the Russian team. When the results were unfavourable to Panin the supporters of the Russian skater issued a second protest. Neither was accepted. Panin later wrote that

> the composition of the judges was unfavourable for me since among them were two Swedes, a personal friend of Salchow named Hugel from Austria, and Wendt from Germany and Sanders from Russia – in all, five judges. Wendt and Sanders gave me first place in the compulsory figures, the Swede, Grenander, gave me second place, nine points lower than Salchow and twenty-three points above the Swede, Per Thoren, who gained third place in the compulsory part of the match. But the remaining judges, the Swede Herle and Salchow's friend Hugel, gave me fourth place. They fulfilled their task of ruining me since by the rules of that time, victory was decided by the least number of place points.[72]

Panin refused the second-place honour and withdrew from the remaining free figures part of this event, allegedly because of an illness but in fact out of protest. Later a group of Swedes, including judges, sent a written apology to Panin for the 'unworthy conduct of Salchow'.[73]

When Panin competed in the special figures contest the following day, Salchow decided not to compete. His claim of illness did not prevent him from completing the free figures later the same day to win the gold medal in the first event. *The Times* had reported a week earlier that Salchow might decline to participate in the special figures contest, lending support to the Russian claim that he simply recognized Panin's superiority in this area.[74] Panin easily defeated the rest of the field to win the gold medal, the first for a Russian competitor in any Olympic contest. Panin was described by the London press as 'undoubtedly the best performer in the world at this form of skating.'[75] The *Official Report* of the British Olympic Committee recorded the Russian skater as 'far in advance of his opponents, both in the difficulty of his figures and the ease and accuracy of their execution; he cut the ice in a series of the most perfect intaglios with almost mathematical precision'.[76]

The Russian press related even less of the story. The principal newspaper in Moscow, *Moskovskie Vedomosti*, did not yet have a sports column and the gold medal victory of Panin went unreported in the *Russkie Vedomosti* of St. Petersburg. *The New York Times* did not report the contests in figure skating, and while popular sporting magazines such as *The Outing* of New York and *Bailey Magazine* of London carried articles on the London Games, nothing was reported on the ice skating events. Other newspapers in St. Petersburg contained only very short summaries of the Olympic results, including Russia's first gold medal. *Novoe Vremia* did mention the unfavourable composition of the judging panel, and *Rech* mentioned that Panin retired 'without a place' from the compulsory free figures competition with no reference to his illness or protest.[77] A small item in *Rech* ten days later suggests some foundation for the controversy when, in describing the post-Olympic winter Games in Berlin, the article says that, 'Regrettably, the victor of the special figures in London, the St. Petersburg resident, Nikolai Panin, did not participate at Berlin.'[78] Perhaps Panin wished to avoid a repetition of the unpleasant contest with Salchow, who then took the skating honours in Germany. One Russian sportswriter was forthright four years later when, discussing Russia's undistinguished results at the Stockholm Games, he accused the Swedish judges of favouritism toward their own athletes and wrote that biased judging against Russian athletes was not unusual.[79] Albeit belatedly, perhaps national pride was piqued by the Panin–Salchow affair.

Panin is the subject of another dispute. Without exception, Soviet sport historians referred to the upper class domination of sports in the pre-revolutionary era. As in all countries, working-class athletes had hurdles to overcome but in the West somewhat greater leisure time in maturing industrial societies enabled workers to become more active in athletics by the turn of the century. By contrast, Russia's industrial movement was barely in its infancy. Notwithstanding the long hours, some Russian industrial managers introduced western-style sports for their workers. There is some indication that elitism and class discrimination were less noticeable in winter sports.[80] Never-theless, Panin related that disdain and mockery of sporting activities was so common among his university friends that he decided to 'hide his family name and take a pseudonym', a not uncommon practice for many athletes. Hence Nikolai Kolo-menkin became Nikolai Panin.[81]

Although Panin's class origins are uncertain, he may have come from a common background. He was born in the village of Khrenova in the Voronezh region in 1872 and is often mentioned in Soviet accounts as one who overcame deplorable conditions of life to achieve fame for the Russian people, despite the absence of physical training for commoners. He is referred to as part of 'only a rare few, the most gifted ones who came from the people', or as 'one of the self-made men whose shining successes were achieved only thanks to their own persistence'.[82]

Nevertheless, doubt remains about his alleged humble origins. His family ties enabled him, for example, to use the privileged facilities at the Yusupov Garden skating fields.[83] While wrestler Ivan Poddubnii was referred to as the 'Poltava farmer' and Ivan Zaikin was called the 'Volga freight loader', such a common occupation was never attributed to Panin. He even became a teacher in the department of physical chemistry at the University of St. Petersburg.[84] It is noted that he was, for many years, one of the premier pistol shooters of the Russian nation. After his victory in London in 1908, Panin went to Paris where he won several medals in shooting matches before returning home to St. Petersburg. Four years later he was a member of the Olympic shooting team at Stockholm. He finished eighth out of 54 in the individual competition with revolver and pistol at a distance of 60 metres. This time he was identified in the official records by the name 'Nikolai de Kolomenkin.'[85] Not only did he revert to his earlier last name but the addition of 'de' indicates that he was regarded among the privileged class. Ten times Panin-Kolomenkin won the national pistol shooting title. Shooting, like tennis, yachting and fencing, were regarded as aristocratic sports and shooters were long restricted to officers and gentry.[86]

But there is more to question his humble status. A well-rounded athlete, Panin excelled at tennis and football, he was a first class oarsman and yachtsman, and one learns that he even participated in skiing matches and was a member of an ice hockey team in St. Petersburg. One wonders how a working-class fellow could acquire such a wealth of leisure time! Certainty eludes but Panin does not appear to be a hero of the toiling masses.

Controversy also featured in the early history of speed skating. Before he became a figure skater, Alexander Panshin won the world speed skating title at Amsterdam in the winter of 1888–89. There he outperformed the best world skaters from Norway, America, Austria and Holland.[87] He won this title several more times before yielding to his own countrymen: Nikolai Sedov, Nikolai V. Strunnikov and Vasily Ippolitov. Sedov was European and unofficial world champion in 1909.[88] His successor was the most famous speed skater the Russians produced. Strunnikov, called by the Swedes the 'Slavic Marvel', won the European and world title in 1910 and again in 1911. He set the world record for 5,000 metres in a time of 8 minutes, 37 and one-fifth seconds, beating by two-thirds of a second the former record of Jean Eden of Holland in 1894. His speed was such that his record would stand for the next 17 years.[89] He was one of the most celebrated figures in the history of Russian sport. When *Russkii Sport* featured an article and photograph on the Russian ice hockey team from the Moscow Sokol society, only Strunnikov was identified in the caption.[90]

In a story that appeared in virtually all Soviet accounts, when Strunnikov wished to defend his title abroad in 1912 the Sokol society in St. Petersburg would not fund his trip and so he retired from competition in anger.[91] In fact, the society did provide money for his trip but it was insufficient for him to bring an aide to Austria. At that point amateur sportsmen in Moscow and in St. Petersburg raised the additional sums but not before Strunnikov declined to go.[92] Despite this disappointment *Russkii Sport* lauded him for having achieved 'great success for Russian athletes abroad and for the glory of Russia's name', at a time when physical culture was considered a 'stepmother' to Russia.[93] Regretting the incident one writer to *Russkii Sport* concluded discussion of the incident with the phrase: 'Sic transit gloria'.[94] But this was not quite the case since within a year the Sokol society sponsored national ice skating races named after Strunnikov.[95] The winner was Ippolitov, the Russian skater who won the European championships a few weeks later.

Apart from skating Russian athletes had a great reputation in the field of wrestling. Although several Russian wrestlers won Olympic medals in London and Stockholm, Russians might have done better were it not for the fact that many of them had already become professional, like Ivan Poddubnii, a former longshore-man in Feodosy, P.M. Shmarkovskii, and Georgi Hakkenschmidt who finished his career in England. *Russkii Sport* referred to the professionalization of wrestling as a bitter experience for the Russian land.[96] Reputedly, Russia's best amateur wrestler, Rudnev of St. Petersburg, was not entered in 1912 because of his inexperience.[97] Max Klein, who won the silver medal in Stockholm, had to compete in a marathon-like match that lasted eleven hours in the sun before he finally won. So exhausted was he that he declined to participate in the title match that might have given him the gold medal.[98]

Meanwhile, Russian weightlifters like N.E. Lange, Shemiakin, a world champion, and Kulakov were all famous but there were no Olympic events for this sport. Neither was speed skating an Olympic event at Stockholm. What is more, early in 1910 merely sixteenth months after the Russian gold medal triumph in London, figure skating was dropped from the programme at Stockholm despite the pleas of the Italian and Russian delegations at the International Olympic Committee meetings.[99] Winter sports were ruled out in order to minimize the natural advantages granted the more northerly nations. On 30 March the Russians formally proposed the addition of weightlifting but the majority of the delegates dismissed the suggestion owing to the supposed professional character of that sport.[100] Hence, most of the sports in which Russians excelled were not included on the programme for the Stockholm games of 1912. In wrestling, of course, the Russians did win a silver medal although one writer to *Russkii Sport* complained that the selection committee overlooked the nation's best wrestlers, especially those from Odessa.[101] Some critics of the Russian Olympic squad suggested that Russian success in heavy athletics and in wrestling was natural for the powerful physique of the Slav. Likewise, failure in light athletics could be traced to natural Slavic laziness and lack of persistence which could be overcome by the sophisticated special training employed by the Finns, for example.[102]

Finally, it should be noted that if the final medal standings indicate a low ranking for the Russian team, the results should not have been shocking. During the previous winter Dupperron was lamenting the low state of physical development in Russia and complained about the abysmal knowledge of gymnastics among his countrymen. At one point he exclaimed: 'Can anyone imagine that the English think of football as gymnastics?'[103] On the eve of the games *Novoe Vremia* frankly and soberly assessed the chances of the Russian athletes.[104] The soccer team was riddled with dissension; track and field stars were woefully behind the best abroad; there were no prospects in either the pentathlon or fencing. Hope was entertained in tennis, yachting and shooting, although marksmen were severely handicapped by old-style guns and bullets.

In addition to medalists in yachting, rowing, wrestling and shooting, 29 Russian athletes won special diplomas of merit in six different sports.[105] Such performances just fell short of medals. In this respect the Russian team was placed fifth. Other athletes came close to medals. The four-man pistol shooting team which competed at the 50-metre distance took fourth place. Russian horse jumpers, according to the *Official Report*, were 'excellent jumpers who seemed to suffer from the severe system of training employed and which was carried on until the very last moment and for which the heat-hardened training courses were probably not quite suitable'.[106]

Following the Games Dupperron argued that the Olympic results should not strongly offend national pride since Russia's athletes had performed honourably at the Games, adhering to the maxim: 'may the best man win'. How unlike, he argued, the conduct of those other athletes who were guided by the principle that one must 'win at any cost'.[107] *Novoe Vremia* was more explicit, citing the shameful example of biased officiating by the Swedish judges who favoured their own athletes.[108]

Viewed in these respects, the Russian experience at Stockholm should not be regarded as a kind of sporting disaster, notwithstanding the fact that the whole concept of national rankings was contrary to the spirit of the principles laid down by the founder of the modern Games, Pierre de Coubertin. Hence, neither on the level of organization, nor achievement was the sports picture under the last tsar as dismal as Soviet accounts have led us to believe. If the European sports movement constitutes one segment of modernization then the sports phenomenon in early twentieth-century Russia would indicate a not so modest measure of social development and genuine cause for national pride.

NOTES

1. Eugen Weber, 'Gymnastics and Sports in Fin-de-Siècle France: Opium of the Masses?', *American Historical Review*, LXXVI, 1 (Feb. 1971), 70–99.
2. Bernard Jeu, 'What is Sport?', Reprint, *Diogenes 80*, translated by R. Blohm (1980), pp.150–4.
3. Allen Guttmann, *From Ritual to Record: The Nature of Modern Sports* (New York, 1978), p.16.
4. Guttmann, p.16ff.
5. V.V. Stolbov and I.G. Chudinov, *Istoriia fizicheskoi kultury* (Moscow, 1962), pp.79–84.
6. Stolbov and Chudinov, p.84.
7. N.F. Kulinko, *Istoriia i organizatsiia fizicheskoi kultury* (Moscow, 1982), p.78. See also V.V. Stolbov, *Istoriia i organizatsiia fizicheskoi kultury i sporta* (Moscow, 1982), p.64.
8. Kulinko, p.78; Stolbov, p.64.
9. Kulinko, p.84; Stolbov, p.67.
10. Mikhail Lukashev, 'Grenadier Pyotr I', *Fizkultura i sport*, 5 (1972), pp.36–9.
11. Kulinko, p.82.
12. This list, slightly amended by the present writer, is taken from J.W. Riordan, 'The Development of Football in Russia and the USSR; Part I', *New Zealand Slavonic Journal*, IX (Winter 1972), 67.
13. S.L. Akselrod *et al.*, *Fizicheskaya kultura i sport v SSSR* (Moscow, 1957), p.288.
14. This list, amended and augmented by the present writer, is taken from Riordan, 'Football', p.65.
15. Henry Morton, *Soviet Sport* (New York, 1961), pp.157–8.
16. *Entsiklopedicheskii slovar po fizicheskoi kulture i sportu v 3 tomakh* (Moscow, 1961–63), I, 331; also Akselrod *et al.*, p.10.
17. See John D. Windhausen, 'Russia's First Olympic Victor', *Journal of Sport History*, III, 1 (1976), 35–45.
18. *Russkii Sport*, 1 Jan. 1912 (15 January new style), p.4.
19. Stolbov and Chudinov, p.113; also Kulinko, pp.101–2; also V.I. Kizchenko, 'Z istorii rozvitku sportu na Ukraini', *Ukrain'skii ist. zhurnal*, No. 7 (1980), p.94.
20. Stolbov, p.95.
21. Akselrod *et al.*, p.288.
22. Yuri Lukashin, 'Futbol v Rossii', *Sportivnaya zhizn Rossii*, No. 6 (1973), p.20; *Entsiklopedicheskii*,II, 274. The game was played between societies 'Sport' and 'The St. Petersburg Society of Sportsmen', although as early as 1878 the Odessa British Athletic Club demonstrated the game. See Kizchenko, p.98.
23. Vasily Trofimov, 'Khokkei', *Sportivnaya Zhizn Rossii*, 3 (1973), 17.
24. *Entsiklopedicheskii*, I, 92.
25. *Entsiklopedicheskii*, III, 118.
26. *Entsiklopedicheskii*, II, 97.
27. Stolbov, p.95.
28. *Entsiklopedichesikii*, I, 274.
29. Trofimov, p.17.
30. *Entsiklopedicheskii*, I, 222.
31. Akselrod *et al.*, p.242; Stolbov and Chudinov, p.123.
32. *Entsiklopedicheskii*, II, 145.
33. Akselrod *et al.*, p.222; *Russkii Sport*, 6 March 1911 (20 March , new style), pp.5–6.

34. F.A.M. Webster, P.A.S.I., *The Evolution of the Olympic Games, 1829 B.C.—1914 A.D.* (London, 1914), p.180.
35. *Olympic Review*, 84 (Oct. 1974), 558.
36. Ibid.
37. Ibid.
38. Webster, p.195.
39. Theodore Andrea Cook (ed.), *The Fourth Olympiad: Being the Official Report of the Olympic Games of 1908* (London, 1909), p.656. This report mentions eight Russian contestants but lists the names of only seven.
40. Erik Bergvall (ed.), *The Fifth Olympiad: The Official Report of the Olympic Games of Stockholm, 1912*, translated by Edward Adams-Ray, Swedish Olympic Committee (Stockholm, 1913), p.889.
41. *Novoe Vremia*, 13 June (26 June, new style) 1912, 5.
42. *Russkii Sport*, 25 Feb. (9 March, new style), 5.
43. The information about German and Norwegian public support for athletes comes from the respective papers of Arnd Krüger, 'On the Origin of the Notion That Sport Serves as a Vehicle for National Representation', and Matti Goksøyr, 'International Sport in the Twentieth Century: A Norwegian Arena for National Assertion', both delivered at the History of European Ideas conference in Leuven, Belgium, 6 Sept. 1990.
44. Bergvall (ed.), *The Fifth Olympiad*, pp.256-7.
45. Ibid., pp.970-1.
46. Ibid., p.165.
47. *Russkii Sport*, 10 March (23 March, new style) 1912, 5.
48. *Russkii Sport*, 10 March (23 March, new style) 1912, 5, and 3 June (16 June new style) 1912, 5.
49. Bergvall (ed.), pp.266-7.
50. Ibid., p.272.
51. Ibid., p.995.
52. *Revue Olympique* (July 1914), 103, 2nd Series, 104.
53. Kulinko, *Istoriia I organizatsiia*, p.103.
54. Stolbov and Chudinov, pp.121-2.
55. *Olympic Review*, 84 (Oct. 1974), 559.
56. *The Times* (London), 19 March 1912, 15. Nationalistic promotion by the host city is explored in a recent discussion of 'Cultural Chauvinism and the Olympiads of East Asia' by James L. McClain in *The International Journal of the History of Sport* , 7, 3 (Dec.1990), 388-404.
57. Kulinko, p.102; Akselrod *et al.*, p.113; Stolbov and Chudinov, p.113. The story of Kesiur is told in Kizchenko, p.99.
58. Akselrod *et al.*, pp.10 and 302; see also *Entsi-klopedicheskii*,I, 331; and Kizchenko, p.102.
59. Riordan, p.69.
60. Akselrod, p.288.
61. Mikhail Lukashev, 'Pervoi champion Rossii', *Fizkultura i sport*, 3 (1974), 347.
62. V. Kudriatsev, 'Championka staroi rossii–sportsmenkam novoi strani', *Sportivnaya zhizn Rossii*, XIII, No. 1, 3-4.
63. Akselrod *et al.*, p.169.
64. Kizchenko, pp.101-2. The pages of *Russkii Sport* during the years 1910-1912 frequently featured articles on this sport.
65. Bergvall (ed.), p.675.
66. Anatoly Yusin, 'Instead of an Introduction', *Vek rossiiskikh skorohodov*, ed. L.V. Rossoshik (Moscow: Fizkultura i sport, 1990), pp.6-7.
67. Ibid. p.8.
68. Ibid., p.9.
69. Ibid., p.10.
70. Kradman and Kharabuga, p.47.
71. *The Times* (London), 24 Oct. 1908, 18.
72. B. Chesnokov, 'Pervoe zoloto Rossii', *Sportivnaia zhizn Rossii*, XII, 10 (1968), 32.

73. Ibid.
74. *The Times* (London), 24 Oct. 1908, 18.
75. *The Times* (London), 30 Oct. 1908, 5.
76. The British Olympic Association, *The Fourth Olympiad: Being the Official Report of the Olympic Games of 1908*, drawn up by Andrea Cook (London, 1909), p.292.
77. *Novoe Vremia*, 31 October (13 Nov., new style) 1908, 5; *Rech*, 25 Oct. (7 Nov., new style) 1908, 6.
78. *Rech*, 4 Nov. (17 Nov., new style) 1908, 6.
79. *Novoe Vremia*, 17 July (30 July, new style) 1912, 6.
80. J.W. Riordan, 'The Development of Football in Russia and the USSR', Part I, *New Zealand Slavonic Journal*, IX (Winter 1972), 66–7.
81. Yusin, p.10.
82. *Entsiklopedicheskii slovar po fizicheskoi kultura i sportu* (Moscow, 1961), I, 331; S.L. Akselrod *et al.*, *Fizicheskaia kultura i sport v SSSR* (Moscow, 1957), p.10.
83. Yusin, p.11.
84. L. Gorionov, 'Dorozhite sportivnoi chestiu Rossii', *Sportivnaia Zhizn Rossii*, XVI , 11 (1972), 33–4.
85. Bergvall, p.919.
86. *Entsiklopedicheskii slovar*, III, 117.
87. Vitaly Vasilievich Stolbov, *Istoriia fizicheskoi kultury* (Moscow, 1989), p.113.
88. Stolbov and Chudinov, p.119.
89. Ibid.
90. *Russkii Sport*, 1 Jan. 1912 (15 Jan., new style), 1.
91. See Stolbov and Chudinov, p.119; and Kradman and Kharabuga, p. 75; and Akselrod *et al.*, p.195.
92. *Russkii Sport*, 12 Jan. 1912 (25 Jan., new style), p.12; and 22 Jan. 1912 (3 Feb., new style), 15.
93. *Russkii Sport*, 13 Feb. (27 Feb., new style) 1911, 5–6.
94. *Russkii Sport*, 22 Jan. (5 Feb., new style) 1912, 15.
95. *Russkii Sport*, 15 Jan. (29 Jan., new style) 1912, 15.
96. *Russkii Sport*, 13 Feb. (27 Feb., new style) 1911, 5.
97. *Novoe Vremia*, 4 June (17 June, new style) 1912, 5.
98. Bergvall (ed.), p.763.
99. Ibid., pp.53–4, 60.
100. Ibid., p.60.
101. *Russkii Sport*, 29 July (11 Aug., new style) 1912, 6.
102. *Russkii Sport*, 3 June (16 June, new style) 1912, 5. The author, Ludwig Chaplinsky, was the leader of the Russian wrestling team at Stockholm.
103. *Russkii Sport*, 20 Feb. (5 March, new style) 1912, 3.
104. *Novoe Vremia*, 13 June (26 June, new style) 1912, 5; and 14 June (27 June, new style) 1912, 5.
105. Bergvall (ed.), p.888.
106. Ibid., p.601.
107. *Russkii Sport*, 8 July (21 July, new style) 1912, 1–2; and 15 July (28 July, new style) 1912, 6.
108. *Novoe Vremia*, 17 July (30 July, new style) 1912.

'Buying Victories is Positively Degrading' European Origins of Government Pursuit of National Prestige through Sport

ARND KRÜGER

The following essay examines the origin of the idea that elite sports serve the purpose of national or political representation. Although, like so many other things, this concept can be seen to some extent in Greek antiquity,[1] this piece will study modern sports. Betts claimed that 'by 1920 sport had become associated in the minds of millions of Americans, with local and national prestige and with democratic society',[2] yet not until the *Amateur Sports Act* of 1978 did the American government and Congress provide money to enhance this prestige.[3] This underlines the problem of associating 'in the minds of millions' with political action. As it was not until 1935 that public opinion surveys were used in the context of sport,[4] it seems all the more necessary to look for concrete events which demonstrate that there was not only talk about national representation through sports, but also action.

This study will therefore try to find 'hard' evidence that the idea of national prestige through elite sports was publicly accepted and that something was done about increasing or maintaining such prestige. Very little was done to prepare American teams for international events by national bodies even after 1952 when competition against the Soviet Union was connected with such prestige, as it was supposed to be the touchstone for the efficacy of the socio-economic system.[5] The costs of sending the team abroad were met by the member organizations of the US Olympic Committee, the revenue of the Olympic trial meets and public appeals. Although state and local authorities did invest heavily in sporting activity, this essay will concentrate on national support for international representation, an area in which the United States has almost invariably been isolationist, caring very little about international sports.[6] The former Soviet Union used the sports system effectively to show off its strength and relied heavily on state funds to do so,[7] but it was not the first.

In the case of the former Eastern Block one can also see the absurdity of the claim that there is a positive correlation between the national strength and efficacy of a political or socio-economic system and the outcome of athletic contests such as the Olympic Games, since the system collapsed after the greatest athletic successes.[8]

In the minds of many, the Olympic Games of 1936 stand out as a major event used by a government and a political party to enhance national prestige through sport.[9] The Nazi government invested heavily in staging the Games, improved the infrastructure of Berlin and created the first Olympic Games as a mass spectacle; it was transmitted by radio worldwide and more than tripled the previous spectator record for an Olympic Games. Over three million attended the various venues of the Nazi Olympics while the Los Angeles Games of 1932 had been celebrated as the first to have more than one million spectators.

When discussing the question of state sponsorship of elite sports, the Nazi Olympics of 1936 are a favourite choice. The German organizers, however, wanted to demonstrate organizational power first and athletic power only second.[10] Hitler himself had intimated the importance of being an impressive host in order to curry favour from world public opinion.[11] This made perfect sense, as the United States had so completely dominated the Games in Los Angeles, winning more than half of all possible medals, while Germany had been placed only seventh. No one, therefore, could reasonably expect Germany to finish in first place in 1936, as it eventually did. As Germany had been second in the unofficial national scoring table in 1928, however, second place at home could have been anticipated – a tremendous improvement for which the new government could take due credit. Hitler knew very little about sport and dealt more with the organizers of the Games than with coaches and sport directors; hence little is known of his personal ambitions as far as the German team is concerned. He was, however, an ardent fan who could not get enough of rooting for German victories in the stadium.[12]

In preparing the athletes for national representation several new elements were introduced, which were partly the realization of what had previously been planned for 1916, partly adopted from fascist Italy, and partly put forward by capable athletic organizers keen to co-operate with the new regime, as it seemed to fulfil all of their dreams.[13] The German elite sports system was to some extent a copy of the Italian fascist system which gave athletes substantial support to demonstrate to the Italian population and to the world the strength of fascist Italy.[14] The results were second place in the 1932 Olympics for the 'Mussolini Boys' and winning the Soccer World Cup in 1934 and 1938. The Italian fascist government's financial support for sport in the interests of national representation was, however, not the first example of such support.

National prestige through elite sports requires international competition in which to demonstrate superiority. Although some international championships took place prior to the revival of the Olympic Games in 1896,[15] they were not structured in such a way as to enhance national reputation.

The first international bids for national prestige – other than fighting wars – were the international exhibitions. The first World Exhibition took place in London 1851, and there were others in: Paris 1855, 1867, 1878, 1889, 1900; Vienna 1873; Philadelphia 1876; Sydney 1879; Melbourne 1880, 1888; Chicago 1893; Brussels 1897, 1910; Saint Louis 1904; Liège 1905; Milan 1906; Turin 1911; Gent 1913; and San Francisco 1915. St. Louis (1904) had the largest site, Paris (1900) the most spectators,[16] both incorporated Olympic Games as a demonstration of the world's best performances in sport, human athletic performance, just as they tried to assemble many other outstanding achievements in other fields.[17] In other sections of the exhibitions other records were attempted, such as the construction of the largest glass building, the highest tower, and so forth. This was the age of breaking records for national prestige.[18] The Berlin conference laid down the conditions under which these exhibitions were to take place, how they were to be classified (as 'world' or 'regional' expositions), and established rules and tax exemptions, and so on. As international sporting competitions were codified, so were the expositions.[19] John Astley Cooper,[20] Coubertin's immediate predecessor in reviving the Olympic Games, had seen the connection between the Games and international expositions, and Coubertin took advantage of the opportunity this presented. He had planned the first Olympic Games for the year 1900 in connection with the Paris World Exhibition – Athens had already applied for 1896.[21] Although, for Coubertin, the individual athlete was at the centre of sport, the victory ceremonies which he invented, with flags and hymns, indulged the nationalistic sentiments of the time.[22]

We shall not go into the costs of staging international exhibitions or championships as a measure of organizational ability and hospitality, although investing more in international championships than can be recouped from spectators could be defined as a key element when estimating prestige value. The construction of the stadium and staging of the first modern Olympic Games in Athens are one of the first such cases in sport.[23] The Olympic stadium of 1912 was purpose built, introducing a new element in the pursuit of international prestige.

The Olympic Games of 1916

The Olympic Games of 1916 were supposed to have taken place in Berlin. While Germany had not done too well in the previous Games, it placed only fifth or sixth,[24] it hoped to do better in Berlin. The German government had previously given a small subsidy to its Olympic squad: in 1896 from the Emperor himself; and in 1900 and 1904 as part of the World Exhibition funds. In 1906 and 1908 the German Empire paid 12,000 Marks each from the disposition fund of the Secretary of the Interior and in 1912 gave 25,000

Marks to equip and send the squad.[25] Yet the teams' preparation had been entirely financed by the athletes themselves or their clubs.

I have suggested elsewhere[26] that Franco-German rivalry had been responsible for the German government's decision to increase its funding in preparing for the 1916 Olympics. Now that the archives of the former GDR are fully available for research[27] it is clear that this Franco-German competition was only marginally important, while the rivalry with Great Britain was crucial. This can be traced back to the British–American controversy during and after the 1908 Olympic Games in London, in which even President Roosevelt became involved.[28] While the British public had taken its domination of amateur sports, and athletics in particular, for granted, the US team had fought a tremendous battle (see Table 1). It later emerged that the American system for selecting and developing talent was much superior to the British one, and that 'it is not necessary for the American Olympic Committee to 'create' an interest in athletics as it already exists.'[29]

TABLE 1

MEDALS AT THE 1908 OLYMPICS IN LONDON

Rank	Country	Gold	Silver	Bronze	Male Participants	Female
1	UK	56	48	37	676	34
2	US	23	12	11	121	–
3	Sweden	7	5	10	154	2
4	France	5	5	9	220	–
7	Germany	2	4	4	81	–

In 1912 the Swedish team performed even better at home than the United Kingdom and the United States (Table 2), thus creating considerable concern in Britain about national strength, as the Stockholm Olympics were considered a British defeat.[30] This resulted in the concentration of the British Olympic Committee in a much smaller and more effective *Special Committee* in 1912 at the suggestion of Sir Arthur Conan Doyle.

TABLE 2

MEDALS AT THE 1912 OLYMPICS IN STOCKHOLM

Rank	Country	Gold	Silver	Bronze	Male Participants	Female
1	Sweden	24	24	17	459	23
2	US	24	19	19	121	–
3	UK	10	15	16	283	10
5	France	8	5	3	100	2
6	Germany	5	13	7	180	5

The dramatic result of the national defeat in Stockholm was the committee's appeal, in August 1913, for £100,000 to fund the preparations of the 1916 Olympic team. This was immediately taken up by *The Times* which did not only subscribe an instant £500, but supported the appeal with an editorial and offered to publish the donations. The committee considered Stockholm 'a national disaster'. 'The appeal for funds is made in order that every possible care may be taken to avoid a similar misfortune happening in Berlin.'[31]

For *The Times* the argument was very simple:

> There is also the consideration that the national reputation is more deeply involved than perhaps we care to recognize in the demonstration of our ability to hold our own against other nations in the Olympic contests... Whether we took the results very seriously ourselves or not, it was widely advertised in other countries as evidence of England's 'decadence'.[32]

The purpose of the 'Appeal for National Subscription' was the 'discovery of new athletic talent' which 'will necessitate careful and elaborate organization'. This was done with two aims: '(1) the worthy representation of Great Britain, (2) the improvement of national physique'. The team of 1912 was remembered in this respect as one which was 'quite unable to do justice either to themselves or to their country *owing to the lack of sufficient funds* [emphasis added]... The money available was quite inadequate for the purpose of finding out our best men, or giving them real preparation or even caring for them properly in Sweden.' It was therefore considered 'a national duty to provide funds'.[33]

While the first reaction was very favourable – the Duke of Westminster and Lord Northcliffe each donated £1000 immediately[34] – the appeal did result in a major discussion about whether a sporting event was so important. In letters to the editor of *The Times* Frederic Harrison and Newill Smith pointed out that 'the newpaper advertisement and the £100,000 fund for buying victories are positively degrading...We are not a nation of pot hunters'.

In another editorial, *The Times* accepted the point, but argued that:

> ...our national reputation as well as our national pride make that [the success at the Olympic Games] an object of real importance ... Lord Grey, Lord Harris, Lord Roberts, Lord Rothschild, Lord Stathcona, and the Duke of Westminster are sober and responsible men ... We believe that the prestige is worth recovering ... without undue glorification of athleticism ... The hope expressed by the king that every effort will be made to ensure that the United Kingdom is

represented by its best athletes in the forthcoming Olympic Games ...
Victory, as he says, means efficient organization and training, and both
cost money.[35]

'National efficiency' was the watchword of the day. The government had set
up a commitee to review the question of racial deterioration. The British
were particularly anxious about Germany's economic penetration and its
growing naval strength. In this situation sport was seen ambivalently as a
means of increasing and at the same time testing national strength. It could
boost national morale in case of victory, but in defeat bear out the
decadence everybody was talking about. This was the time when Social
Darwinism determined much political thinking.[36]

In another letter to the editor of *The Times*, Sidney Abrahams, who had
participated in the Stockholm Olympics, pointed out that '...for the
foreigner the Olympic games have become a national affair ... To Sweden
the games were a great historical and patriotic event uniting every branch of
that people with a strong band of enthusiasm.'[37] Like many others, therefore,
he supported the fund.

Although the appeal of the King on behalf of the fund may be considered
as good as government funding,[38] it is obvious from the whole discussion
that this was a private appeal for public support and that no government
money at all was expected or even involved in the selection, preparation and
sending of the team to Berlin. £100,000 was an enormous sum. The
committee had at first estimated the necessary costs at £40,000, but when it
launched the appeal it chose the much larger sum.

By the end of 1913 the special committee dissolved itself as it had not
reached its target of £25,000 for the first year. It had, however, received
£10,664 of which £2,335 was in conditional pledges.[39] The first full list
published by the fund, by then called the 'Duke of Westminster Fund', as
the Duke acknowledged all the receipts, contained only 241 donors who
after one month had given a total of £7,000.[40] It included one of the first
examples of industrial sponsorship as Richard Burbridge subscribed £100
per year for four years for Harrods 'under the condition that no fewer than
ten other firms in the United Kingdom will do the same'.[41]

The public discussion about the value of financial support for amateur
sport was being dealt with at great length. The British Rowing Association
'officially declined to be associated with the fund'.[42] It also pointed out 'the
fact that under Amateur Rowing Association rules oarsmen are no longer
amateurs if their expenses are paid by funds raised outside of their own
rowing clubs'[43] – which was in fact what the British Olympic Association
was intending to do with the money collected. The British IOC member
Theodore Cook responded that 'I am unable to understand an attitude which

apparently desires ... that those privileges enjoyed as a matter of course by all Public School and University men should not be given to anybody else...'[44] This discussion led *The Times* to editorialize about the value of professional sports:

> Men are apt to speak about 'the taint of professionalism' as if professionalism were one of the deadly sins. Yet if we think of the professionals that we know – in golf cricket, rackets, tennis and practically every other form of sport – we realize at once that they are deservedly one of the most respected classes in the community ... The Olympic authorities are fully aware of the dangers of veiled professionalism, and that true professionalism in practically every branch of sport is one of the most satisfactory and characteristic features in athletic life of the nation.[45]

At a time of the general discussion about the value of the Empire, it was also argued from an Australian that an Empire team should compete in the next Games and that Australians should add to the fund as it would 'have an appreciable influence in deepening the growing sense of Imperialism among our farflung people'.[46] This discussion eventually supported the creation of separate Empire Games in which every colony had the chance to compete against the home country on equal terms.[47]

The public discussion, particularly in *The Times*, gave space to every argument for and against national representation through sport. A wide variety of opinions was voiced which can be heard today as well:

> If our country is represented by its best men and those men are afforded every facility to do their best for their country, however unpleasant defeat might be, it would not be humiliating.[48] Competition of this character under the conditions which obtain should play no part in securing national fame. They are a false standard of national efficiency. Success in the Olympic games proves little but that the youth of one nation has devoted more time to unproductive effort than the youth of another.[49]

The major consequence of the *Appeal* seems to have been the hiring of the first ever full time national coach in British athletics. The Canadian Walter R. Knox received a three-year contract in 1914. As the next British national coaches in athletics were hired almost fifty years later, this fact has been more or less forgotten.[50]

The situation in Germany was different. It was a union of different states of which Prussia was the largest and it also contained rich cities which did a lot for sports.[51] Germany had been selected to stage the Olympic Games in Berlin. For this a new stadium was to be built which was, however, privately funded. Victor von Podbielski, a cavalry general and president of the prominent Berlin Union Club which owned most of Berlin race horse tracks, was president of the German Olympic Committee (DRAfOS) and offered to have the Olympic stadium built in a small valley in the middle of the Grunewald racetrack. The permanent DRAfOS, which was in the process of becoming the sports governing body for all bourgeois amateur sports, was to pay just the interest for the construction costs. For this it asked for subsidies from the Reich, the Prussian government and the city of Berlin. The upper half of the stands had to be temporary, as after the Olympics the spectators of the race track wished to see the opposite straight again.[52] The 'super stadium for super-Germans'[53] contained an unusually long (and thereby fast) 600 metre running track and even a 666.67 metre bicycle race track. It was opened by the German emperor himself, thus stressing the importance of sport.[54]

Von Podbielski asked the *Reichschancellor*, von Bethmann-Hollweg, in an indirect way for government support in that he wished to be 'entitled to stage the [Olympic] Games'. He received an immediate reply: 'I cannot empower you to start with the preparations for the Games, as this is entirely a *private affair* [emphasis added] ... considering the public importance, I am, however, willing to support the matter through commissioners ... and you should, therefore, contact the Secretaries of the Exterior and the Interior.'[55]

The responsible officer of the Secretary of the Interior (RMI), *Geheimer Oberregierungsrat* von Stein, acted immediately. He was quoted by the national press in the annual assembly of DRAfOS on the same day, saying that the *Herr Reichschancellor* considered the Olympic Games a national action of the first priority. 'Sweden, England and America are already preparing themselves for the Olympic Games. Germany should not fall behind.' He asked for immediate intense training under German coaches, and suggested that a 'special American coach' should be hired in the following year.[56]

At this assembly the member organizations were asked to quantify how much such preparation would cost above their regular annual expenses. Carl Diem, the secretary general of DRAfOS, added this up and arrived at a sum of between 300,000 and 350,000 Deutschmarks (M). This amount was to be used in 1913 for selection, in 1914 and 1915 for training and in 1916 for final selection and Olympic success. It included the salary of a national Olympic coach and of Diem himself as first full-time secretary of a German sports governing body. The justification for this was:

> we will be successful at the Olympic Games...it will also give such a strong impuls to all of our physical training that we will have a leading role in all future Olympic Games which will be the proof of our

physical abilities.[57]

As the budget for the following year had to be prepared by 10 June,[58] there was some hectic activity to do the necessary sums. Eventually von Stein produced the figures and wrote to the Emperor for approval:

> Germany has not had the position in these international championships which it should have had considering the ability of its youth ... We should do better as the *Deutsche Turnerschaft* has not taken part yet ... About the future developments I will keep you informed from time to time.[59]

The German emperor accepted the recommendation of M 200,000 from the Empire and another M 100,000 from Prussia, assuming that additional money would come from Bavaria and the other smaller German states. The crown prince accepted an invitation to be the patron of the Olympic Games. The financial agreement needed, however, parliamentary approval.

Before this approval was given by parliament the RMI granted M 14,000 for 1913 from their funds of immediate necessities, permitting Carl Diem[60], Martin Berner (a journalist), Walter v. Reichenau,[61] and Joseph Waitzer (national coach for track and field) to make a fact-finding tour to the United States in August and September 1913.[62] In a booklet, which was widely distributed, they recommended changes in the German system away from *Turnen* towards more specialization and sports.[63] It is obvious that they saw only what they wanted to see as sportsmen who were vigorously against *Turnen*.[64] The German *Turner* teachers[65] and the *Turner* federation reacted violently to this approach,[66] but not to the public money to be spent on them. Diem also hired the American coach (Dr) Alwin Kraenzlein. The fantastic salary of $50,000 (= £10,000 or M 200,000) over five years, allegedly stipulated in his contract, inflamed the public discussion about the feasibility of top level sports.[67]

Comparison with what the other countries were doing and their governments were paying did not take place in the German press. In the RMI, however, such a comparison was attempted to check how realistic the demands of the DRAfOS were. The desired £100,000 (= M 2,000,000) in Great Britain was so much out of proportion with the M 300,000 (= £15,000) of Germany that they were pleased to find out that the French sports authorities had asked from their parliament 400,000 francs (= £16,000 or M 320,000) and that Sweden had collected M 150,000 (= £7,500) in 1912.[68] Later Basil Zaharoff, owner of the French newspaper *Excelsior*, gave $100,000 to the French Olympic Committee to prepare the athletes for Berlin.[69]

The imperial government proposed to parliament M 200,000 for the budgets of 1914–16, starting with M 46,000 for 1914. This sum was explicitly for the committee to prepare the Games of 1916 and 'to show to the world coming to Berlin the beauty of the homeland in its industrial, economic, and military might'. It was claimed that it would be important 'to show the ability of the German youth as an eternal source of strength ... youth which is not afraid of anybody in the world'.[70] Various newspaper articles explained what was expected of German sports: '1916 we have to win!' For this Diem proposed a talent selection process among all men in compulsory military service and argued that

> what is taking place here on behalf of the Olympic Games is in the best interest of the army itself ... We are aware of the fact that we are not as much accepted abroad as we deserve. The knowledge of the importance of German economic life and industry, but also of Germany's military power has not spread fast enough. The Games of 1916 will be and are supposed to be a medium to convince the people of our worldwide importance.[71]

Martin Berner was even more direct:

> The Olympic Games are a war, a real war. You can be sure that many participants are willing to offer – without hesitation – several years of their life for a victory of the fatherland ... The Olympic idea of the modern era has given us a symbol of world war, which does not show its military character very openly, but – for those who can read sports statistics – it gives enough insight into world ranking.[72]

To lobby successfully for government support the DRAfOS had more than M 5,000 in its 1913 budget and used it.[73] Diem played an important role in this as he was one of the links between the Olympic Committee and the pre-military *Jungdeutschland Bund* (Young Germany Union), being the secretary of both and editing the publications of both. The *Jungdeutschland*, under the presidency of General Fieldmarshal von der Goltz, advocated youth training in *Turnen* and sport to make sure that a higher proportion of each age group passed the requirements for compulsorary military service. Von der Goltz's main motto was *Viel Feind, viel Ehr!* (Many enemies – much honour!).[74] In the *Jungdeutschland, Turnen* and sport co-operated for the first time, thus paving the way for their co-operation in DRAfOS. To have the *Turners* as part of the team for 1916 was considered the main prerequisite of doing far better than in 1912.

The budget commission of the Reichstag turned the request down, however.[75] This came as a general surprise as the government had a majority in the commission and in parliament. The argument of the commission was twofold: the government had committed contempt of parliament having already granted the M 14,000 without parliamentary approval in 1913 and the central government should not become involved with sports as this was in the field of culture, one of the few rights the German states had not given up to the central Reich.[76] Prussia could pay M 100,000 and see how much the other states would contribute. There was no need to hurry as the Olympic Games would not take place before 1916. It was also feared that if one such amount of money was granted for four years, the demands would not stop but continue annually thereafter.[77] In addition, the opposition Social Democrats, were against the grant anyway, as their workers' sports organizations would not receive a share. They did not participate in bour-geois international sports and were, therefore, formally excluded from the grant proposal.[78]

In the budget commission von Stein explained the distribution of the money: *Turnen* M 50,000, athletics M 40,000, weight sports M 20,000, cycling M 20,000, rowing M 20,000, swimming M 20,000, tennis M 10,000, football M 10,000 and the rest for the minor sports and the Olympic committee. M 14,000 in 1913, M 46,000 in 1914, M 70,000 in 1915, and again M 70,000 in 1916 was the distribution for the four years. He pointed out that the actual value of the sports movement was not the achievement of top performances but a rise in general interest and the standard of physical training.

The decision of the budget commission created a national sensation. It resulted in sports making the front page headlines in the German press for the first time. The *Turner* and sport press lobbied in favour of the money for the Olympic Games as they had made their plans to use the money.[79] Von Podbielski circulated a petition on behalf of the Olympic Committee claiming that the Olympic Games were a means of propaganda for national fitness to achieve a strong nation.[80] Diem and Kraenzlein went on a lecture tour through Germany to raise public interest and assure that the press took up the matter day after day.[81] The press generally argued on the following lines:

> Last year the Reichstag passed several resolutions asking for support of any measure which helped improve the fitness of our youth as the increase in the size of the imperial army makes this a national necessity ... All athletic endeavour goes hand in glove with the desire to improve the military preparedness of our country ... The withholding of these funds creates a similar impression to that of a host who orders the servants not to offer wine and food too often as the party would otherwise become too expensive.[82]

The public discussion resulted in a lengthy parliamentary debate over the benefit of the Olympic Games and elite sports in the full house. This debate was preceded by three resolutions to restitute the M 200,000[83] and by two members of parliament who interrupted their actual speech to add that they and their political friends were in favour of restituting the original M 200,000.[84] Although this was probably done to draw the attention of the press to the particular member of parliament, it did show that a heated debate would follow.

In the debate on 14 February 1914 it became obvious why the Social Democrats had opposed the bill. The money would be exclusively for the benefit of elite sports in the bourgeois sports organizations and would leave out labour sports, which had to suffer the random harassment of the authorities anyway.[85] As the money was supposed to be for the member organizations of the Olympic Committee, and the labour movement did not join this, it was obvious that they were left out. But even if they had joined, the standard of performance in the labour organizations was lower than that in most of the bourgeois organizations; as for the former, top performances were less important than class consciousness. Weight lifting and wrestling were the only exceptions. Only six months later the situation changed. With the beginning of the war, workers' sports joined in the general war effort for physical readiness. As the Olympic Games were a national affair, it is obvious that the candidates of the Danish minority in the north of Schleswig were against the bill, too.[86]

In the budget commission, the *Zentrum*, a Catholic party of the centre, had voted against the bill, as a matter of state rights. Theodor Lewald, then representative of the RMI in parliament, could show a precedent of 1899, however, when it was accepted by the *Zentrum* that not only German cultural representation abroad, but also the preparation for such representation, was a matter of the central government to deal with and therefore for the Reichstag to decide.[87] Lewald, who had been responsible for the German exhibitions in Paris and St. Louis, was a supporting member of DRAfOS,[88] became v. Podbielski's successor in 1919, and a member of the IOC as of 1925.[89] As the Reich paid so much for 1916, most of the other states did indeed pay less than in 1912. Apart from Prussia and Alsace-Lorraine (M 4,000) none of the other states contributed as much as they had done previously. Some of the larger German cities, including Berlin, did, however, with M 66,500.[90]

The arguments in favour of preparing for the Olympic Games were very similar to those mentioned in the newspaper articles. The Olympic Games were of national importance as the athletes were going to bring 'victory to themselves and to our flag – black – white and red'[91] – a statement that caused loud applause and shouts of 'hurrah' in parliament. The Olympic Games were considered a matter of national representation.[92]

The connection was clearly made, that preparing for the Olympic Games would increase the fitness of youth and thus provide a better basis for military readiness. This argument had already convinced the Prussian army one year before that it should encourage intermilitary competition for the selection of talent in conjunction with DRAfOS.[93] The logic of the matter was presented by a representative from southern Germany, Müller:

There are no Olympic Games without a strong nation, and a strong nation will have Olympic victors. This makes for the connection of physical training and physical competition. There will be a tremendous educational impulse so that more and more young people participate in sports ... and thus being physically ready for other endeavours as well.[94]

The Olympic Games were considered particularly useful for this, as each athlete could maintain his national identity and show his national feelings. The laurels were won for the fatherland, representing a competition of country against country.[95] Finally, the bill passed without the votes being counted.[96] The *Turner* and sport press reprinted most of the parliamentary debate *verbatim* as it was the first time that *Turnen* and sports had been dealt with at such length and so positively in the national parliament.[97]

DRAfOS would have been in a very awkward position, had it been otherwise, as it had already started to operate an Olympic budget of M 2 million, including hiring Carl Diem as the first full-time top administrator for German sports (M 8,000 p.a.), four national coaches for track and field, headed by Alvin Kraenzlein, the then 36-year-old former coach of Princeton University and four times Olympic champion of 1900. Kraenzlein organized national training courses, selection competitions, training camps, coaching clinics, etc. As he was of German parentage, born in Nürnberg, he was able to improve his German speaking ability quite fast, and fulfilled his contract until the beginning of the War.[98]

The proposed budget did look very impressive with its systematic approach to the selection and preparation of high calibre athletes. It did show a trend, however, which has been visible in all top sports which are state sponsored: a trend towards bureaucratization. The share for 'administration', 'representation' and other items for the sports administrators rather than the athletes increased considerably. While the amateur rules did not permit the athletes to be reimbursed for breaking records, paid administrators started to take over in sports. Was this why Coubertin termed the sports functionaries the 'leprosy' of sports[99] and prohibited the lists comparing the success of countries to be printed in the *Olympic Review* after 1912?

The Olympic Games of 1916 did not take place. The First World War, for which the athletes had to prepare themselves, substituted reality for a mere sporting contest. It is not surprising that in the aftermath the question of world supremacy examplified through the Olympic Games no longer played a part in the German discussion until the Nazis took the question up again. In the meantime, the Games were not considered a test of national readiness in Germany. It was enough to take part, to be back on the international stage.[100] In those years national representation had a different meaning. National representation through sport is primarily fostered by countries which expect to do very well, but for the others, participation, displaying one's flag at the opening and closing ceremonies, are what matters most.

It would seem that Germany was the pioneer in using sports for national representation and investing government money in the performance of its athletes. A more detailed analysis of the situation in Sweden, however, may reveal that the Swedish effort for 1912 was an even earlier example. The arguments about the sense of national representation through sport were less sophisticated in Germany than in England. But in accordance with the emphasis Germans put on the state in contrast to the role of the private individual, it is not surprising to find Germany to the fore in contributing government money to what at first seems to be a perfectly private matter.[101]

NOTES

1. According to M.J. Finley, H.W. Pleket, *Die Olympischen Spiele der Antike* (Tübingen, 1976), pp.161ff. The rich cities even bought up winners between victory and victory ceremony in order to be better represented.
2. J. R. Betts, *America's Sporting Heritage: 1850–1950* (Reading, Mass.: Addison-Wesley, 1974), p.191.
3. United States Olympic Committee (ed.), *Constitution and By-Laws* (Colorado Springs, 1981); see J. Hutslar, 'Das Sportgesetz der USA von 1978 und seine Auswirkungen', in *Leistungssport*, 9 (1979), 525–30; *The Final Report of the President's Commission on Olympic Sports, 1975–1977*, 2 vols. (Washington, DC US Goverment, 1977); J. Falla, *NCAA: The Voice of College Sports. A Diamond Anniversary History, 1906–1981* (Shawnee Mission, Kan.: NCAA, 1981).
4. The first one was conducted in the United States over the question whether the American team should participate in the Nazi Olympics, cf. A. Krüger, *Die Olympischen Spiele 1936 und die Weltmeinung* (Berlin: Bartels & Wernitz, 1972), p.95.
5. See M.L. and R. Howell, 'The 1952 Helsinki Olympic Games: Another Turning Point?', in P.J. Graham and H. Ueberhorst, *The Modern Olympics* (West Point, NY: Leisure Press, 1976), pp.187–98; V. and J. Louis, *Sport in the Soviet Union* (Oxford: Pergamon, 1980), pp.3–8; J. Riordan, *Soviet Sport. Background to the Olympics* (Oxford: Blackwell, 1980), pp.143ff.; H. Lathe, *Geheimnisse des Sowjetsports. Hintergründe internationaler Erfolge* (Düsseldorf: Econ, 1979); W. Gloede, *Sport die unbekannte Größe im Spiel* (Munich: Goldmann, 1980), pp.141 ff.; R. Espy, *The Politics of the Olympic Games* (Berkeley: University of California, 1981), pp.3ff.; A. Krüger, *Sport und Gesellschaft* (Berlin: Tischler, 1981), pp.31ff.
6. See A. Krüger, 'Amerikanischer Sport zwischen Isolationismus und Internationalismus', *Leistungssport*, 18 (1988), 1, 43–7; 2, 47-50.
7. J. Riordan, *Sport in Soviet Society: Development of Sport and Physical Education in Russia and the USSR* (Cambridge: Cambridge University Press, 1977).
8. For the GDR's illicit means of achieving superiorty in the Olympic Games, such as doping,

see B. Berendonk, *Doping-Dokumente. Von der Forschungs zum Betrug* (Berlin: Springer, 1991). For an inaccurate account of how GDR sport was misled by the apparent effectiveness of the system see D. Gilbert, *The Miracle Machine* (New York: Coward, McCann & Geoghegan, 1980); for the Soviet Union see N.N. Shneidman, *The Soviet Road to Olympus: Theory and Practice of Soviet Physical Culture and Sport* (Toronto: The Ontario Institute for Studies in Education, 1978).

9. R.D. Mandell, *The Nazi Olympics* (New York: Macmillan, 1971).

10. A. Krüger, 'Deutschland und die Olympische Bewegung. 1918–1945', in H. Ueberhorst, *Geschichte der Leibesübungen*, Vol.3/2, (Berlin: Bartels & Wernitz, 1982), pp.1026–47.

11. 10 Oct. 1933, see Krüger, *Die Olympischen Spiele 1936*, p.12.

12. U. Popplow, 'Adolf Hitler–Der Nichtsportler und der Sport', in H. Nattkämpfer (ed.), *Sportwissenschaft im Aufriß* (Saarbrücken: DSLV, 1974), pp.39–55.

13. With an infrastructure of state sport, with systematic training, and state amateurs Italy had its best ever results in 1932 in Los Angeles when it was placed second overall with 12 gold, 12 silver, and 13 bronze medals, one medal more than 28 years later when the Games were held in Rome. See M. Di Donato, 'Italien. Die Tradition der Leibesübungen', in Ueberhorst, *Geschichte*, Vol.5 (1976), pp.239–64. For the fascist influence on early Nazi sports see A. Krüger, 'The Influence of State Sport of Fascist Italy on Nazi Germany', in J.A. Mangan and R.B. Small (eds.), *Sport, Culture, Society: International Historical and Sociological Perspectives* (London: Spon, 1986), pp.145–65; J.M. Hoberman, *Mortal Engines: Scientific Ambition and the Dehumanization of Sport* (New York: Free Press, 1991, pp.131 ff.) suggests that doping might also have played a role.

14. A. Krüger, 'Fascie e croci uncinate', in *Lancillotto e Nausica. Critica e storia dello sport*, Vol 8 (1991), 88–101; R.Bianda and G.Leone, *Atleti in Camicia nera. Lo sport nell'Italia di Mussolini* (Rome: Volpe, 1983).

15. A. Krüger, 'Neo-Olympismus zwischen Nationalismus und Internationalismus', in H. Ueberhorst (ed.), *Geschichte*, Vol.3/1 (Berlin, 1980), pp.522–68.

16. *Meyers Lexikon*, Vol.1 (Leipzig: Meyer 1924), p.1193.

17. R. D. Mandell, *Paris 1900: The Great World's Fair* (Toronto, 1967).

18. See R. Mandell, 'The Invention of the Sports Record', in *Stadion*, 2 (1976), 250–64; for a critique of this concept see J.M.Carter and A. Krüger (eds.), *Ritual and Record* (Westport: Greenwood, 1990).

19. In charge of the conference was Theodor Lewald who later became IOC member for Germany and the president of the Organizing Committee of the 1936 Olympic Games, see DZA, Potsdam, *Nachlaß Lewald*, Vol.136, *Conférence Diplomatique relative aux Expositions Internationales* from 10 to 25 Oct. 1912.

20. K. Moore, 'A Neglected Imperialist: The Promotion of the British Empire in the Writing of John Astley Cooper', *International Journal of the History of Sport*, 8 (1991), pp.256–69.

21. J. A. Cooper, 'The Proposed Periodic Britannic – Contests', in *Greater Britain*, 30 Oct. 1891, pp.596–601. For a detailed discussion see Krüger, 'Neo-Olympismus', pp.526 ff.

22. J.H. MacAloon, *This Great Symbol. Pierre de Coubertin and the Origins of the Modern Olympic Games* (Chicago: Chicago University Press, 1981).

23. R. D. Mandell, *Die ersten Olympischen Spiele der Neuzeit*, (Kastellaun: Henn 1976); J. A. Lucas, 'Baron de Coubertin and the Formative Years of the Modern International Olympic Movement' (dissertation, University of Maryland, 1962); P. de Coubertin, *Einundzwanzig Jahre Sportkampagne* (Ratingen: Henn, 1974); for an overview of the literature see R. D. Mandell, 'The Modern Olympic Games. A. Bibliographical Essay', in *Sportwissenschaft*, 6 (1976), 89–98.

24. France won 8 gold, 5 silver, 3 bronze medals, Germany 5-13-7, so many statistics had France ahead of Germany for having had more victories, see E. Kamper, *Enzyklopädie der Olympischen Spiele* (Dortmund: Harenberg, 1972), pp.322ff.

25. Deutscher Reichstag, *Stenographische Berichte*, Vol.292, p.7340; see A. Krüger, *Dr. Theodor Lewald* (Berlin Bartels & Wernitz, 1975), pp.21ff. For 1912 the *Reich* had paid M 25,000 (= £1,250), about one half of the cost of sending the team, see C. Diem, *Die Olympischen Spiele 1912* (Berlin: Selbst,1912), pp.12ff. The *Deutsche Turnerschaft*

wanted to compete against only Germans, no matter where they lived in the world, therefore the *Turners* of St. Louis had succeeded in explaining that they were in charge of the gymnastics there, so the German *Turners* came, headed by F.A. Schmidt, M.D., a prominent leader of the *Turner* movement.
26. A. Krüger, 'Sport, State, and the Olympic Games. The Origin of the Notion of Sport as a Medium of Political Representation', in B. Kidd (ed.), *5th Canadian Symposium on the History of Sport and Physical Education* (Toronto, 1982), pp.369–79.
27. I acknowledge the generous help of the staff of the former *Deutsches Zentralarchiv (DZA),* Potsdam, now *Bundesarchiv Abt. Potsdam.*
28. See J.A. Lucas, 'Theodore Roosevelt and Baron Pierre de Coubertin: Entangling Olympic Games involvement 1901–1918', in *Stadion,* 8/9 (1982–83), 137-50; idem, 'Early Olympic Antagonists. Pierre de Coubertin versus James E. Sullivan', in *Stadion,* 3 (1977), 258–72.
29. *The Times,* Letter to the Editor by Robert Thompson, President of the American Olympic Committee, 2 Sept.1913, 11:2.
30. The discussion on the decline of the British self-consciousness and its consequences on sport has been started by J. Lowerson, 'Sport and National Decay – The British and the Olympics before 1914', in N. Müller and J. Rühl (eds.), *Olympic Scientific Congress 1984. Official Report. Sport History* (Niedernhausen: Schors, 1985), p.384 (abstract).
31. *The Times,* Letter to the Editor from the British Olympic Committee, 5 Sept. 1913, p.11:6.
32. *The Times,* Editorial, 18 Aug. 1913, p.7:4.
33. *The Times,* Letter to the Editor by the British Olympic Committee, 18 Aug. 1913, p.7:1.
34. *The Times,* Report of the British Olympic Committee, 22 Aug. 1913, p.4:3.
35. *The Times,* Editorial, 27 Aug.1913, p.7:4.
36. R. Holt, *Sport and the British: A Modern History* (Oxford: Oxford University Press, 1989), pp.274ff.; for the situation in Germany see A. Krüger, 'A Horse Breeder's Perspective? Scientific Racism in Germany. 1870–1933', in D. Schirmer and N. Finzsch (eds.), *The Invention of Identity and the Practice of Intolerance. Nationalism, Racism and Xenophobia in Germany and the United States* (Cambridge: Cambridge University Press, 1995).
37. *The Times,* Letter to the Editor by Sidney Abrahams, 28 Aug. 1913, p.11:1.
38. From 1914 onwards George V began the tradition of royal attendence at the FA Cup Final, see R. Holt, *Sport and the British,* p.269.
39. *The Times,* 16 Jan 1914, p.53:6, has the detailed account for 31 Dec.1913.
40. The largest sum had come from Lord Northcliffe with £2,000. The exact sum was £7,073 7s. 3d. *The Times,* 11 Sept. 1913, p.13:3.
41. *The Times,* 10 Sept. 1913 p.6:5.
42. Report of the Special Committee, *The Times,* 5 Sept. 1913, p.11:6.
43. *Morning Post* (London), 24 Sept.1913, p.5:2.
44. *Morning Post* (London), 25 Sept.1913, p.5:6.
45. *The Times,* 13 Sept. 1913, p.7:5, 'Professionalism and Sport'.
46. *The Times,* 2 Sept. 1913, p.11:2; for a full account of this discussion see I.F. Jobling, 'The Lion, the Eagle and the Kangaroo: Politics and Proposals for a British Empire Team at the 1916 Berlin Olympics', in G. Redmond (ed.), *Sport and Politics* (Champaign: Human Kinetics, 1986), pp.99–107.
47. K. Moore, 'Sport, Politics and Imperialism. The Evolution of the Concept of British Empire Games from 1891 to 1930', in D. Benning (ed.), *Proceedings of the Fourth Annual Conference of the British Society of Sports History* (North Staffordshire Polytechnic, 1986), pp.46–57.
48. *The Times,* Letter to the Editor by the British Olympic Committee, 5 Sept. 1913, p.11:6.
49. *The Times,* Letter to the Editor by H.E. Morgan, 6 Sept. 1913, p.5:6.
50. P. Lovesey, *The Official Centenary History of the AAA* (Enfield: Guinness, 1980). He received £400 per year for three years plus £150 for travelling. His seven part-time training assistants were hired for £100 per year each, see *The Times,* 16 Jan. 1914, p.53:6.
51. E. U. Hamer: *Die Anfänge der 'Spielbewegung' in Deutschland* (London: Arena, 1989).
52. Letter by von Podbielski to the Secretary of the Interior, 4 Feb.1913. DZA Potsdam 07.01. Reichskanzlei, Nationalfeste pp.24a (now on microfilm 1355).

53. *Daily Mail* quoted in the *New York Times*, 9 June 1913, p.3:3.
54. *New York Times*, 8 June 1913, part III, p.2:8.
55. Letter from von Podbielski to the Secretary of the Interior, 4 Feb. 1913 and his reply, 19 Feb., DZA Potsdam 07.01.Reichskanzlei, Nationalfeste pp.24a (now on microfilm 1355).
56. *Lokalanzeiger Berlin*, 19 Feb.1913. Sweden had hired the American coach Ernie Hjertberg (formerly of the Irish AC New York) who was of Swedish descent, see *New York Times*, 2 July 1914, p.11:2.
57. C. Diem on behalf of DRAfOS to the RMI , 1 March 1913, DZA, op.cit.,
58. DZA Nachlaß Th. Lewald, Vol.35, order of the RMI of 9 May 1908.
59. Denkschrift des Herrn Reichskanzlers an den Deutschen Kaiser, 2 June 1913 DZA Potsdam 07.01. Reichskanzlei, Nationalfeste pp.24a (now on microfilm 1355).
60. For a photo of the four on board of the ship to America, see C. Diem, *Ausgewählte Schriften* (St. Augustin: Richarz, 1982), Vol 3, p.48.
61. Responsible for sports in the army, a sprinter, from 1938 onward IOC member for Germany, as *Generalfeldmarschall* the commanding general of the German invasion of Belgium and Poland in the Second World War.
62. The *New York Times* is full of reports of the activities of this group. For an interview and photo see *New York Times*, 24 Aug. 1913 part IV, p.1:5.
63. Deutscher Reichsausschuß für die Olympischen Spiele (ed.), *Sport und Körperschulung in Amerika. Bericht über die Sport-Studienreise nach den Vereinigten Staaten im August-September 1913* (Berlin: DRAfOS, 1913).
64. A. Krüger, '"We are sure to have found the true reasons for American superiority in sports". The reciprocal relationship between the United States and Germany in physical culture and sport', in R. Naul (ed.), *Turnen and Sport. Cross-Cultural Exchange* (New York: Waxmann, 1991), pp.51–82.
65. Von Diebow (for the Deutsche Turnlehrerverein)(ed.), *Das deutsche Schulturnen und die Studienkommission des deutschen Reichsausschusses für Olympische Spiele. Eine Erwiderung* (Spandau: Selbst, 1913).
66. The *Deutsche Turnzeitung* is full of the discussion which eventually led to a large-scale fact-finding tour of the DT itself, see 'Eine Fahrt deutscher Turner, Turnlehrer und Lehrer nach Amerika', in *DTZ*, 59 (1914), 42–4; W. Eichler, 'Einiges über Turnen und Sport in den Vereinigten Staaten', ibid., pp.44–51; A. Siebert, 'Sport und Turnen an den amerikanischen Universitäten', ibid., pp.51–2; 'Das Neueste', in ibid., p.113. Even the *New York Times* was not sure in its editorial whether the learning process should not be reversed and the Americans should learn from the German *Turners* as they were well trained and placed no emphasis on winning, see *New York Times*, 22 Aug. 1913, p.8:4.
67. The *Times*, 6 Sept. 1913, p.5:6. Kraenzlein had a dental degree and was therefore often referred to as Doctor. I doubt the accuracy of the sum, which may have been half of that figure. In his will he left $25,000 to his daughter, see *New York Times*, 7 Jan. 1928, p.9:4.
68. DZA Potsdam 07.01. Reichskanzlei, Nationalfeste pp.24a (now on microfilm 1355)., *Aktennotiz* at the occasion of the translation of the editorial of *The Times*, 18 Aug. 1913.
69. *New York Times*, 25 April 1914 p.16:8.
70. Deutscher Reichsausschuß für die Olympischen Spiele (ed.), leaflet, reproduced in Carl-Diem-Institut (ed.): *Die VI Olympischen Spiele Berlin 1916* (Cologne: Barz & Beienburg, 1978), pp.58–60.
71. C. Diem, 'Aufgaben für 1916', in *Fußball und Leichtathletik*, 14 (1913), 465 ff.
72. M. Berner, 'Der olympische Gedanke in der Welt', in ibid., pp.495ff.
73. Generalsekretariat für die VI. Olympiade, *Voranschlag für die VI. Olympiade und Kassenbericht für das Rechnungsjahr 1913/14* (Berlin, 1914), see Carl-Diem-Institut, op.cit., pp.76 ff.
74. Von der Goltz, 'Jungdeutschland 1912', *Jungdeutschland 1913. Kalender des Jungdeutschlandbundes* (Berlin: Süsserott, 1912), p.4.
75. C. Diem, *Weltgeschichte des Sports* (Stuttgart: Cotta, 1971), pp.970 ff.
76. *Kommission für den Reichshaushaltsetat. 13. Legislaturperiode. 1 Session. 119. Sitzung.*
77. Dr Hoch, MP, was right. Under the same Kap.3, title 40 of the Minister of the Interior

German elite sport has been financed ever since.

78. A. Krüger and J. Riordan, *Der Internationale Arbeitersport* (Cologne: Pahl-Rugenstein, 1985).
79. See 'Zur Ablehnung des Reichsausschusses', in *DTZ*, 59 (1914), 94.
80. Deutscher Reichsausschuß für die Olympischen Spiele, 'VI. Olympiade Berlin 1916', in *Akademische Zeitschrift für Leibesübungen*, 1 (1914), 31–3.
81. 'Propagandavortrag in der Alberthalle am 31.1.14', in ibid., pp.42f.
82. See *Göttinger Zeitung*, 27 Jan.1914, p.1:1.
83. *Deutscher Reichstag*, op.cit.,Vol.303, res.no.1289, 1290, 1308 by the Conservative Party, the Progressive Party (DFV) and the National Liberal Party, pp.2558, 2580. For the curricula of the responsible men see M. Schwarz, *MdR. Biographisches Handbuch der Reichstage* (Hanover: Madsack, 1965).
84. Keinath (Nat.Lib.) on 19 Jan. 1914, *Deutscher Reichstag*, 292, 6612 A; Albrecht von Graefe (Conservative), ibid., 6618 C.
85. Otto Rühle (Social Democrat), ibid., 293, 7333–5; Wolfgang Heine (Social Democrat), ibid., 7344–8; for the attitude of *Turners* to their worker brothers see E. Wolf, 'Ein wichtiges Urteil', in *DTZ*, 59 (1914), 98–9. They hated each other.
86. Hans Peter Hanssen (Danish minority), *Deutscher Reichstag*, op. cit., 7343ff.
87. Theodor Lewald, ibid., .7339–7341; reprinted in A. Krüger, *Lewald*, pp.91 ff.
88. Lewald payed DM 50 on 19 Jan. 1913 to join. Nachlaß Lewald, *DZA* Potsdam, Nr. 157.
89. For a full biography see A. Krüger, *Dr. Theodor Lewald. Sportführer ins Dritte Reich* (Berlin Bartels & Wernitz, 1975); for a more recent study, see R. Pfeiffer and A. Krüger, 'Theodor Lewald: Eine Karriere im Dienste des Vaterlands oder die vergebliche Suche nach der jüdischen Identität des "Halbjuden"', in *Menora. Jahrbuch für deutsch-jüdische Geschichte* (Munich: Piper, 1995), pp.233–65.
90. Nachlaß Lewald, op cit., Nr. 157. For the 1912 Olympic expedition Prussia had provided M3,000, Bavaria M2,000, Saxony M1,500, Elsass-Loraine M200, Free City Hamburg M2,000, Free City Bremen M600, and the three smaller states M300 each, see Diem, *Olympische Spiele 1912*.
91. Stöve, (Nat.Lib.), *Deutscher Reichstag*, 292, 7336.
92. Ludwig v. Massow (Conservative), ibid., p.7337.
93. 'Auszug aus der Verfügung des kgl. Preußischen Kriegsministeriums vom 19. Juni 1913. Bestimmungen', in Carl-Diem-Institut, op.cit., p.136.
94. Dr. Müller (Progressive Party), *Deutscher Reichstag*, op.cit., 7339.
95. Erich Mertin (DRP), ibid., 7342.
96. 17 Feb. 1914, ibid., 293, 7386.
97. *DTZ*, 59 (1914), 157–68; *Akademische Zeitschrift für Leibesübungen*, 1 (1914), 53–7; 70–75; 104–6; 116–19.
98. C. Diem, *Ein Leben für den Sport* (Ratingen: Henn, 1974), pp.78–98. For his return *cf. New York Times*, 25 July 1914, p.4:4.
99. Y.-P.Boulogne, *La vie et l'oeuvre pédagogique de Pierre de Coubertin* (Ottawa: Leméac, 1975), p.168.
100. In this respect it can be argued that it was also a matter of national representation, see A. Krüger, 'Turnen und Turnunterricht zur Zeit der Weimarer Republik.-Die Grundlage der heutigen Schulsportmisere?', in A. Krüger and D. Niedlich (eds.), *Ursachen der Schulsportmisere in Deutschland* (London: Arena, 1979), pp.13–31; *id.*, 'Gesinnungsbildung durch Turnunterricht-oder "pro patria est dum ludere videmur"', in R. Dithmar and J. Willer (eds.), *Schule zwischen Kaiserreich und Faschismus* (Darmstadt: Wissenschaftliche, 1981), pp.102–24.
101. See H. Böhme, *Prolegomena zu einer Sozial- und Wirtschaftsgeschichte Deutschlands des 19. und 20. Jahrhunderts* (Frankfurt: Suhrkamp, 1968).

In Search of National Identity: Argentinian Football and Europe

EDUARDO P. ARCHETTI

This essay will present some general ideas on how a particular discourse on the character of the Argentinian style of playing football developed in this century. It is an attempt to depict a social and historical process wherein the identification of a framework of meaning, values and symbols makes possible the construction of a 'self-identity' (for whatever moral, economic, cognitive, or political purpose). Two concepts of identity will be considered: one is 'essentialist', with identity as 'something' (an attribute, entity, thing) which an individual or a group has in and of itself, an identity that is subject to growth and decline, to continuity and change, to health and sickness. Obviously, this perspective adopted by the actors themselves is also built up in a context of oppositions and relativities.[1] However, secondly, social anthropology takes a relativist position and perceives identity as positional and strategic: a group has no *one* identity, but a variety (and in theory a potentially very large variety) of possibilities. However, the point to be stressed is that in both the essentialist and the contextual framework there is a possibility of change and variation. But, in the essentialist perspective changes can be accepted only if key values and meanings are somehow maintained. Therefore, the essentialists are more concerned with decline and crisis.

The search for identity in football is tied to style, both in the sense of individual and collective style. This implies the achievement of a difficult balance between individual characteristics and communal belonging in a game that is basically collective. The great players can transcend the style of given teams, but, nevertheless, in the quest for identity the great heroes are always associated with the success of teams; they need each other. This study will argue that the Argentinian discourse and practice of football has developed in two directions: one essentialist, the search for the 'typical' style represented by 'mythical teams' and 'model players'; and another contextual, in which opposition of styles is open to a relativist representation. In the relativist representation it is common to accept that Argentinians play a kind of 'Latin American style', close to the way Uruguayans play, or that the contemporary Argentinian style is an attempt to combine European discipline with Latin American improvisation.

Since its beginning Argentinian football has been a part, and a very important one, of a kind of general history of football uniting the periphery (new nations) and the centre (Europe). This general history is not only related to the growing internationalization of competition but, in the specific case of Argentina, to the 'foot drain' to Europe which has been continuous since mid-1920s. This history has created a twofold process: a reinforcement of the ideal model symbolized by the success in Europe of Cesarini, Orsi, Di Stéfano, Sivori, Kempes, Ardiles, and more recently, Maradona (the 'typical' players representing the 'essential' style); but at the same time a relative picture of the conditions for success (the necessity of physical strength and continuity, and team discipline). In the Argentinian mythology Di Stéfano represents the 'universal player' combining some essential aspects of Argentinian style (technical skill and the creation of unexpected events) with some properties of European style (tactical discipline, courage, leadership and a winning mentality). Maradona, on the contrary, is closer to the 'essential' style based on technical virtuosity.[2]

This essay will describe a historical process that creates a stock of values, events and meanings . This symbolic capital constitutes the core of the representations and in this sense is very close to the essentialist perspective. These key elements permit:

1. a process of *self-definition* that includes players, managers, journalists and public in general;
2. a specific way of registering given events that will constitute 'crucial events' (victories, teams, players);
3. a rethinking of past events from the perspective of the present and finally
4. the production of a narrative that is a mixture of 'real' history, pseudo-histories and mythologies.[3]

However, both the history and the narrative are open, and, therefore, allow for the growth of oppositions and alternative interpretations. The contemporary Argentinian football scene is represented by the 'conflict' between two 'schools': one identified with Menotti and the other with Bilardo. Both coaches achieved worldwide recognition and prestige through Argentinia's World Cup victories in 1978 and 1986. However, Menotti's victory was achieved at home, in the World Cup of 1978 celebrated in Argentina, while Bilardo's victory was in Mexico in 1986. In the world of football the victory of Bilardo is much more prestigious because his team did not have the 'home advantage' of 1978. Menotti's second attempt, in the World Cup of 1982 in Spain, was not a success: Argentina did not pass the quarter-finals. Bilardo's second World Cup, in 1990 in Italy, brought Argentina to the final and the silver medal after losing against Germany. Menotti, explicitly and in a very articulate form, defends the essentialist position while Bilardo represents a kind of 'bastard' product in which discipline and tactical dispositions are considered of extreme importance.

The Origin of Football in Argentina

The spread of football was caused by Britain's world power status and active presence in commerce, industrial production, territorial control and international finance.[4] In the case of Argentina, the rapid expansion of the game and its internationalization was also related to the importance of the British colony in the last half of the nineteenth century. By 1890 there were 45,000 British nationals living in Buenos Aires and small cities close to the capital. The Buenos Aires Football Club, a division of the Buenos Aires Cricket Club, was founded in 1867. The first recorded match was played that year by two teams from the same club; the 'Reds' had as captain Tomas Hogg and the 'Whites' William Held. Many clubs were founded after 1880 and the majority of them sprang out of British schools. In the period 1890–1900 the Lomas Athletic Club won five titles. All the players had been students in the Lomas de Zamora School, a prestigious British boarding school. Alumni, the great Argentinian club of the beginning of this century, was originally the Buenos Aires Higher School. After 1900 it was decided that the clubs change their English names for Spanish ones. However, the first association had an English title: the Argentine Football Association. This association kept English as its official language until 1906. In 1912 the Association was divided and for the first time Spanish was partially used: Federación Argentina de Football and Asociación Argentina de Fútbol. Not until 1934 was 'football' replaced by the Spanish 'fútbol' when the new and definitive association was created: Asociación de Fútbol Argentino.[5]

Not only was the game a British export but so too were the standards and the quality of play. In the first decade of the twentieth century Argentinian football grew under the influence of the great British teams that came to play in Buenos Aires and in Rosario. Southampton arrived in 1904 and won all the matches (3–0 against Alumni, the Argentinian champions). In 1905 Nottingham Forest played several matches and returned to England undefeated. The first home victory, in 1906, was over a team of British nationals living in South Africa. It was celebrated in Buenos Aires as a glorious event. The winners were Alumni and this success consolidated the image of Alumni as a great team. Before the First World War, Everton and Tottenham visited Argentina with great success, and in 1923 Chelsea played several matches and won all of them. The myth of British invincibility in football was then created,[6] and was intelligently manipulated by the British themselves, and not only in relation to the Argentinians. Tony Mason writes:

The British belief that their football was best remained a plant of sturdy growth despite unpredictable frosts...Defeat in the World Cup of 1950 by the United States could also be forgotten in a pre-television era as an inexplicable aberration. Even the famous defeat at Wembley in 1953 by Puskas's Hungarians, whose manager turned the knife by insisting that not only were they amateurs but the players had given up their annual holidays to come over and play the match, seemed to matter less than the home victories under the new floodlights and on BBC Television, of Wolverhampton Wanderers over Moscow's Spartak and Budapest's Honved. British claims to superiority at club level provoked *L'Equipe* into initiating the moves which led to the establishment of the European Cup in 1955. It was twelve years before a British club won it'.[7]

It was almost a century after the establishment of the game in their country before the Argentinians defeated England in a tournament in Rio de Janeiro in 1964.

From 1895 onwards football spread all over the country. By 1910 there were clubs and provincial leagues as far as Santiago del Estero in the North. However, Buenos Aires, Rosario and La Plata remained the main centres of the new game. The rapid growth of Buenos Aires due to the arrival of one million immigrants from Europe at the beginning of this century determined the character of the national league. Buenos Aires and small industrial cities close to the capital, like Avellaneda (with the great teams of Racing Club and Independiente), Quilmes, Banfield and Lanus, dominated organized football. At the same time, the close contact with Montevideo and the regular games between Argentinian and Uruguayan teams since 1902 (for a trophy donated by the world famous 'tea baron' Sir Thomas Lipton) created a core of football in the Rio de la Plata basin. In addition, the success of Uruguay and Argentina in the Olympic Games of 1928 and in the first World Cup in 1930, when the two teams played in the finals, made possible the creation of the concept of 'fútbol rioplatense' (football from the river, Rio de la Plata, which separates Argentina from Uruguay). This style was based on a superb technique, keeping, with endless touches, possession of the ball, and on rapid changes of rhythm in the attack. With the main aim of surprising the opponent, Argentinians and Uruguayans played the game at different tempos: very slow in the middle of the field and very fast in approach to goal. It is, perhaps, necessary to remind the reader that the national teams of Argentina and Uruguay dominated the South American Cup from its first year, 1916, until the late 1950s. During this period, Argentina won 12 titles, Uruguay 8 and Brazil only 3.

It is possible to imagine that the 'original' style of Argentinian football was British, a kind of kick-and-run way of playing where physical strength and continuity dominated. However, in the early 1920s some teams from Central Europe played in Buenos Aires. The Argentinian mythology recorded especially the visit of the Hungarian Ferencvaros in 1922. No kick-and-run is remembered. The Hungarian players were liked due to their technical skills and ability to dribble. In the 1920s and 1930s the myth of a 'typical Central European style' was created in Argentina. Argentinians believed that their style of playing was very much like the football played in Austria and Hungary.[8]

For Argentinian football the 'foundation myth', namely the emergence of a style of its own, is located in the 1920s and is associated with the following aspects: the cult of 'dribbling', the appearance of symbiotic partnerships of players in a team (forward-wing) and the crystallization of a style defined as elegant, skilful, cheeky and lively. It is interesting to note that Argentinian players were credited with the development of certain skills: Pedro Colomino with the 'bicycle kick'; Juan Evaristo with the 'marianella'; and Pablo Bartolucci with the 'flying header'. Only in an essentialist recreation of history is it possible to imagine that these stunts, recorded as key developments, were an original creation of Argentinian players. However, a style must be seen and perceived in opposition to others. For Argentinian football the turning point in international (European) recognition was the 1928 Olympic final in Amsterdam. Nevertheless, history has recorded the famous tour of Europe of Boca Juniors in 1925 as the founding myth. Boca's way of playing – the elegant and fluent movements of the players, absolute control of the ball, skill in dribbling and a move to an acrobatic, spectacular and artistic style – astonished Europeans. In addition, it is said that Argentinians demonstrated that it was possible to play and to win with less continuity and physical strength. In contrast to kick-and-run football, this style was associated with two qualities: play at different tempos, and possession of the ball, even if this meant back passing. What the game lost in intensity and continuity, it gained in precision. At the same time, and closely related to the two defeats against Uruguay in 1928 and 1930, the essentialists created the myth of the generosity of Argentinian football, as opposed to tactical considerations that could guarantee a victory. Victories are ephemera, everything is style. Brera comments on the final of the World Cup in 1930: 'Argentina plays football with a lot of fantasy and elegance but the technical superiority cannot compensate for the abandonment of tactics. Of the two 'rioplatense' national teams, the ants are the Uruguayans, the cicadas are the Argentinians' [author's translation].[9]

The historical record registered Uruguay's two victories; the mythology, the superiority of the Argentinian way of playing. The myth was transformed into history when, after the final, the Italians bought the most skilful 'cicada' of the Argentinians: the left-winger Raimundo 'Comet' Orsi. Juventus offered him what at that time constituted a privileged contract: 8000 lire per month, a beautiful house and a car with chauffeur. The Argentinians considered the purchase an outrageous assault on national dignity: heroes were not for sale. It took one year before Orsi could leave Argentina. His emigration was the beginning of a continuous exodus of 'Rioplatense' and Brazilian players to Italian football. The players of football's periphery were suddenly integrated into European football. Moreover, the internationalization of the players' market provoked a rapid change in the Argentinian football. In the years 1930–31, professionalism was introduced in the Argentinian League to combat, among other things, the emigration of star players.

In Argentinian football of the 1930s there was a lot of space between defenders and forwards. The forwards had not only plenty of space for their movements but also quite a lot of time to think about what to do with the ball. Defenders never tried to close down the space with co-ordinated movements and never practised man-to-man marking. This kind of football invited an offensive way of playing. The greatest Argentinian players of this epoch were forwards. The Italians knew it, and, consequently, bought insiders, wingers and centre-forwards. The only exception in the case of Argentinian star players was Luis Monti, a centre-half, who joined Juventus in 1931. This movement constituted a kind of 'world market' of players in which the attacking offensive and creative players came from the periphery. This historical fact permitted the crystallization of the essentialist image of Argentinian football. Both Europeans and Argentinians created a mythology around these exceptional players.

In 1934 Italy won the World Cup, with three Argentinian stars playing an outstanding role in the Italian national team: Luis Monti and the two brilliant wingers, Guaita and Orsi. They qualified on the basis of Italian descent. It is believed in Argentina that the Italian 'revolution' was made possible by the combination of great physical strength (a typical English attribute) with a renewed technical skill (the Argentinian contribution). The athletic power of the Italians was fed by the talent of Monti, Guaita and Orsi, and due to them Argentinian football was considered a decisive component of this change.[10] Hence, the Italian victory was also an Argentinian victory. Again, in the historical record Argentinians felt dispossessed. Earlier, the main cause had been the tactical ability and audacity of Uruguayans; this time it was the existence of a world market of players and rules that permitted the sons of Italians to play in the Italian national team. It is important to keep in mind that the consolidation of an Argentinian style occurred in a context of international defeat for the national team. The myth of Argentinian superiority was never history. The history of Argentinian victories was related to something abstract – 'a style', 'a way of doing', 'a way of playing', or to concrete names, the great players in exile. Thus, the exile and the existence of a world market of players contributed to the isolation of the Argentinian national team: Argentina decided to stay away from international competition. The country's return to the World Cup in 1958 in Sweden represented the most traumatic moment in the history of Argentinian football.

From the 1930s until the second half of the 1950s, Argentinians chose to stay in South America. In addition, the Second World War interrupted the expatriation of great players. During these years great national and club teams were constantly produced and many of them dominated the South American arena. The Brazilians and the Uruguayans developed a kind of 4-2-4 system in order to counteract the flair of the Argentinian forwards. In the 1940s the Uruguayans discovered that the inside-left should play a more defensive role, and they began to play with four backs.[11] Both midfielders represented in this period the creativity of the team and, at the same time, the capacity for scoring. They were offensive players, never occupied with the boring task of regaining the ball for the team. They were perceived, and they behaved in the field, as eccentric aristocrats. The 'essence' of the Argentinian style was then associated with the names of great midfielders: Nolo Ferreira, De la Mata, Méndez, Labruna, Simes, Martino, Moreno, Farro, Baéz y Grillo. The contribution of Argentina to the Italian national teams until the 1960s consisted mostly of midfielders: Cesarini, Maschio, Sivori, Lojacono and Montuori. Even Angelillo, a classical centre-forward, played for the Italian national team as a midfielder.

It is interesting to note that Juan Carlos Lorenzo and César Luis Menotti, who in theory and in practice represent two different ideologies in the history of Argentinian football, agree on the fact that this period and the style related to it can be defined as 'typically Argentinian'. Lorenzo writes that during this epoch the Argentinian way of playing was characterized by an attitude that advocated great offensive vitality and an incredible lack of discipline in defence.[12] According to Menotti this style produced many great players and over time consolidated a kind of ethos that must be protected.[13] Lorenzo will argue that this great advantage was, at the same time, a negative factor which prevented the changes that were needed in Argentinian football before the World Cup of 1958 in Sweden. Menotti, on the contrary, points out, from an essentialist perspective, that this style should be preserved, and in this sense any change is a sign of decay and, therefore, a loss of self.

The Argentinian football ethos was maintained and reproduced as a myth after San Lorenzo de Almagro's famous tour of Europe of in 1946.

This great team had a 'small chamber orchestra' in the attack composed of a violin (Farro), a viola (Pontoni) and a cello (Martino).[14] On the 15 January 1947 they defeated the Spanish national team 6–1 in Madrid. This tour, which included some matches in the Basque country, is still remembered in Spain. Panizo, the great inside-left of Athletico Bilbao, said:

> When I started out as a football player you could do marvellous things but if you did not score enough goals or continued to run in spite of the fact that a defender took your shirt, everyone said that you were slow. I was very happy, therefore, when the Argentinians of San Lorenzo de Amagro, who at that time were one of the best teams of the world, visited the San Mames stadium. The people were astonished to see them play, and they commented: 'Look, all of them play like Panizo'...I never understood that some fans preferred you to send the ball to nowhere instead of playing safe and passing it back... Now it is different, but then the people did not understand, they said that I was slow, that my way of playing hindered the team [author's translation].[15]

So strong is the myth of Argentinian football that Segurola, a Spanish journalist, writes in an article on Panizo:

> But then came San Lorenzo de Almagro...a team that was able to play on equal terms with the River Plate 'machine', at that time the best team in the world. And everyone played like Panizo. Never again was his quality in the San Mames stadium questioned... There was general agreement among the fans that Panizo, so much criticized during his early games wearing the Athletic shirt, would revolutionize Spanish football after the Second World War, and that following San Lorenzo's masterful demonstration, every player should play like him [author's translation].[16]

First, San Lorenzo de Almagro was revolutionary because play at quick tempo was replaced by the search for space through keeping possession until an attacking opportunity was created. Second, it is accepted in Spain, even today without discussion, that San Lorenzo de Almagro and River Plate were the world's two best teams.

Between 1938 and this key point in the 1940s international contacts with European football almost disappeared. During this period, Argentinians developed, in isolation from Europe, the idea that they played the best football in the world. This idea was confirmed by the team's success in the South American competitions. From 1941 to 1947, the National League was dominated by River Plate with the famous team 'la máquina' (the machine). This team still belongs to the imaginary world of beauty, excellence and superiority, to the epics of Argentina's 'golden age', a time that will never return. It is a kind of unchallenged mythology because River Plate never played in Europe against the best teams and therefore vanished from history undefeated. Every Argentinian fan will still remember the name of the five in the attack: Muñoz, Moreno, Pedernera, Labruna and Loustau. River Plate lost its best players after a strike in 1948 when most of them, left Argentina for Colombia in search of better wages. Among the travellers was a player who never had the opportunity to play regularly in the first team, Alfredo 'the Blond Dart' Di Stéfano.

The great success of Di Stéfano in the victorious Real Madrid of the 1950s reaffirmed the myth of the superiority of Argentinian football: the best player in the best European team was an Argentinian. Moreover, during his time with River Plate he was ignored, eclipsed by the other stars. Hence, Argentinians could say with confidence that if a 'second class star' had become the best player in the world, then what if Moreno, Pedernera or Labruna could have had the same opportunity?

Argentinians continued to believe in their superiority. The South American Cup of 1957 confirmed it. Argentina won easily in Peru, defeating the Brazilians 3–1 in the final. In this team a new 'small chamber orchestra' performed: the teenagers Maschio (20), Angelillo (17) and Sivori (19), 'los ángeles con la cara sucia' (angels with dirty faces). After the victory, all of them were bought by Italian clubs: Maschio by Bologna, Angelillo by Inter and Sivori by Juventus. They became great players and, due to their Italian ancestors, they also played in the various Italian national teams of the 1960s. Again, as in 1930, Argentinians felt both dispossession and pride at the same time. They lost successful players, young players in their prime, to a better life in Europe. The opening of the world market, after the interruption due to the depression in Europe during and after the Second World War, again put Argentinian football on the periphery, providing rich European teams with young talented players.

The Crisis of 1958

In 1958 the Argentinians decided to take part in the World Cup in Stockholm. This date was considered a privileged opportunity to transform the myth of superiority into historical reality. 'The encounter with history' developed into the most traumatic and tragic event in the history of Argentinian football, only comparable in intensity with the Brazil's national frustration after the defeat in the World Cup Final in Maracená in 1950.[17] The humiliation suffered at the hands of Czechoslovakia, a decisive 6–1 defeat, put the whole nation into a state of shock and transformed the players from heroes into a bunch of traitors. The team was supposed to represent the typical style of slow tempo and great technical ability. At the symbolic level, the presence of the great inside-left Labruna, a survivor of the great 'máquina' of River Plate, close to his forties, was a guarantee of confidence and historical continuity. The débâcle was rapidly rationalized by the coach Guillermo Stábile, top scorer of the Argentinian team in the World Cup of 1930 in Montevideo and later professional player in Italy: the best Argentinian players, 'los ángeles con la cara sucia', had been stolen by 'our bad brothers of Italy' and 'the best centre-forward in the world is playing in Milan and his name is Angelillo'.[18] Brera comments on Stábile's rationalization in the following way: 'the Argentinians were presumptuous in a masochistic way: they believed that they were superior to all, they did not take the time to study a tactical scheme suited to their actual resources: moreover, their bad Italian and Spanish brothers have always stolen their best players' [author's translation].[19]

Symbolically, for the makers of public opinion this crisis was a reflection of a general decadence in Argentinian football in a national context of deep economic crisis. A model of growth, based on self-sufficiency and isolation from the world market, went into crisis. This metaphor was used to explain the defeat of 1958: the isolationism of Argentinian football had to change. The political and socio-economic decay of Argentina after 1955 was related to football: the Argentinian style could no longer be considered invincible. The 'golden age' of football had been associated with a continuous growth in the economy since the depression of the 1930s. New influences from European football were needed. It is interesting to note that Brazil's victory in the World Cup also influenced changes in the way football was perceived. From Europe it was necessary to import physical strength, from Brazil the famous 4-2-4 formation. Argentina began to buy defenders from Brazil. The great players Orlando and Dino arrived at the beginning of the 1960s, so the Argentinians could learn to play with four defenders and adopt the style of zonal marking.

During these years Argentinian football entered the wilderness, with very few successes at international level. National heroes were playing in Spain (Di Stéfano) and in Italy (Sivori). They symbolized the victories that the national team never achieved. Real Madrid and Juventus were suddenly transformed into 'national teams'. In the case of Real Madrid this was even more understandable because, in addition to Di Stéfano, there were two other Argentinians in the side: Dominguez and Rial. By this *tour de force*, characteristic of crisis in national identities, Di Stéfano represented a new type of player, the synthesis of two styles: the Argentinian and the European. Menotti writes:

I maintain that Argentina's style at international level has always depended on highly talented players. For various reasons we never realized this at the team level...but it is fantastic to realize that it was Di Stéfano who showed Europe that there was another style, another way of playing football. When he travelled, Di Stéfano, had a great heritage in his suitcase, the heritage of 'la máquina' of River Plate...To this he added his temperament, and his dynamics, but it must be made clear that he did not win just because of these qualities...He had great drive, he imposed his style [author's translation].[20]

This description of Di Stéfano coincides with a European perspective:

[In Paris]...journalists of all countries and players of all origins chose Di Stéfano the all-time best European player... The winner, a man with a menacing look, a third-generation immigrant and educated in the lush fields of River Plate, had proved that football is a *nationless* emotion and a pluralistic force in which both ability and impetus can coexist. In the spirit of the old blond gaucho...the Muses and the Devils were powerfully reunited. Such a powerful coalition provided him with a mixed style: he added to a cold nordic inspiration a refined Southern malice [author's translation].[21]

In Search of a New Identity

In the 1960s Juan Carlos Lorenzo represented the 'European revolution' in Argentinian football. He had an active career as player in Italy (Sampdoria), France (Nancy) and Spain (Atlético Madrid and Rayo Vallecano). He worked successfully as coach in Spain and Italy (Lazio and Roma) and was in charge of the Argentinian national team in the World Cups of 1962 and 1966. He was strongly opposed to the 'typical Argentinian style', which he characterized as very slow, without discipline in defence and over-preoccupied with ball skills. He defined this style as 'anachronistic traditionalism producing stagnation'.[22] He emphasized that this ideology produced excellent jugglers but incomplete footballers. He tried to combine ability with speed and tactical discipline. His model was the German team of 1954. They lost in the preliminaries against Hungary but eventually defeated them in the final. According to Lorenzo, the Germans understood that 'art' could be destroyed by physical power, and they had shown this in the final. He writes: 'Germany won due to its physical capacity, spirit of sacrifice...and a strong and intelligent tactical discipline'.[23] Moreover, he argued that the Brazilian victory of 1958 was closely related to an ideal combination of ability, speed and tactical discipline in defence. His philosophy was summarized in a slogan: 'Before we played football, now we run football'.[24]

It is easy to understand that in the 1960s, after the catastrophe of

Sweden, Lorenzo was a charismatic 'pioneer' of a 'needed revolution' in Argentinian football. He was considered, and became, a national figure, enjoying for a long period the total support of the Argentinian Football Association. However, he did not succeed as coach and Argentina did very poorly in the World Cups of 1962 and 1966. His most important contribution was, without doubt, to question the traditional style of play. He emphasized that the model players were the Argentinians who had triumphed in Europe: Orsi, Monti, Guaita, Di Stéfano, Sivori and Angelillo. They were, in a way, jugglers, but above all they were real, disciplined professionals. The national teams he coached symbolized the transitional years, a period of deep identity crisis: they abandoned the 'rioplatense' slow tempo, and tactical discipline was interpreted not only as running faster but also as tackling harder and without mercy. The image of Rattin, the captain, leaving Wembley in 1966 while one hundred thousand English fans cried 'Animals Animals' is still remembered as the symbol of his epoch.

Argentinian teams did not get the recognition they deserved. At club level, the 1960s produced Estudiantes de la Plata, where Carlos Bilardo was a player, one of the most physical teams in the history of Argentinian football. The coach, Zubeldia, represented the victory of Machiavellianism and pragmatism. The matches against English, Scottish and Italian teams in the finals of the Intercontinental Cup were 'violent struggles': football became war. For the essentialists, Estudiantes de la Plata and Lorenzo stood for the denaturalization of a style based on generosity, still, art, inspiration, beauty and individualism. In this perspective, the success of the great players in Europe was related to these values. Orsi, Di Stéfano and Sivori were always perceived as very skilful players who imposed their art in spite of collective discipline and the physical game. It was the time of H.Herrera and Inter in Europe. The essentialists saw Lorenzo, Zubeldia and H.Herrera as the 'enemies' representing greediness, force, graft, boredom and team discipline. They accused them of teaching players pragmatic amoral standards: any means are valid if victory is achieved. In addition, they argued that proper behaviour on the field could only be achieved by maintaining the values of generosity and beauty. This was the 'real and everlasting Argentinian style'.

The debate in Argentinian football was related to a concrete historical crisis: neither the typical way of playing nor the 'modern' had enabled Argentina to win the World Cup. Argentinians were profoundly frustrated by the lack of victories during a period in which they believed that they had produced the most outstanding players in the world. Some essentialists never understood that the best players always play in the best teams. The relativists in their turn, like Lorenzo and Zubeldia, put Argentinian players in a difficult position, stressing the importance of discipline, intelligence and 'smart tricks'. These two approaches divided the cultural world of football, reproducing over time the same identity crisis that they were trying to solve. Argentines are generally as divided now as they were in the 1960s.

The Age of National Success

Football and sport in general are exceptional in being privileged areas as far as patriotism is concerned. Argentinian football created a symbolic and practical male arena for national pride and disappointment, happiness and sorrow. Women were excluded from this field of discourse and practice. The question of national identity in sport and politics seems to be a domain reserved for the male imagination. In this process, the image of a national identity is chosen from a manifold reality; it is a kind of arbitrary selection and, therefore, it is always open. The debate between essentialists and relativists illustrates this problem: a national identity, irrespective of the perspective assumed, is always 'imagined'.[25] For the essentialists, it is continuity that counts, defending the 'essence' of a style; for the relativists, it is the relation to other styles, the adaptation to a moving international context, what matters. The essentialists, however, accept changes, as we have seen, but they are always functional and 'tactical' and help to keep the imagined football traditions alive.

The 1978 World Cup, in Argentina, was the ideal occasion for confronting history, for transforming the myth into reality: Argentinians were the best footballers in the world. The political context invited a revival of traditions. From 1976, the military Junta tried 'to extirpate the cancer of guerrilla revolutionaries who had infiltrated the body of Argentinian society'. The nationalist language of the military, fighting against 'the influence of foreign ideas and communism', created a positive atmosphere for an essentialist discourse in football. History produces unexpected coincidences. In this case, the presence within the same symbolic field of the reactionary generals and a 'progressive' essentialist: César Luis Menotti. This coincidence in turn produced paradoxes that Argentinians are used to: the victory of a style in football was transformed into 'the victory of the race' over foreign influences and powers. This was not the language, but the tragedy of Menotti.

Menotti was a talented inside-left: slow, tall, elegant, very technical, visionary and a great goal-scorer. He began his career in Rosario Central with great success. Later, he played in two of the five 'great' teams of Argentina: Racing Club in 1964 and Boca Juniors in 1965. His stay at Boca Juniors was very problematic. His languid style based on elegant touches did not fit very well with the kick-and-run method that has always characterized Boca Juniors. Like many Argentinian players, he went abroad. In 1967, he played in New York for The Generals and in 1969 for the famous Brazilian club Santos.[26]

He was always known as being very articulate, with contacts in radical university milieux, and sympathetic to left-wing ideas. At the end of his playing career he began a short stint as a journalist and in 1973 was appointed coach of Huracán, a Buenos Aires club of some prestige but without a single league title to its name. In that year he built up a great team which easily won the league title at the end of the season. After further failure for Argentina in the 1974 World Cup, he was appointed national team coach for the 1978 World Cup in Argentina. Argentinia's victory in 1978, followed by the success of Maradona, Diaz, Barbas, Simon and Calderón among others in the Under-21 World Cup in Tokyo the following year, made him a national hero. It is easy to imagine that for Argentinians these victories were the realization of a national dream, nurtured since the beginnings of organized football. It was the historical confirmation of an 'imagined' and elusive superiority.

For the Junta it was clear: the victories demonstrated the excellence of the 'race' and the importance of unity, like that of the national team, in the face of all types of enemy. Menotti desperately tried to rationalize the success, searching the history of football rather than political history for categories and concepts with which to interpret the happy events. He developed a simple ideological theory: society and politics are based on hypocrisy and deception; 'his philosophy of football' tries to demonstrate the importance of playing with generosity, creativity and honesty, without tricks. Football, then, in a difficult period of Argentinian history could be seen as an arena dominated by 'permanent' values of decency. He says:

> Many people could say that I have coached teams during a time of dictatorship, in an epoch when Argentina had governments whose views I did not share and, even more, contradicted my way of life. And I ask, what ought I to have done? To coach teams which played badly, which based everything on tricks, which betrayed the feelings of the people? No, of course not...We were conscious all the time that we played for the people. A people who at that time in Argentina needed a new point of departure for doing something different together...We tried to play in the most attractive way because we understood that we were obliged to give back the spectacle of football to the people. To give it back through victory, if this was possible, but, above all, through the pleasure of playing honest football. Each of us had an order when we took to the field on the day of the final: to look at the people in the stand. We are not going to look at the box occupied by the officials. I told the players, 'We are going to look at the stand,

to all the people, where perhaps sits the father of each of us, because there we will find the metal workers, the butchers, the bakers and the taxi drivers.'[27]

Menotti recreates a history of purity through an explicit cult of heritage, the heritage of the great players of Argentina, many of whom are named in this study, who sought success without tricks. He advocates these qualities to counteract the contamination produced by other ways of interpreting football. Menotti tell us that tricks have no place in his essentialist perspective. In this way he contrasts the 'pure' Argentinians with the 'impure', the contaminated and, therefore, the contaminators of essential Argentinian identity. In his discourse on football 'the real enemy' is the Estudiantes de la Plata team coached by Zubeldia, for which, coincidentally, Carlos Bilardo played during his active period a as footballer. According to Menotti, Zubeldia and his team developed a football based on the systematic use of tricks and, therefore, represented the 'other football', a way of playing that must be opposed.[28] In this kind of discourse, the Argentinian 'real style and identity' is always threatened and, therefore, in spite of the importance of tradition, is also perceived as ephemeral. To be Argentinian in football, according to Menotti, then, is to feel vulnerable and at risk, for one has defined oneself in terms of a national style and/or a set of qualities that can never be regarded as fully secure. From this perspective, 'Argentinianness' is the very opposite of 'Brazilianness' or 'Englishness', which are defined as stable and solid. It is said in Argentina that the Brazilians and the English have maintained the purity of their style despite tragedies and failures. If we follow this logic we can conclude by saying that from an essentialist perspective the fragility of identity needs support and requires constant re-creation.

Neither in 1978 nor in 1986 did the Argentinians played in a such a way as to eclipse the mythical Brazilian teams of 1958, 1970 or 1982, the Hungarian team of 1954, the Dutch team of 1974, or the French team of 1982. They entered into the historical record but not the mythology of football. Even the victory in 1978 was obtained at home, in a terrible political climate, with some players practising a very physical style of play, and with a dubious victory against Peru in the quarter-finals. Nevertheless, Menotti insisted that he recreated in 1978 a team based on a tradition. Bilardo will never argue in such a way, for him football is a game, it is not a privileged arena for discovering national qualities. In his estimation what matters is victory and not philosophy or the proof of moral qualities.

The problem is that for most Argentinians national feeling is always a matter of contrast; it presupposes other countries and other styles. The 'imagined' community, the 'imagined' style is always thought of as unique.

In this sense, football appeals to a sense of collective belonging: nations need traditions, great teams and great heroes. And in addition they need their qualities to be recognized by others. Menotti repeated, over and over again, that his two victorious teams, the senior in 1978 and the junior in 1979, produced many players who achieved great success in European football. This fact was a measure of his triumph as a coach and as defender of the 'ancestral tradition'. He ironically commented: 'I laughed when one day I heard the coach of the national team, Bilardo, saying that we left no legacy. He should travel around Europe, he should ask, and he would find out what Argentinian football was like before Menotti and his team, and what it was like after us...if only he could achieve twenty per cent of what we accomplished in our day.'[29]

Bilardo's team of 1986 did not capture the imagination of millions of fans. Even in Argentina after the victory in Mexico it was said that the team depended on one genius (Maradona), two excellent players (Burruchaga and Valdano) and eight disciplined 'Japanese' who worked the whole time for the others. Therefore, what did enter into the mythological world of football? The image of Maradona, the man who in Mexico 'won singlehandedly', explodes the idea of a team with a style of its own.[30] He was variously described in the following terms: 'a hero', 'the creator of luck', 'the intrepid robber', 'the omnipresent', 'strong as a bull', 'as quick as a missile'; 'the star of the century'; 'in his blood doctors will find not blood, but missile fuel'; 'moving like wind through a crevice'. The style is that of a man, a lonely individual like Orsi, Di Stéfano and Sivori formerly. In this sense, the great heroes are appropriated by others: they do not evoke national associations in neutral spectators because 'they elevate football to the level of a musical abstraction, to the most absolute purity'.[31] They had the capacity to recreate and to re-actualize the beauty of the game.

The problem, from the Argentinian point of view, is not only the fact that heroes are universalized in a context where football belongs to a kind of 'world global culture', but that they are perceived as 'historical accidents', as 'products of an arbitrary nature'. Maradona, in this kind of interpretation, is not associated with a tradition, or a national style – he is himself, he is unique, and, therefore, his nationality is accidental. After Mexico it was said, that any team could have won if they had had Maradona. Any national Brazilian team will always be defined as 'the team to beat', as 'the favourite' before each World Cup, and, consequently, they are treated with an almost religious respect and consideration. The same could be said of the German national team. This has not been and will not be the case for Argentinian teams. Maradona, however, understood this very well. He does not perceive himself as the continuation of a great national tradition, his talent is a 'divine gift'. He maintained that: 'My faith helps me in each moment of my life. God is with me and my family, with my parents, my sisters, my brothers, with every one. I always say that God plays with me. I realize this when I am on the football field and when I am not, in the street, or in my house.'[32]

Therefore, his explanation of the first goal against England in Mexico, 'I scored with the hand of God and the head of Maradona', is logical. He is touched by the magic of God and not by the power of his football ancestors. He is not the continuation of a great tradition. He is himself; he is simply Maradona alone before God. He must not be compared with other human beings. He is not the product of a cultural heritage; he has been created as a divine, religious subject.[33]

Conclusion

In this study I have developed two main ideas. The first is related to the question of how national identity is represented as 'an ideological construct' where given qualities are associated with a 'typical Argentinian way' of playing football. In the search for essential features, given teams and players are recorded and their characteristics are transformed into 'ahistorical traits'. Football is used as a symbolic arena for producing discourses about an 'imagined and limited' national membership. However, this essay has tried to demonstrate that Argentinians believed for a long period of time, until the crisis of the 1958 World Cup, that they played the most creative and beautiful football in the world. This could be interpreted in different ways: as a deep complex of superiority, as a very provincial perspective, or as a manifestation of insecurity. This 'image' was reinforced by the presence of international stars who achieved great success in European football. In this respect, national identity was heavily dependent on the role played by outstanding individuals. If a style depends so much on given heroes, who are also mortal human beings, identity is then transformed into something ephemeral and problematic. History, then, is not only a question of continuity, as the essentialists maintain, but of lucky accidents and unexpected events. I believe, although it is not possible to develop this idea here, that one may find the same logic in the Argentinian interpretation of a stormy and difficult history as an unrealized modern nation on the periphery of the world. This history is dominated by two 'unique' groups, the Radical and the Peronist, unlike those that exist in the modern political world, whose ideologies are related to the cult of ancestors (Irigoyen and Perón). Hence a diffuse tradition permits the legitimation of beliefs through the exceptional role of unusual individuals. The Argentinian football tradition is, essentially, an adjunct of individual heroes and their marvellous performances. The style is thus a myth; the individuals are the real history. You can invent a tradition, but never concrete individual lives.

The second idea is very simple: football is an arena dominated by the conflict of interpretations. It is a kind of theatre in the world; it is a field made of 'realities and masks'; it is a stage dominated by dissimilar meanings; it is a beautiful game that invites us to think about reality as the product of different skills and tricks. The actual division between Menottists and Bilardists illustrates this remark and permit us to see identity, values and meaning as a complex field of analysis. Again, the divisions represented by different schools question the idea of an 'unchanged' national style.

NOTES

This essay was originally presented at the conference 'Football and Europe' organized by the European Culture Research Centre, European University Institute, Florence, Italy, 3–5 May 1990.

  1. 'Introduction' in M. Chapman, M. McDonald and E. Tonkin (eds.), *History and Ethnicity* (London, 1989), p.17. In an analysis of Brazilian football undertaken by R. Da Matta and other anthropologists, it is postulated that football is a privileged arena that permits a discussion of identities and dramas in social life. See R. Da Matta *et al.*, *Universo do futebol:esporte e sociedade brasileira* (Rio de Janeiro, 1982).
  2. For Argentinian football history see: E. Escobar Bavio, *Historia del fútbol en el Rio de la Plata* (Buenos Aires, 1923); E. Olivera, *Orígenes de los deportes británicos en el Rio de la Plata* (Buenos Aires, 1932); and P. Ramírez, *Historia del fútbol profesional* (Buenos Aires, 1977).
  3. See E. Ardener, 'The Construction of History: "Vestiges of Creation"' in M. Chapman, M. McDonald and E. Tonkin (eds.), *History and Ethnicity*, p.26.
  4. See T. Mason, 'Football' in T. Mason (ed.), *Sport in Britain* (Cambridge, 1989).
  5. A. Scher and H. Palomino, *Fútbol: pasión de multitudes y de elites* (Buenos Aires, 1988), p.25.
  6. H. De Marinis, 'La pasión furbolística' in *La vida de nuestro pueblo*, 33 (Buenos Aires, 1981, p.6.
  7. T. Mason, *Sport in Britain*, pp.177–8.
  8. J.C. Lorenzo and J. Castelli, *El fútbol en un mundo de cambios* (Buenos Aires, 1977), p.37.
  9. G. Brera, *Storia critica del calcio italiano* (Milan, 1978), p.98.
 10. J.C. Lorenzo and J. Catelli, *El fútbol*, pp.36–7.
 11. Ibid., p.38.
 12. Ibid., p.41.
 13. C.L. Menotti, *Fútbol sin trampa* (Barcelona, 1986), p.63.
 14. D. Lucero, *Siento ruido de pelota* (Buenos Aires, 1975), p.140.
 15. P. Unzueta, *A mi el pelotón* (San Sebastian, 1986), p.39.
 16. *El País Deportes*, 19 Feb. 1990, 7.
 17. Obdulio Varela, the renowned centre-half and captain of the Uruguayan team, remembered this day as follows: 'After the match I went out with the masseur to a friend's bar. We did not have a single penny and we asked for credit. We sat in a corner and saw all the people. All of them were crying. It was like a lie: everyone had tears in their eyes... We had ruined everything and what had we got? We got a title, but what was it in relation to this sadness? I thought about Uruguay. There, perhaps, the people were happy. But I was here, in Rio de Janeiro, in the middle of so many unhappy people... If I had to play the final over again, I would score an own-goal, yes, Sir'. See O. Soriano, *Artistas, locos y criminales* (Buenos Aires, 1984), p.78.
      A fan at Maracaná on that day remembered: 'At times of sadness all the people were united. It is like this also in moments of happiness. The same happened in a moment of sadness.

Everyone was suddenly a Brazilian. It was Brazil that lost. It was our country that was defeated.' A. Vogel, 'O momento feliz. Reflexoes, sobre o futebol e ethos nacional' in R. Da Matta *et al.*, p.90.

18. G. Brera, *Storia Critica*, pp.280–6.
19. Ibid., p.286.
20. C.L. Menotti, *Fútbol sin trampa*, p.63.
21. J.C. Iglesias, *El País Deportes* (Madrid, 8/1-1990) p.24.
22. J.C. Lorenzo and J. Castelli, *El fútbol*, p.31.
23. Ibid., p.44.
24. Ibid., p.49.
25. B. Andersson, *Imagined Communities. Reflections on the Origin and the Spread of Nationalism* (London, 1983), p.11.
26. See Gasparini-Pónsico, *El director técnico del proceso* (Buenos Aires, 1983). Gasparini and Ponsico, well-known Argentinian journalists, have written the most militant pamphlet against Menotti. They describe him as a very ambitious person with double standards and as a political opportunist. The title of the book indicates their message: 'the coach of the "process".' In military junta jargon the dictatorship installed in 1976 was baptized 'the "process" of national reorganization'.
27. C.L. Menotti, p.27.
28. Ibid., pp.29–30.
29. *El Gráfico*, 7 July 1988. Bilardo thinks differently. For him the exile of Argentinian players is a sign of deep crisis and not of success. He asks himself: 'Which football nation in the world could stand the fact that 150 top players had left its country the last two years? If this happened in Italy, its teams would consist of second division players... Under these conditions the existence of Argentinian football is a miracle'. *El Pais Deportes*, 8 Jan. 1990, 9.
30. M. Darwish, 'Maradona. Plegarias al héroe de nuestro tiempo', *El País Domingo*, 14 Dec. 1986, 18.
31. M. Darwish, op. cit. p.15.
32. *Corriere della Sera* (Milan), 11 Nov. 1985.
33. Italian journalists and Napoli's fans understand this 'religious dimension' in Maradona. They can write and think about miracles and magic. The day after Napoli's victory over Juventus, Gregori writes: 'This is a field of miracles, a chest which cannot be opened by anyone: yesterday Maradona had revealed diamonds, rubies, emeralds, topazes. With a simple gesture, a simple movement of his muscles, he has resuscitated a moment of enchantment. The two goals were created by magic... Maradona is always the same: unbelievable, untouchable, untrustworthy, superb and arrogant when he is in possession of Beauty, laying waste to all the other football stars who happen to be near him', *La Gazzetta dello Sport* (Milan), 26 March 1990, 3. Paolo Forcolin is even more enthusiastic: 'Half an hour of the game, two goals, two magic inventions of "Bambin Gesú" [young Jesus Christ – Maradona's Italian nickname], him, Diego. This was the end of the match', *La Gazzetta dello Sport*, Milan, 26 March 1990, 5. Belmonte, in a passionate monograph of a small neighbourhood in the slums of Naples, found out that Neapolitans preserve a Catholic ritual façade but prefer their many saints and Madonna-goddesses to Christ and maintain an active belief in myriad local house-spirits (*The Broken Fountain* [New York, 1979], p.141). In this context one might expect Maradona to become 'Bambin Gesú'; he is transformed into a local saint, into a young Jesus Christ himself.

Nationalism and Sport in Latin America, 1850–1990: The Paradox of Promoting and Performing 'European' Sports

JOSEPH L. ARBENA

Although nearly all of the 'Latin' countries of Latin America had achieved nominal independence by the 1820s, it is generally agreed that that political step was not accompanied in any area by a broad-based, deeply felt spirit of nationalism. Only after the mid-1800s, and then very slowly, did certain Latin Americans – statesmen, educators, intellectuals, businessmen – begin to pursue programmes aimed at stimulating nationalism. The present century has seen more deliberate efforts at nation building and jingoism, but on balance, long-term, emotional and functional nationalism remains relatively weak in most Latin American countries, a problem compounded by the tension between a search for national identity and one for regional or even hemispheric identity.[1]

By nationalism, here and later, we refer to at least three distinct but not mutually exclusive senses of the term at the nation-state level. First is the building of loyalty to the national state or government (the *patria grande*) through a reduction in traditional loyalty to local or (sub-national) regional areas (the *patria chica*). Second is the cultivation of pride in the positive achievements and creativity of citizens, groups, or agencies who seem to express the shared needs and feelings of that larger national community as opposed to citizens of other countries. Third is the promotion of negative images of 'foreigners' so as to create a sense of who 'we' are by distinguishing 'us' from the undesirable characteristics of 'them'. There are few, if any, national groups in the ethnic sense in Latin America today, though there is considerable ethnic diversity which, like class and regional differences, can hamper national integration. As Rodolpho Stavenhagen has argued, 'In political and cultural terms, the idea of a nation in contemporary Latin America is based on the denial of indigenous cultures',[2] even if indigenous communities and some indigenous cultural expressions remain: for nowhere is as indigenous culture, or that of any other identifiable ethnic group, the basis for cultivating the national identity of the region's two dozen post-colonial countries.[3]

In effect, then, strengthening nationalism in Latin America has meant creating a psychic identity to coincide with somewhat artificially delineated political borders, and the construction of features suitable to that end has meant drawing on a wide range of cultural and historical models and experiences, many inspired by European much more than indigenous or African influences.[4] Consciously or not, the implicit objective in the best of cases is greater political stability, national self-determination, and the basis for improvement in overall socio-economic conditions, though in fact the ultimate objective may be to preserve the power and privileges of dominant/ hegemonic political, economic and social groups. Nationalism, therefore, may itself be as much a mechanism for social control as for social change.[5]

In that context we can ask what role sport has played in Latin America since the late nineteenth century in helping or hindering the move toward stronger nationalistic institutions and feelings and, implicity, in maintaining or changing social institutions. This study presents a summary of selected impressions of those questions and of potential answers made in the course of long-term study of sport and the pursuit of national identity in Latin America from about 1850 to the present. My thinking thus far focuses on several issues.

With little debate it seems fair to follow Bale, Guttmann and others in concluding that the history (and language) of 'modern' organized sport in Latin America is the history of the diffusion, adoption and manipulation of sports invented and/or codified and institutionalized by Europeans, mainly the British and Anglo-Americans.[6] One need spend only a weekend in Buenos Aires (or perhaps Montevideo or Santiago) to appreciate the pervasiveness today of such sports as soccer, rugby, polo, cycling, boxing, horse-racing, rowing, tennis, golf, auto racing, even (though less important than a few decades ago) fencing and athletics. In a few places, several Iberian sports, such as bullfighting and derivatives of the Basque ball game family, persist at a lower level, while indigenous survivals are mere anthropological or recreational curiosities. Basketball and volleyball are now widely played from north to south. Regionally, in Anglo-Caribbean areas cricket fills the top sporting spot, while among many circum-Caribbean hispanophones, both Indo and Afro, baseball is 'el rey de los deportes' ('the king of sports').

Elsewhere this author has speculated on why it was that these changes, which were already visible long before the end of the last century, occurred so rapidly in Latin America and with what consequences. No doubt it was a combination of both the 'intrinsic ludic properties' and the 'extrinsic cultural associations' which led Latin Americas increasingly to play European games.[7] Likewise, those imported sports had a partially imperialistic impact in that they helped to shape local elites and their values in ways at least initially beneficial to the Europeans and that those sports made the Latin Americans just a bit more 'dependent' on the dominant European world.[8] They also had a strong influence on the languages (i.e. Spanish and Portuguese) of the recipient countries. In particular, imported sports vocabulary produced what some critics consider a corruptive effect, as foreign (especially English) words increasingly penetrated both written and spoken communication, in the form of either direct adoptions or phonetic transcriptions; eventually, also, sports images came to permeate much of political and daily discourse even when these were totally unrelated to sports themes or contexts.[9]

The irony, then, is that while Latin American societies were gradually trying to strengthen nationalistic feelings, they were often doing so along with, and at times by means of the increasing presence of imported European culture, strong indications of which were the increasing practice of foreign sports and the intrusion of an accompanying vocabulary. Consequently, even at the end of the twentieth century, and despite alleged attempts to define for themselves new identities and perhaps new ideologies, Latin Americans still basically define their economic, political and cultural goals, whether of the left or the right, in terms set by the experiences, standards, values and institutions of the global centre's capitalist or socialist systems.[10]

In many cases those sports came inextricably intertwined with other European (or North American) institutions, such as schools, athletics and social clubs and commercial enterprises. To the extent that sport, as many Victorian proponents hoped, also conveyed values and models, they likewise offered a potential means to modify traditional Latin American society, be it some remnant of indigenous culture or more likely some creole or mixed variety.[11] Following the oft-cited teachings of the Argentine politician and educator Domingo F. Sarmiento, that the only way for any country of Latin America to progress was through a major acceptance of European behaviour, leaders in different parts of the hemisphere began to embrace European sports and physical education, along with other cultural forms, as a viable means of developing their own national societies, displacing – at times by force – the cultural and recreations practices of Latin America's 'folk' communities.[12]

In Porfirian Mexico (1877–1911), for example, the growing popularity of both competitive and recreational cycling paralleled and reinforced the acceptance of values and behaviour associated with industrialization and so-called modernization in Europe and the United States. Part of this was mere imitation of a European fad, aimed at proving that Mexicans could behave like the 'best' people of the civilized world, but some of it derived from cycling's connection with technology, physical fitness, precision in measuring time and distance, and commercialization. To some degree the acceptance of baseball, horse-racing, and a bullfighting revival can be attributed to similar motives. So Mexico was being 'developed' and a sense of Mexicanness being stimulated, however incidentally, by means of imported cultural forms. The resulting tensions would burst forth as part of the post-1910 Mexican Revolution.[13]

In Argentina the approach was much more structured both inside and outside those institutions linked to the conspicuous foreign presence.[14] Before the end of the nineteenth century, Argentines were regularly engaged in athletic competitions involving the newer sports, with foreigners resident in the Southern Cone, with visiting teams from Europe, and with clubs of both foreigners and locals in and around Montevideo across the Río de la Plata estuary.[15] By the 1910s Argentina had established a national institute for physical education and was participating in the international Olympic movement.[16] At least among an elite, there was an early perceived value in promoting sport both to build Argentina within and to gain it respect without. César Viale, lawyer and politician and president of the Argentine Boxing Federation and the Argentine Olympic Committee, held that Argentina should join those civilized nations that promote 'the muscular' in pursuit of what is 'noble, worthy, and beautiful'. Physical and athletic development would eventually serve as 'expression of power, a guarantee of virility', and the basis of those triumphs which would be enjoyed by tomorrow's generations.[17]

In the twentieth century the use of sport for intended nationalistic purposes has tended to follow three paths:

The Establishment of Domestic Physical Education Programmes, Sports Competitions, and the Permanent Institutions Necessary to Oversee Athletic Programmes

Either building on the small foundations laid in the late 1800s, or, more commonly, starting from scratch, Latin Americans have tried to expand their domestic facilities and institutions for promoting physical education, recreation and competitive sports. Repeatedly the argument has been made that physical education and sports can teach constructive values, improve health and morals, aid the economy, reduce vice and crime, develop a sense of community and co-operation, and, of course, promote patriotism and nationalism. Typical of many Latin Americans, the former president of the Venezuelan Instituto Nacional de Deportes expressed his belief that sport 'constitutes an integral part of man's formation and a fundamental element in the concept of the Fatherland'. Sport is, for him, essential for the country's development, while athletic successes can likewise earn it respect and prestige.[18]

That these efforts have mostly failed is obvious. Not only have the institutions and activities usually been grossly understaffed and underfunded, but in countries where regionalism remains a viable force, the holding of 'national games' may intensify rather than soften the sectarian identities and rivalries. This was the case, for example, with the National Sports Games held in Quito, Ecuador, in November 1974. One objective of the games was to stimulate friendship and build national unity among all Ecuadorians. Yet, in covering the event, newspapers around the country tended to support athletes from their regions and to criticize both the national government and the athletes from other areas.[19] Such competition may also highlight traditional regional inequities which will intensify rather than diminish hostility toward the national metropolitan centre, as smaller communities in, let's say, Peru find that they cannot compete with the clubs in the larger cities, especially (Lima), because they lack adequate training facilities, or if professional, the funds to pay players salaries sufficient to keep them in town.[20]

The Preparation of Individuals and Teams Capable of Competing Successfully at the International Level

In theory not inconsistent with the efforts to bring more sports to the general population, but often in conflict for scarce resources, programmes have been aimed at preparing athletes and teams to win at international level and thus bring prestige to governments and pride to the people. All Latin American countries today have a hierarchy of federations and Olympic committees designed to promote their respective sports.[21] Most of these, however, are no better situated than those assigned to fostering physical education or national games, and their leaders sometimes appear more interested in serving their own interests rather than those of the athletes. Analysing recent experiences in El Salvador, Augusto Antonio Cornejo lamented that various national sports agencies 'became instruments which, at the service of their directors, functioned merely as means to achieve status and benefits', producing only disagreements and fights. 'The Salvadoran Olympic Committee finds itself in similar conditions, having served just to represent the country but not to aid the growth of Salvadoran sport.'[22] Such an assessment echoed observations of the Colombian sporting scene a generation ago.[23]

Even when funds are relatively more abundant it has been suggested that Latin Americans often lack an adequate support structure and the necessary 'sporting mentality' to produce a proportionate number of high-level athletes.[24] Peruvian journalist Abelardo Sánchez León, who has written extensively on the few successes and many failures of his country on the international sporting scene, while citing a lack of finances and facilities, likewise wonders if his fellow Peruvians have the proper attitude towards training, teamwork, and style of play to ever gain more than isolated athletic respect abroad.[25] A late Chilean professor, himself a former soccer player and coach, may have summed up the essence of the issue: 'In the Chilean case, the atmosphere does not aid the athlete, in that it neither motivates him nor provides him with the elements which sport requires to develop. In addition, its structure is not clearly defined; everything is unpredictable, conforming only to the wishes of the men who control soccer.'[26]

In the end, victories are rare and more often the function of private rather than public labours. Such was the case, for example, of the Mexican walker, Raúl Gonzáles Rodríguez, who won three world championships, two Olympic medals, and various other national and international competitions. In his autobiography Gonzáles Rodríguez recounts the difficulties of achieving excellence in a non-professional sport in a Third World country, where lack of administrative and financial support forced him to raise funds and develop a training regimen virtually on his own.[27]

But we are still left with the question of whether those successes which have been achieved by Latin American athletes have done more than gain momentary attention and provoke pleasant emotions. While nearly everyone once knew that Pelé was from Brazil, it is hard to agree with the claim that soccer across the years has brought 'recognition and prestige' to Costa Rica.[28] And Andrés Gómez may be a hero to many Ecuadorians, but his status surely means less in day-to-day functional terms than the traditional tension between Quito and Guayaquil.[29]

Janet Lever contends that sport generally and, in Brazil, soccer specifically have the 'paradoxical ability to reinforce societal cleavages while transcending them', 'to create social order while preserving cultural identity', thus promoting rather than impeding goals of national development.[30] By extension, however, the case could also be made that international competition can likewise diminish nationalism in favour of a greater sense of transnational community, if only through a sense of shared experiences and the consequences of operating within similar institutions and regulations.[31] Alan Klein demonstrates the highly ambivalent reactions of Dominicans to their relationship with United States baseball – an ambivalence apparently shared by baseball lovers throughout the circum-Caribbean region – and describes how difficult it is to determine if sport and its institutions, in this case at least partially 'foreign', contribute to exploitation or development, to colonialism or nationalism, to hegemony or resistance. For how should Dominicans react when their local heroes leave them behind to become highly paid stars in the United States and when North American clubs establish camps in the Dominican Republic to harvest the best of the amateur players for uncertain futures in organized baseball?[32] Thus generalizations about the contributions of successful athletes and teams to a country's state of nationalism are at best problematical.[33]

There is also the interesting case of the Anglophone Afro-Caribbean where cricket is such an integral part of the post-colonial culture. Virtually everyone who writes on the subject concedes that learning the game and the ethic of cricket may have initially made West Indian blacks better colonial subjects, but eventually their enthusiasm for and skill at the sport made it easier for those blacks to challenge the foundations of racism, to prove their social and mental worth, and to pursue more confidently the road to national independence and self-government. It has also helped bring together islands that are physically separated and peoples who are at times more different than one might first believe.[34] Nevertheless, even here the process of homogenization is not complete and sport has provided opportunities for the expression of both ethnic and class divisions, if only in muted ways. Kevin Yelvington explains how a test match between India and West Indies in 1976, coinciding with national elections in Trinidad and Tobago, stimulated the open expression of long-standing ethnic cleavages. The local East Indian population, which feels itself a 'subjugated' people, tended to cheer for the visitors, while Caribbean blacks vocally supported the home team.[35] The Mandles, also focusing on Trinidad and Tobago, have shown how basketball has allowed poor, deprived people, at least on the 'micro' level, 'an increase in its opportunity for achievement and recognition, for expressiveness and enjoyment', in a social context which traditionally denies them so much.[36]

The Hosting of International Sporting Events

In the short run, among the most visible sporting policies which governments have used to win favour, as well as to make a profit,[37] and which might have nationalistic impact is the hosting of international sporting events on any of several levels. As early as 1930, for example, Uruguayans gained great satisfaction from both hosting and winning the inaugural soccer World Cup, leading the journalist and sportsman José María Delgado to wax poetic about his country's latest heroic exploit, as Montevideo became the centre of the earth and 'Uruguay, once again and even more clearly than before, was champion of the world'.[38] In later years Brazil (1950), Chile (1962), Mexico (1970 and 1986), and Argentina (1978) would pride themselves on their ability to organize this increasingly complicated affair.[39] Still, the hosting of these events was never without major critics, and, by contrast, few Colombians were seriously upset when their government opted not to sponsor the 1986 festival.[40]

In addition, Mexico hosted the 1968 Olympic Games, which likewise generated official efforts to promote Mexican pride at home and a more positive image of Mexico around the world. National leaders clearly hoped to win favour among their people and both to gain political acceptance abroad and to attract foreign investment and tourism to Mexico itself. No doubt some of this was achieved, but much of the potential goodwill was lost when the government felt compelled a few weeks prior to the Games to crack down on students and workers who were protesting about political and economic conditions.[41]

Other examples of more modest attempts at using such events to stimulate national pride and regime legitimacy include Mexico's inauguration of the Central American and Caribbean Games in 1926, the convening of the first Bolivarian Games in August 1938 in conjunction with the 400th anniversary of the founding of Bogotá, Colombia, Peronista Argentina's invitation to launch the Pan-American Games in 1951, and Guatemala's hosting, in 1950, of the sixth edition of the games begun in Mexico in 1926. The last is instructive because it permitted a self-styled revolutionary regime to present itself at home and abroad as competent, democratic, peace-loving and worthy of popular support. 'Doing sport, we build the Fatherland' became a much publicized motto of the Games, and Guatemalans were encouraged to take national pride in what they had accomplished, while remembering their ties to other brown-skinned and dark-eyed peoples of America. Guatemala was 'on the march', and the efforts its people demonstrated in hosting the Games and that its athletes put forth in competition were not only a testimony to the success of the revolution but also a contribution to international solidarity.[42]

But, again we ask, to what effect? Whatever the short-term satisfaction and honour earned for the Guatemalan revolution and government in 1950, it was not enough to prevent internal splits and external pressures which overthrew the incumbent regime in 1954; it also contributed little to building a broad-based sport and physical education programme within the country.[43] Both hosting and winning the 1978 Mundial did not save the Argentinian generals, nor bring economic prosperity, nor establish domestic social and political tranquillity. For all of Mexico's visibility as global host, Mexican nationalism today may be as much in crisis as it ever was.[44] And Colombia's years of violence (1946–63) and the current interconnected drug and guerrilla crises hardly suggest a united society at peace with itself.[45]

As a special case, we might mention the record of Cuba since 1959 in these three areas of nationalistic sports policy. Though not without dispute, based on the costs if not the facts, most students of Revolutionary Cuban physical culture contend that Cuba by now has been the most successful of all Latin American countries in constructing an egalitarian sports and recreation system for its citizens and in training athletes to compete in international arenas. Both the reported levels of mass participation in domestic programmes and the number of victories from regional to international competitions suggests that this is probably true. The Castro regime has been less adept at bidding to host international games, in part no doubt because of diplomatic pressures directed by the United States, though the 1991 Pan-American Games were held in Cuba. While all of this has enhanced Cuba's image in some foreign circles, it remains unknown – given the number of defections and the lack of internal openness – to what degree it has strengthened Cuban nationalism[46] or even Castro's popularity, though those goals are certainly part of the government's objectives.[47] In the context of a changing world scene and of refocused Soviet priorities, even the 1991 Pan-Am Games were seen by the Cuban leadership both as a means to trumpet their socialist achievements and as a way to reduce Cuban isolation and attract tourism.[48]

Almost certainly, the ability to compete equally with the United States has added spice to a traditional Cuban anti-Americanism and has won some sympathy among other Latins who like to see Uncle Sam suffer periodic setbacks or to observe a dependent country display significant development in an area which suggests both domestic progress and international power. After calculating the results of the 1970 Central American and Caribbean Games, one Salvadoran cleric expressed amazement at the way a country of eight million people could so dominate countries representing some 100 million. Here was evidence that Cuba had engaged the majority of its youth in sport, not only producing champions, but also promoting the spiritual and corporal well-being of all its people. Cuba was using sport to build its future.[49]

Other Latin American countries have obviously followed Cuba's lead, but none with the same breadth and long-term commitment of resources, and consequently none with the same visible and consistent results. The most obvious was Nicaragua during the decade of Sandinista rule. Here, as in Cuba, professionalism was abolished and structures were established with the purpose of broadening popular participation in an expanded number of sporting and physical activities. Some attention, though less than in Cuba, was given to producing a national sports industry and more championship calibre athletes. Due, however, to a lack of ideological clarity and of trained personnel and to the demands of the war against the US-backed Contras, only limited progress was made, though certainly the situation, with help from Cuban experts and domestic volunteers, had changed markedly between 1979 and 1990 along lines suggesting a Nicaraguan model, not an imported one.[50]

Interestingly, neither the Cubans nor any other 'revolutionary' or nationalist movement proposes the abandonment of 'European' or 'North American' sports as a way to flaunt national identity and independence. Nevertheless, there have been situations where nationalists, officially or unofficially, have displayed indigenous or creole sports/games as part of efforts to promote an appreciation for their countries' cultural heritage, but always within the larger context of the continued practice of the pre-eminent Western sports. For example, on the programme of the Juegos Deportivos Nacionales de la Revolución (November 1941), Mexican organizers scheduled competitions in some 25 sports for male and female amateur athletes to celebrate the 31st anniversary of the Mexican Revolution. But to add to their nationalistic and folkoristic nature the festivities included, on a demonstration basis only, the performance of several 'autochthonous' sports/games as well as typical dancing.[51]

Earlier in the century, Chilean educator Daniel Aeta Astorga tried to promote health, morality and nationalism among his countrymen through expanded programmes of physical education, games and sports in general. But he made a special point of encouraging the inclusion of native games and Spanish/Chilean vocabulary in such programmes in order to enhance the nationalistic objective.[52] As part of their efforts at promoting mass, revolutionary sports the Sandinistas also tried to revive 'traditional values and popular expressions' by linking sports/games to activities associated with traditional festivals.[53]

In the Argentine case, at least one folk sport – the gaucho game of pato – which had been discouraged during the half-century of most intense Europeanization (roughly 1880–1930), has been revived as an expression of 'Argentineness'. But pato – try to imagine a game of basketball on horseback! – has been so stylized or rationalized and the costs are so high that it is much more of an elite diversion than a truly popular activity, tending to appeal to the same class that supports polo. Today's sport may have its roots in the pre-industrial Argentina pampa, but its performance context has been dramatically changed. And efforts to promote the sport in Europe have brought only minimal success.[54] So, for Latin America, imported sports still dominate, and exported sports rarely catch on elsewhere.

If sporting competition has helped build friendly bridges across national boundaries, we should also ask if sport in Latin America has contributed to promoting friction among peoples and their governments across those same frontiers. There is, of course, the oft-cited case of the 'Soccer War', the rather short (100 hours) armed conflict between El Salvador and Honduras which broke out on 1969 after a series of regional matches in the elimination round prior to the 1970 Mundial. The truth is that even here the name is a misnomer in that events on the pitch were at best a catalyst, at worst an excuse, the causes of the conflict residing in much deeper socio-economic and political factors which were likely to have provoked some confrontation whatever the final goal tally.[55]

Beyond that, except for occasional complaints about the comportment of a player on the field or the decisions of certain officials, there is little evidence that the emotions associated with sporting competitions have exacerbated international tensions or deepened negative feelings towards outsiders, though the Cuban factor has provoked a few unpleasant incidents at the sites of international competitions.[56] While United States athletes did compete in the August 1991 Pan American Games in Cuba US spectators and US cash were excluded to the extent that American officials could control them; and it became difficult for Games officials to import the required US manufactured drug-testing equipment and to train the necessary technicians.[57] In short, within Latin America sporting problems rarely alter serious political routines.

However, sporting events may be modified or suspended because of political considerations. For example, neither Venezuela nor the Dominican Republic sent delegations to the 1950 Central American and Caribbean Games in Guatemala City. Those two governments were then headed by military dictators – Marcos Pérez Jiménez and Rafael Leonidas Trujillo respectively – who were clearly at odds politically with the Guatemalan regime of Juan José Arévalo which, as noted above, was using the event in part to promote its own idelogical image.[58] Always anxious to display their independence of Washington, the Cubans went to the Moscow Olympics in 1980, joined the Soviet boycott of the 1984 Los Angeles Games, and strongly supported North Korean claims to share in hosting the 1988 competitions.[59] In contrast, some conservative Guatemalans attended the Moscow Olympics precisely because they wished to express their dislike of what they considered Jimmy Carter's excessively liberal policies towards El Salvador and Nicaragua.[60]

Throughout this essay has noted the paradox evident in the efforts of Latin Americans to employ basically European cultural forms (sports etc.) to implement a fundamentally European concept – the construction of a nation-state with a more nationalistic society – all for the purpose of distancing and differentiating themselves from Europeans, North Americans, and perhaps each other. The same problem plagued the nationalist movement in Latin American music: Latin American composers did develop 'nationalistic' themes through various techniques. But the concept of nationalistic music was borrowed from Europe; the compositional idiom was likewise usually imported from Europe; in some operatic and choral works the language was non-Iberian European, and often the primary intended audience (or market) was European.[61] Even after rejecting such over European influences as Italian 'bel-canto', 'musical nationalism in Latin America was more a product of Western art than of American folk culture; it was the product of an art that discovered in folk music a fresh source with which to rejuvenate itself'. Later, in an attempt to create a broader base for a truly national culture, the bourgeoisie in certain Latin American countries resorted to folklore for inspiration, but again they ended up producing 'folkloristic' music (and art) which were more attuned to foreign or international values than any valid national folk culture.[62] Of course, as noted above, in the realm of sports there has hardly ever been an attempt to find a source for nation building in peasant or folk traditions.

That Latin Americans are aware of this dilemma is seen in the authoritative pronouncements of one of Mafalda's ever wise friends:

> My father says that our problem is that here people live imitating what is fashionable in Europe and the United States. But fortunately the solution is very simple: we have to begin being ourselves and not like the Europeans and North Americans, because they don't give a hoot about us. This is what we have to do: be like them who are only concerned about themselves, because they day we cease imitating them and succeed in being like them, we will begin to be ourselves.

Mafalda replies that it is indeed fortunate that the solution is so simple, which may explain why it has not worked.[63]

There appear to be two other paradoxes confronting those who would use sport, or any other cultural form, to promote nationalism within Latin American countries in the late twentieth century. To the extent that national unity and identity require some degree of ethnic and cultural homogeneity within fixed political boundaries, William McNeill argues that the European nation-state model has become plainly obsolete. Statesmen and others may well now be wasting their time in pursuing nationalism except in the most limited and superficial political or legal sense. The tendency, he concludes, is for people increasingly to transfer their 'loyalties from a smaller to a larger unit by drawing the boundaries between "us" and "them" on a more inclusive basis'.[64]

Secondly, within the Latin, or at least Hispanic world, there is the question of a common language and the relative ease of transnational communication. Consequently, contends Mexican essayist and Nobel laureate Octavio Paz, a true literary and cultural nationalism within individual countries is unlikely since, despite whatever differences, they share the same linguistic, literary and cultural traditions which do much more to bind than to separate.[65] They also frequently share athletes, mainly soccer players. For while the national team (*'selección nacional'*) is composed only of citizens of a single country, the standing professional teams are regularly stocked with foreigners. Consequently, Argentines often cheer for the Bolivians or Peruvians who carry the club's banner, while Colombians have Argentine and Chilean heroes, various South Americans often lead Central American squads, and so on.[66]

Returning to the general proposition that sports can build nationalism, recent events in eastern Europe and the former Soviet Union may also provide additional lessons. Despite some incredible international sports achievements, the leaders of East Germany could not cultivate among their people a sense of unique national identity strong enough to supersede the desire for larger German reunification under West German sponsorship. The painful travails of Mikhail Gorbachev in dealing with the national minorities within the Soviet Union showed that the collective athletic programmes of perhaps the world's leading sports country were insufficient to overcome deeper nationalistic loyalties.[67] Why, therefore should we expect the most limited sporting successes of Latin American athletes to form the basis for long-term, viable nationalistic sentiments in their societies?

Conclusion

If, in balance, the above assessments are correct, we are left with the conclusion that the efforts of the last hundred years to use sport to build 'nations' in Latin America have been relatively ineffective. Sport and physical culture *may* have helped to advance selected political agendas, or to promote 'development' in selected ways, to give many people pleasures as well as pains.[68] Through winning medals and championships, the successful sponsorship of international competitions, and the periodic defeat of teams and athletes from the European and North American sporting powers, Latin Americans have probably also gained in self-confidence and pride.

But that sport has contributed significantly and uniquely to the construction of national identity and cohesiveness – to the building of 'nations' – seems questionable in any long-term context; nor has it completely removed some feelings of weakness, dependency, perhaps even inferiority within the region which derive from Latin America's historical marginality. At best, sport has merged with other social, political, economic, regional, ethnic, religious and institutional forces to aid the nation-building process. At times, however, sport has worked against that process and/or has been easily overwhelmed by the destructive and divisive impact of those same complex and volatile pressures.[69] Yet, perhaps because of a naive faith in the efficacy of sport or perhaps because of the perceived benefits which sport has provided many 'advanced' countries of Europe and North America, Latin Americans and others in the Third World seem committed to continuing the application of sporting models imported from the metropolitan centres.[70]

NOTES

1. Arthur P. Whitaker, *Nationalism in Latin America* (Gainesville: University of Florida Press, 1962); Leopoldo Zea *et al.*, *El problema de la identidad latinoamericana* (Mexico, D.F.: Imprenta Universitaria de la UNAM, 1985).

2. Rodolfo Stavenhagen, 'Human Rights of Indigenous Peoples', *Voices of Mexico*, Nos. 8–9. (June–Nov. 1988), 56–62 (quote is from 58–9).

3. Anthony H. Richmond, 'Ethnic Nationalism: Social Science Paradigms', *International Social Science Journal*, 111 (Feb. 1987), 3–18. Richmond provides an excellent review of existing paradigms which seek to explain ethnic identity, its relationship to nationalistic movements, and its capacity for action. He argues that not all ethnic political activity is nationalistic, nor are all nationalistic movements based on ethnicity. 'States may consist of one or more nations. These nations may also, in turn, be polyethnic' (4).

4. Frederick B. Pike, *Spanish America, 1900–1970: Tradition and Innovation* (New York W.W. Norton & Co., 1973).

5. Drawing on Raymond Williams's concept of dominant, emergent, residual and (less significantly) archaic cultural forms, I discuss various examples of sport, including concurrent nationalistic appeals, as mechanisms and expressions of social conflict across the broad spectrum of Latin American history, in Joseph L. Arbena, 'Deporte y cambio social en América Latina', *Pretextos*, I, 1 (Aug. 1990), 77–90; this is part of a larger analysis of 'Sport and Social Change in Latin America' on which I am currently working. Peter Donnelly, inspired by Williams as well as Antonio Gramsci, is especially impressed by sport's ability to serve as a site for resistance or opposition to dominant cultural and political regimes; among many, he also cites a few examples from Latin America in 'Sport as a Site for "Popular" Resistance', in Richard B. Gruneau (ed.), *Popular Cultures and Popular Practices* (Toronto: Garamond Press, 1988), pp.69–82.

6. John Bale, 'International Sports History as Innovation Diffusion', *Canadian Journal of History of Sport*, XV,1 (May 1984), 38–63; Allen Guttmann, '"Our Former Colonial Masters": The Diffusion of Sports and the Question of Cultural Imperialism', *Stadion*, XIV,1 (1988), 49–63.

7. See Guttmann, '"Our Former Colonial Masters".'

8. Joseph L. Arbena, 'The Diffusion of Modern European Sport in Latin America: A Case Study of Cultural Imperialism?' *South Eastern Latin Americanist*, XXXIII,4 (March 1990), 1–8.

9. Allen Guttmann has gone so far as to assert, 'with a bit of exaggeration that the language of modern sports is English'; 'Our Former Colonial Masters', 49. Earlier Américo Barabino found among selected examples of English influence on the language of both sides of the Río de la Plata that 'sports have been the richest source of foreign words'; 'English Influence on the Common Speech of the River Plate', *Hispania*, 33,2 (May 1950), 163–5. For more specific examples of this linguistic modification and for Latin American reactions, see my 'Sports Language, Cultural Imperialism, and the Anti-Imperialistic Critique in Latin America' (Paper presented at the annual meeting of the Southeastern Council of Latin American Studies, Jacksonville, FL, March 1991). An excellent survey of the problem with a focus on Spain and Argentina, but with broader applications, is provided by Juan José

Alzugaray Aguirre, *Extranjerismos en el deporte* (Barcelona: Editorial Hispano Europea, 1982).

10. H.C.F. Mansilla, 'Latin America Within the Third World: The Search for a New Identity', *New World: A Journal of Latin American Studies*, 3,1–2 (1988–89), 9–27.

11. The term creole ('criollo' in Spanish) here refers to the predominantly white descendants of Latin America's European conquerors and colonial settlers. In turn, it denotes their evolving culture which is 'American', but with somewhat stronger Iberian than either Amerindian or African qualities.

12. E. Bradford Burns, *Poverty of Progress. Latin America in the Nineteenth Century* (Berkeley: University of California Press, 1980). For an example drawn from the world of sport and recreation, see Richard W. Slatta, 'The Demise of the Gaucho and the Rise of Equestrian Sport in Argentina', *Journal of Sport History*, 13,2 (Summer 1986), 97–111.

13. William H. Beezley, *Judas at the Jockey Club and Other Episodes of Porfirian Mexico* (Lincoln: University of Nebraska Press, 1987).

14. In principle, 'sports' were made a requirement in Argentine schools in the late 1890s; in contrast, in Mexico a similar step was not taken till the 1930s.

15. José Luis Buzzetti and Eduardo Gutiérrez Cortinas, *Historia del deporte en el Uruguay (1830–1900)* (Montevideo: Talleres Gráficos Castro & Cía., 1965); Ernesto Escobar Bavio, *El football en el Río de la Plata (desde 1893)* (Buenos Aires: Editorial Sports, 1923); Eduardo A. Olivera, *Orígenes de los deportes británicos en el Río de la Plata* (Buenos Aires: Talleres Gráficos Argentinos L. J. Rosso, 1932).

16. Enrique Romero Brest, *El Instituto Nacional Superior de Educación Física. Antecedentes, organización, resultados* (Buenos Aires: Cabaut y Cía, 1917); Enrique C. Romero Brest, Alberto R. Dallo, and Simón Silvesttrini, 'Los deportes y la educación física en la República Argentina', in Horst Ueberhorst (ed.), *Geschichte der Leibesübungen*, Vol.6: *Perspektiven des Weltsports* (Berlin: Bartels & Wernitz., 1989), pp.846–86.

17. César Viale, *El deporte argentino (contribución a su desarrollo y prosperidad)* (Buenos Aires: Librería de A.García Santos, 1922). By the same author also see *La educación física obligatoria impulsaría la grandeza nacional* (Buenos Aires: Talleres Gráficos de la Penitenciaria Nacional, 1924).

18. Carlos Felice Castillo, *El deporte institucional* (Caracas: Tipografía Remar, 1973). Similar comments from Mexico and Ecuador are found respectively in Luis Felipe Obregón Andrade, *Recreación física para escuelas y comunidades rurales* (México, D.F.: Secretaría de Educación Pública, 1935), and José Silva Romo, *Teoría y práctica del deporte* (Quito: Imprenta Cevallos, 1973). Additional examples are cited in Joseph L. Arbena (comp.), *An Annotated Bibliography of Latin American Sport: Pre-Conquest to the Present* (Westport, CT: Greenwood Press, 1989).

19. Gilberto Mantilla Garzón *et al.*, *Los terceros Juegos Deportivos Nacionales y la prensa* (Quito: Secretaría Nacional de Información Pública, [1975]).

20. 'FBC Melgar: una selección nacional', *Debate* (Peru), 17 (Nov. 1982), 73–5.

21. Institutional histories or descriptions of sports entities in Latin America are rare. Some exceptions include the club 'histories' cited in Arbena (comp.), *An Annotated Bibliography of Latin American Sport* and the contents of several of the 18 essays devoted to Latin American countries in Horst Veberhorst (ed.), *Geschichte der Leibesübungen*. A useful exception which emphasizes political intervention by various Argentine governments in the operations of the country's soccer administration is Ariel Scher and Héctor Palomino, *Fútbol: pasión de multitudes y de elites. Un estudio institucional de la Asociación de Fútbol Argentino (1934–1986)* (Buenos Aires: Centro de Investigaciones Sociales sobre el Estado y la Administración, 1988). For a brief description of the organization and inter-relationships of national sports institutions n Venezuela, see *Historia y organización del deporte en Venezuela* (Caracas: Instituto Nacional de Deportes, 1984?).

22. Augusto Antonio Cornejo, 'Historia de la educación física y el deporte en El Salvador', in Horst Ueberhorst (ed.), *Geschichte der Leibesübungen*, pp.1070–8 (quote is from p.1077).

23. Ernesto Vidales, *Nos dejó el tren . . .* (Bogotá: Editorial Kelly, 1961).

24. '20 años de atraso', *Veja*, No. 557 (9 May 1979), 69–76. Conrad Phillip Kottack likewise concludes, based on his experiences with youth swimming programmes in the United States

and Brazil, that cultural differences help to explain the differences in performance records of national athletes; see his 'Swimming in Cross-Cultural Currents', *Natural History*, 94,5 (May 1985), 2–11.

25. Among his many columns and essays, see 'El deporte al instante: el Perú en el mundo', *Debate*, 18 (Dec. 1982), 65–8, and 'Laboratorio', *Debate*, IX,51 (July–Aug. 1988), 67.

26. Luis Alamos Luque, *El hombre y el fútbol* (Santiago: Editorial Universitaria, 1988), pp.152–3.

27. Raúl Gonzáles Rodríguez, *Así gané; mi espíritu de lucha .... y voluntad de triunfo* (Monterrey, México: Ediciones Castillo, 1986). For another comment on the lack of Mexican interest in the labours of their champion walkers, see the comments of Olympic gold medalist Daniel Bautista in Dave Prokop *et al.*, *1976 Olympic Games: A Close-up Look at the Track & Field Events* (Mountain View, CA, 1977).

28. Fernando Naranjo Madrigal, *Epoca de oro del fútbol en Costa Rica* (San José: Editorial Costa Rica, 1988), p.11.

29. For a laudatory, anecdotal picture of Gómez, with strong nationalistic overtones, see Fausto Zambrano Zúñiga, *Mi poder en la raqueta. Memorias de un trotamundos (Andrés Gómez)* (Quito: Consejo Provincial de Pichincha, 1985).

30. Janet Lever, *Soccer Madness* (Chicago: Univesity of Chicago Press, 1983), pp.6, 22. For a reasoned critique of Lever's thesis, see Alan Klein's review in *Sociology of Sport Journal*, 1,2 (1984), 195–7.

31. I think this is one of the implications of the argument in Eric A. Wagner, 'Sport in Asia and Africa: Americanization or Mundialization?', *Sociology of Sport Journal*, 7,4 (Dec. 1990), 399–402.

32. Alan M. Klein, 'American Hegemony, Dominican Resistance, and Baseball', *Dialectical Anthropology*, 13 (1988), 301–12; Alan M. Klein, 'Baseball as Underdevelopment: The Political-Economy of Sport in the Dominican Republic', *Sociology of Sport Journal*, 6,2 (June 1989), 95–112; Alan M. Klein, *Sugarball: The American Game, The Dominican Dream* (New Haven: Yale University Press, 1991). For the larger context see John Krich, *El Béisbol: Travels Through the Pan-American Pastime* (New York: Atlantic Monthly Press, 1989).

33. That sport has the potential to both integrate or disrupt societies is a point advanced by L. Fleming, 'The Contribution of Sport to the Integration of Society', in Ommo Grupe (eds.), *et al., Sport in the Modern World – Chances and Problems* (Berlin: Springer-Verlag, 1973), 82–86.

34. Recent sources include: Christine Cummings, 'The Ideology of West Indian Cricket', *Arena Review*, 14,1 (May 1990), 25–32; Brian Stoddart, 'Gary Sobers and Cultural Identity in the Caribbean', *Sporting Traditions*, 5,1 (Nov. 1988), 131–46; Keith A.P. Sandiford, 'Cricket and the Barbarian Society', *Canadian Journal of History*, XXI (Dec. 1986), 353–70.

35. Kevin A. Yelvington, 'Ethnicity "Not Out": The Indian Cricket Tour of the West Indies and the 1976 Elections in Trinidad and Tobago', *Arena Review*, 14,1 (May 1990), 1–12.

36. Jay R. and Joan D. Mandle, 'Open Cultural Space: Grassroots Basketball in the English-Speaking Caribbean,' *Arena Review*, 14,1 (May 1990), 68–74. By the same authors, see also *Grass Roots Commitment: Basketball and Society in Trinidad and Tobago* (Parkersburg, IA: Caribbean Books, 1988).

37. Emiliano Villalta, 'El Fútbol es una industria', *La Nación* (Guatemala), I,28 (21 March 1970), 28. Villalta was a Guetamalan journalist assigned to Mexico City who commented critically on the extent to which the Mexican organizers of the 1970 World Cup were openly pushing the event as a way to promote commercial sales and make big money.

38. Background on Uruguayan negotiations to organize the 1930 Mundial is provided by Enrique E. Buero, *Negociaciones internacionales* (Brussels: Imp. Puvrez, 1932). Expressons of Uruguayan pride in the results of those efforts are in Arturo Carbonell Debali, *Primer Campeonato Mundial de Football* (Montevideo, 1930). Delgado's oft-cited poem is printed in Carbonell Debali and in José Luis Buzzetti, *et al.*, *El fútbol (antología)* (Monevideo: Centro Editor de América Latina, 1969).

39. Argentina's role in hosting the 1978 Mundial while under the leadership of a brutal military dictatorship provoked many unfavourable comments at home and abroad. The relatively

peaceful atmosphere which surrounded the Cup and the final victory by the home squad temporarily reduced the criticism on both fronts. Ultimately, however, revelations about the military leaders and their usavory behaviour led to renewed allegations and bitterness toward the Mundial. See Joseph L. Arbena, 'Generals and *Goles:* Assessing the Connection between the Military and Soccer in Argentina', *International Journal of the History of Sport*, 7,1 (May 1990), 120–30.

40. 'Contra el reloj', *Semana* (Bogotá), No. 421 (29 May–5 June 1990), 124–6. One critic of the decision by President Belisario Betancur to withdraw from hosting the 1986 Mundial is Christina de la Torre who attributed the change to unfair actions on the part of FIFA, all part of an international plot engineered by Henry Kissinger and others who wanted to shift the site, probably to the United States; see her essay '¿Qué pasó con el Mundial?', in Christina de la Torre, *et al., Las cinco maravillas millionarias de Colombia* (Bogotá: Editorial Oveja Negra, 1982), pp.11–64.

41. For a discussion of Mexico's use of international sporting events in pursuit of domestic and foreign policy goals, see Joseph L. Arbena, 'Sport, Development, and Mexican Nationalism, 1920–1970', *Journal of Sport History,* 18, 3 (1991), 350–64.

42. Among many sources on the Guatemalan case are Carlos A. Paz Tejada, *Discurso pronunciado ... en al acto de inauguración de los VI Juegos Deportivos Centroamericanos y del Caribe* (Guatemala City: Tipografía Nacional, 1950) and Benjamin Paniagua S., *et al., Guatemala* ((Guatemala City: Tipografía Nacional, 1950) Extremely useful is the *Boletín de la Oficina de Publicidad de los VI Juegos Deportivos Centroamericanos y del Caribe* (Guatemala City), published irregularly between February and April 1950.

43. Héctor Cifuentes Aguirre, 'Breve reseña del deporte de Guatemala', in Horst Ueberhorst, *Geschichte der Leibesübungen*, pp.1082–92.

44. Roger Barta, 'La crisis del nacionalismo en México', *Revista Mexicana de Sociología*, LI,3 (July–Sept. 1989), 191–220.

45. For a discussion of the connections among Colombia's economic conditions, political corruption, and soccer administration see Juan Ignacio Rodríguez, *Los amos del juego* (Bogotá: Peyre, 1989).

46. Enrico Mario Santí discusses the difficulties involved in trying to trace the sources of an emerging Cuban national identity: 'In the specific case of Cuba, which along with the rest of the Latin American nations lies at the margins of the West, one could further question whether the will to self-knowledge had been comprehensive systematic, or perhaps even radical enough, given the past two centuries of political instability and fragmentation'. Consequently, Santí observes, Cuban identity '. . . emerges from the (often conflictual) interplay of difficult strategies, discourses, and historical moments. That is, instead of a cultural given or assumption, identity here becomes an *effect*, often sparked by the friction between or among claims, interpretations, or ideologies'. A fragile foundation, indeed! See Enrico Mario Santí, 'Introduction', *Cuban Studies*, 16 (1986), 3–7 (quotes are from pp.5–6).

47. Geralyn Pye, 'Physical Culture and the Cuban Revolution: Elitism, Egalitarianism and Socialisation in Cuban Physical Culture', unpublished Ph.D. thesis, The Flinders University of South Australia, 1990; Joseph L. Arbena, 'Sport and Revolution: The Continuing Cuban Experience', *Studies in Latin American Popular Culture*, 9 (1990), 319–28. A recent and highly favourable assessment of what the Castro Revolution has done with sports and physical education to promote both mass participation and elite performance and, in turn, to advance Cuba's socialist ideology, its nationalism, its relations with the great powers, and its claim to global leadership at least in the Third World, is offered by John Sugden, Alan Tomlinson and Eamon McCartan, 'The Making and Remaking of White Lightning in Cuba: Politics, Sport and Physical Education 30 Years After the Revolution', *Arena Review*, 14,1 (May 1990), 101–9. Provocative comments on the Cuban use of sports as part of the 'unconventional' foreign policy of a Third World state are found in Paula J. Pettavino, 'Novel Revolutionary Forms: The Use of Unconventional Diplomacy in Cuba', unpublished manuscript, 1987.

48. 'Game for the Games', *Sports Illustrated*, 74,3 (28 Jan. 1991), 16.

49. Ignacio Ellacuría, 'Medallas para Cuba', *ECA; Estudios Centro Americanos*, 25:259 (April 1970), 228.

50. Brad Whorton and Eric A. Wagne, 'Nicaraguan Sports Ideology', *Journal of Sport and Social Issues*, 9,2 (Summer/Fall 1985), 26–33; Wolf Kramer-Mandeau, 'Occupación, dominación y liberación – La historia del deporte en Nicaragua', in Horst Ueberhorst (ed.) *Geschichte der Leibesübungen*, pp.1039–67.

51. Dirección General de Educación Física, *Juegos Deportivos Nacionales de la Revolución* (Mexico, D.F.: Dirección Nacionale de Educación Física, 1941).

52. Daniel Aeta Astorga, *Juegos de los niños chilenos de ambos sexos a base folklórica, sinonímica i pedagójica* (Santiago: Imprenta, Litografía i Ecuadernación Barcelona, 1913) and *Juegos y deportes con un diccionario de equivalencias* (Santiago: Editorial Nascimento, 1930 [1929]).

53. See Kramer-Mandeau, 'Ocupación, dominación y liberación', p.1042.

54. Guillermo Alfredo Terrera (h), *El juego del pato: reseña socio-cultural* (San Isidro, Argentina, Editorial Patria Vieja, 1971); Juan Pedro Grenón, S.J., 'El juego de pato', *Historia*, I,4 (April–June 1956), 121–46. For a debate over the origins of the game, see Luis García del Soto, 'El pato, la fiesta del coraje', *Todo Es Historia*, No. 127 (Dec. 1977), 62–74.

55. William H. Durham, *Scarcity and Survival in Central America. Ecological Origins of the Soccer War* (Stanford: Stanford University Press, 1979).

56. Cubans themselves comment on both the problems and successes they experienced, athletically and politically, during the Tenth Central American and Caribbean Games held in Puerto Rico (June 1966), in Juan Marrero, *Nos vimos en Puerto Rico (crónicas)* (La Habana: Ediciones Granma, 1966).

57. Keith Kendrick, 'Economic War on Iraq, Back at the Home Front', *The Washington Post National Weekly Edition*, 7,47 (24–30 Sept., 1990). 33.

58. Cifuentes Aguirre, 'Breve reseña del deporte de Guatemala', p.1086.

59. Fidel Castro, *El movimiento olímpico internacional, la grave crisis que se va a generar en torno a los juegos de Seul en 1988 y la única solución posible* (La Habana: Editorial Política, 1985).

60. Augusto López Ramírez, '"Carter jugó una carta sucia; por eso vinimos": delegados guatemaltecos', *Uno Más Uno*, III, 962 (16 July 1980), 31.

61. Gerard Béhague, *Music in Latin America: An Introduction* (Englewood Cliffs: Prentice-Hall, 1979).

62. Juan Pablo González, '"Inti-Illimani" and the Artistic Treatment of Folklore', *Latin American Research Review*, 10,2 (Fall – Winter 1989), 267–86 (see especially 267–8).

63. Mafalda is a popular cartoon character appearing in a strip of the same name. Its creator is Argentine and much of its content reflects an Argentine context, but the strip is known and appreciated throughout Latin America.

64. William H. McNeill, *Polyethnicity and National Unity in World History* (Toronto: University of Toronto Press, 1986), and 'The Peasantry's Awakening All Over the World', *The Washington Post National Weekly Edition*, 8,13 (7–13 Jan. 1991), 24–5 (quote is from p.24). Stanley Hoffmann, without specific reference to Latin America, takes a dissenting view: 'The nation-state as a shelter in a stormy world, national togetherness as the (so far) highest possible bond (indeed, often a liberating force) for the greatest number of people living in a given area, will continue to be among the most fundamental forces in politics ...'; see 'Nations Are Nuisances', *The New York Times Book Review* (7 Oct. 1990), 24–5. For more on the debate, consult Glenn Frankel, 'Is the Nation-State Headed for the Dustbin of History?' *The Washington Post National Weekly Edition*, 8, 3 (19–25 Nov. 1990), 16.

65. Octaviio Paz, 'Spanish-American Literature', *The New Republic*, 176,15 (9 April 1977), 23–7.

66. I allude to this process in my essay, 'International Aspects of Sport in Latin America: Perceptions, Prospects, and Proposals' (Paper presented at the annual conference of the North American Society for the Sociology of Sport, Denver, CO, November 1990).

67. John M. Hoberman, 'The Transformation of East German Sport', *Journal of Sport History*, 17,1 (Spring 1990), 62–8.

68. On the one hand, a well-known Argentine sportswriter, pseudonym Juvenal, concluded that, if nothing else, his country's sports victories over the years had 'granted us a moment of

happiness and a bit of illusion', perhaps even helping 'us to know ourselves better'; Julio César Pasquato, 'El deporte: ¿qué le dió, *Todo Es Historia,* XXI; 242 (July 1987), 204–6. On the other hand, for the painful reaction to Brazil's loss in the World Cup final of 1950, see Paulo Perdigão, *Antonomia de uma derrota* (Porto Alegre: L&PM Editores, 1986).

69. A more positive assessment of the contribution which at least soccer has made to the development of nationalism globally is offered by Jorge Emilio Salazar Monge, *El fútbol en su intimidad* (San José: Servicios Litográficos, 1988), pp.27–59. My own more sceptical, even pessimistic view seems consistent with that of James H. Frey, 'The Internal and External Role of Sport in National Development', *Journal of National Development,* 1,2 (Winter 1988), 65–82.

70. In Jim Riordan's words, 'One thing is certain: far from being a luxury, *sport or, better still, physical culture, in modernising societies is an absolute necessity.'* See his 'State and Sport in Developing Societies,' *International Review for the Sociology of Sport,* 21,4 (1986), 287–303 (quote is from p.299; Riordan's italics).

Notes on Contributors

Joseph L. Arbena teaches Latin American history and geography at Clemson University, South Carolina, USA. In addition to writing numerous papers on sport in Latin America, he edited *Sport and Society in Latin America* (1988) and compiled *An Annotated Bibliography of Latin American History* (1989). He is also editor of the *Journal of Sport History*.

Eduardo P. Archetti is Professor of Anthropology at the University of Oslo, Denmark. He is the author of *El mundo social y simbólico del cuy* (1992) and *Exploring the Written* (1994).

Henning Eichberg is a cultural sociologist and historian at the Research Institute of Sport, Body and Culture (Idrætforsk), Gerlev, Denmark. He is the author of *Der Weg des Sports in die industrielle Zivilization* (1973), *Leistung, Spannung, Geschwindigkeit* (1978) and *Leistungsräume: Sport als Umweltproblem* (1988).

Jean-Michel Faure is Professor of Sociology at the University of Nantes, France.

Matti Goksøyr is Associate Professor of Sports History at the Norwegian University of Sport and Physical Education, Oslo.

Richard Holt is Research Fellow at the University of Leuven, Belgium, and Visiting Professor at DeMontfort University and the University of Brighton. Among his books are *Sport and Society in Modern France* (1981) and *Sport and the British: A Modern History* (Oxford, 1989).

Arnd Krüger is Chair for Sport Science at the George-August University of Göttingen. An International Fellow of the American Academy of Kinesiology and Physical Education and a former Olympic semi-finalist, he has written extensively on the history of sport.

J.A. Mangan is Professor of Education and Director of the International Centre for Socialization, Sport and Society, University of Strathclyde, Glasgow. His recent publications include the edited works *The Cultural Bond: Sport, Empire, Society* (1992) and *The Imperial Curriculum: Racial Images and Education in the British Colonial Experience* (1993).

H.F. Moorhouse is Senior Lecturer in Sociology at the University of Glasgow. He has written many articles and reports on most aspects of football and is the author of *Driving Ambitions: A Social Analysis of the American Hot Rod Enthusiasm* (1991).

Sverker Sörlin is Professor of Environmental History at Umeå University, Sweden. He co-edited *Denationalizing Science: The Contexts of International Scientific Practice* (1993).

Jan Tolleneer is a Professor and Head Librarian at the University of Leuven, Belgium.

Irina V. Tsypkina is a practising psychologist from St Petersburg, Russia, and is a graduate of Leningrad State University.

John D. Windhausen is Professor of Russian History at Saint Anselm College, Manchester, USA. He edited *Sports Encyclopedia North America* (1987–93).

INDEX